What People Ask About The Church
2nd Edition

Answers To Your Questions
Concerning Today's Church

Dale A. Robbins, D.Min.

Victorious Publications
Grass Valley, California – Nashville, Tennessee
www.victorious.org

What People Ask About The Church, 2nd Edition
Copyright © 1995, 2014, Dale A Robbins
Published by Victorious Publications
Grass Valley, California – Nashville, Tennessee
www.victorious.org

First Edition, July 1995
Second Edition, November 2014

ISBN-10: 096480221X
ISBN-13: 978-0964802216

CONTENTS

21. What is a fundamentalist Christian?

22. Why are ministers referred to as "Reverend?"

23. Why are some ministers called "Parsons?"

24. Why do so many churches have splits and problems getting along?

25. What things contribute to the health and stability of a church congregation?

26. How should I decide if or when to change churches?

27. What should I do if I'm not getting fed in my church?

28. How can a person keep from getting hurt or injured in a church fellowship?

29. How should disputes and offenses be dealt with between believers in the church fellowship?

30. What is it like to be a pastor of a church?

31. Should ministers receive pay for their ministry?

32. How come a pastor only has to work one day a week?

33. What is a dysfunctional church?

34. What are the qualifications of ministers and pastors?

35. Why have some churches been accused of teaching cannibalism?

36. Why do churches practice the Lord's Supper?

37. Why are some churches considered nonprofit organizations?

38. Why do many churches have a Constitution and By-laws?

39. Why do some churches require counseling for couples before they will perform a marriage?

40. What is the difference between a Protestant church and a Catholic church?

41. What can I do to be a help to my church?

42. What's the difference between Elders, Bishops and pastors?

43. What are Deacons?

44. What is church government and why is it necessary?

45. What is a Pentecostal church?

46. What is a Charismatic church?

47. What is an Evangelical church?

48. Why do some churches encourage the use of offering envelopes?

49. Why do many churches use the Bible as their sole source of teaching?

50. Why do many churches use different translations of the Bible?

51. What is a liturgical church?

52. What is an ecumenical church?

53. Why do churches stress the importance of authority?

54. Why do churches teach believers to be accountable to spiritual leadership?

55. Why do some churches believe in washing one another's feet?

56. What do churches mean by references to "traditional values?"

57. Why are there so many hypocrites in the church?

58. Why have some churches turned persons over to Satan?

59. Why do some churches forbid women to be preachers?

60. How did followers of Jesus come to be called Christians?

61. Why do many churches have different ways of worship?

62. Is it true that some churches believe in handling snakes and drinking poison?

63. Why do many churches believe in speaking in tongues?

64. Why do churches hold revivals?

65. Why do many churches have conflicting views about spiritual gifts?

66. How can I help the spiritual climate of my church?

67. Why is the celebration of Christmas considered to be controversial in some churches?

68. Why do many churches oppose Halloween?

69. What qualities do churches look for in the selection of lay leaders and workers?

70. What is meant by the Church Fathers?

71. Why is the term Easter considered to be controversial in some churches?

72. Why do most Christian churches meet on Sunday to worship instead of the Sabbath?

73. What does it mean to call for the elders of the church?

74. Why is a church building sometimes referred to as a "House of Prayer?"

75. Why are most church services based around preaching?

FOREWORD

A prominent religious leader once gave me the following advice: "The questions are more important than the answers. It's your job to ask the questions and seek the answers; but ultimately, it's God's job to reveal the answers." But fortunately, God raises up persons like Pastor Dale Robbins to serve as instruments to communicate His answers.

Whenever I read a book, I want to know about the author. I want to know if he or she is writing under the inspiration of the Holy Spirit. I want to know if his or her personal life measures up to a standard of holiness. I want to know if they are motivated by personal gain or by a desire to touch the lives of people.

The writings of Dale Robbins are worth reading, for he is a gifted writer and a servant. He is motivated by a passion to win souls and a desire to enrich the lives of believers.

This book will bless you. It will answer your questions and help you gain a better understanding of the church. Thank you, Dale, for having the courage to write such a book.

— Hal Donaldson
President of Church Care America
Editor of the Pentecostal Evangel

INTRODUCTION

Some years ago a friend said, "one of the problems with today's church is that ministers often try to answer questions that no one is asking." So challenged was I by this statement, that after some thought and prayer I wanted to find out whether this was true of my own ministry. I decided to start a series of Q and A Bible studies one evening each week, inviting the congregation to submit whatever questions they had about the Bible, the Church or related spiritual subjects. I then attempted to answer them the following week.

It sounded like a great idea at the time, to let the congregation set the agenda from their own curiosity, but little did I know where this open-ended adventure would take me. Nor did I foresee the occasional mischief that would inspire some to make this an amusing "Stump the Pastor" night! But despite this, the weekly Q & A night became a quick hit, and everyone enjoyed hearing the questions that began to focus mainly about the Church... some simple, others profound, a few wacky and hilarious. I enjoyed researching and trying to answer each, and it became apparent that we were providing legitimate answers that were helping to open hearts to a deeper relationship with the Lord Jesus Christ.

Eventually, realizing that many questions I frequently heard about the Church were similar, I decided to compile a few of the more interesting or controversial ones into this brief volume. As you will discover, I included a wide range of topics... but be assured that there's also a lot more here than just superficial tidbits, as I deal with many of the more important concepts, philosophies and history of the Christian Church from a Biblical perspective.

I hope you find this book interesting, sometimes amusing, and most of all informative... as you read *What People Ask About The Church*.

May God bless and encourage you in your walk with Christ!

— Dale A. Robbins

—1—
What is the Church?

In the New Testament, the term "church," also sometimes translated as "assembly," comes from the Greek word *EKKLESIA* which means the "called out." The word was used by the Greeks to describe the assembling or gathering of citizens who were called out to meet together for public hearings. The heralds would walk through the streets and literally call for people to come out from what they were doing to gather for public business. In the scriptures EKKLESIA refers to those whom Christ has "called out" from the world to be His own, and to assemble together in His name.

The primary meaning of the church is used in a universal sense, referring to all Christian believers everywhere. Irrespective of denominational or doctrinal differences, all persons who have genuinely placed their faith in Jesus Christ as Savior and Lord are members of His church, also called the body of Christ, over which Christ is the head *(Ephesians 1:22-23)*.

Secondarily, the church also refers to a local congregation of believers. While the scriptures tell us that there is only one true church, yet it is made up of many individual churches. Most of the Apostle Paul's epistles were written to the local churches such as at Rome, Corinth, Thessalonica, Ephesus, Philippi, Galatia, and Colosse, and he makes mention of many other churches which had been established in various cities at that time.

It is important to understand that a church is not a building, although many people frequently use that term to describe the facility built for the use of the church. History shows the New Testament church met primarily in private homes — Christian cathedrals or tabernacles designed specifically for believers to gather for worship did not exist until almost three centuries after the church got started. Unlike the Old Testament temple, in which the presence of God habitated, the new covenant of Jesus Christ made every believer a temple of the Holy Spirit. *"Do you not know that you are the temple of God and that the Spirit of God dwells in you?" (1 Corinthians 3:16)*.

The church is often viewed as an organization, but is actually more of an "organism." It is the united fellowship of all Christians with their God — the wondrous union of Christ's Spirit indwelling the hearts of all true believers.

— 2 —
Why are there so many different churches?

According to estimates by the Hartford Institute for Religion Research, the United States has about 314,000 Protestant churches and 24,000 Catholic and Orthodox churches (not counting the non-Christian religious groups).[1] But despite the numerous individual congregations here and throughout the world, there's really only one true church. Even though many have differences in doctrinal opinions or other characteristics, every church which is based on Jesus Christ as Savior and Lord is a part of the true church.

Amazingly, there are thousands of different denominational and independent Christian churches who, for the most part, agree on the basic fundamentals of Christ, but who maintain their separate groups for relatively minor issues. They may not agree on all other matters of doctrine, interpretation, traditions, or the special emphasis placed on certain beliefs.

Regardless of how closely various churches may agree with each other doctrinally, there still will never be two churches exactly alike. This is largely due to the fact that no two people are alike in every detail. Churches are made up of people. Thus, the combined individual personalities in a congregation, creates a distinct "congregational personality." Sometimes people mistake differences in church personality as differences in belief or doctrine.

A denomination is a cluster of separate congregations, which have unified together due to their agreement on certain issues, and perhaps due to their disagreement with the viewpoints of other churches or denominations.

According to Church Historian, Dr. Bruce E. Shelley, the original usage of the term "denomination" actually stood for unity, not division. It was used to describe cooperation with other churches without compromise of fundamental convictions.

"The idea goes back to a minority wing of the Puritan party in 17th century England. At the Westminster Assembly (1643) was a group of Independents akin to American Congregationalists. These men had come to the conclusion that the sinful condition of man, even Christian men, made the full and clear grasp of the truth of God an impossibility. Consequently, no single body of beliefs can ever fully represent God's total demand upon the minds and hearts of believers, and no single body of Christians can claim to be the true church of God without considering other believers in other groups."

"Thus, in the minds of these Puritans, the word denomination implied that a particular body of Christians (let us say, for example the Baptists) was only a portion of the total Christian church called — or denominated — by its particular name, Baptist." The denominational idea of the church originally stood for an important biblical truth. The church is one. There is only one Saviour, only one Gospel, only one Spirit, so there can only be one church. Divisions, therefore must be within the one body, not from the body. Otherwise Christ would be divided and that is unthinkable (1 Corinthians 1:12-13)."[2]

Some believe that the first trace of denominations emerged in the early church at Corinth over loyalty to different Christian leaders, as some believers had separated themselves as followers of Paul and others of Apollos *(1 Corinthians 3:1-6)*. Paul chided them for their unspiritual, childish behavior as they had allowed division, strife, and envy to rule their behavior. He reminded them that the Lord's servants were only men, mere instruments of God, not the ones to whom credit was due for these persons conversions. *"I planted, Apollos watered, but God gave the increase" (1 Corinthians 3:6)*. It is clear that Paul did not approve of divisions within the body of Christ. *"Now I plead with you, brethren, by the name of our Lord Jesus Christ, that you all speak the same thing, and that there be no divisions among you, but that you be perfectly joined together in the same mind and in the same judgment" (1 Corinthians 1:10)*.

Denominations were probably not Christ's first choice for His church. We recall His prayer that His church would be one *(John 17:20-21)*, and can imagine that He would have preferred for His church to remain fully unified for the cause of Christ. **But denominations came to help serve the purpose of God in many important ways:**

(1) They helped to divide and scatter the influence of the Gospel to a wider spectrum of people.

(2) They helped to filter out the spread of harmful heresies and false doctrines.

(3) They have unified significant portions of the body of Christ, integrating those congregations of similar views. Even though a denomination may not have an organizational affiliation with all other churches, this does not have to represent disunity any more than a local church who seeks to befriend and support its neighboring congregations. Wise denominational leaders have used their influence to help their flock see the larger family picture of Christianity.

Thank God there will be no denominational divisions in Heaven, only those who have agreed upon their faith in the precious atoning blood of Jesus Christ.

— 3 —
How can I tell the difference between a genuine Christian church and a cult?

A genuine Christian church is founded on the life, death, resurrection, and Gospel of Jesus Christ. It bases its doctrine and teachings on the Bible.

In the early church, creeds were often used to identify the basic beliefs of Christians. What is known as The Apostles Creed, has been recognized as perhaps the oldest historic statement of the fundamental beliefs of orthodox Christianity. Whether it was actually composed by the Apostles as some have alleged, it can be traced back as far as the late second century where it was used as a baptismal creed in Rome.[1]

The Apostles Creed
"I believe in God almighty [the Father almighty]
And in Christ Jesus, his only Son, our Lord
Who was born of the Holy Spirit and of the Virgin   Mary
Who was crucified under Pontius Pilate and was buried
And the third day rose from the dead
Who ascended into heaven

And sits on the right hand of the Father
Whence he comes to judge the living and the dead.
And in the Holy Ghost
The holy [universal] church
The remission of sins
The resurrection of the flesh
The life everlasting."

Creeds of this kind were helpful in giving a short summary of the basic essentials of Christianity, and were brief enough to be easily committed to memory. Today, most all churches have a similar expression, sometimes called a "Statement of Faith," which summarizes their basic beliefs and theological views.

The following is such a statement, typical of a modern evangelical church. Any legitimate Christian church or ministry will believe and support at least some variation of the following fundamental truths:

(1) That the Bible is the inspired and only infallible, authoritative written Word of God — It is used exclusively as the source for teaching and doctrine, not in conjunction with any other alleged sacred writings or scriptures *(2 Timothy 3:15-17, 1 Thessalonians 2:13, 2 Peter 1:21, Galatians 1:8)*.

(2) That there is one God — who is eternal and exists in three persons: God the Father, God the Son, and God the Holy Ghost *(Deut. 6:4, Isaiah 43:10-11, Matthew 28:19, Luke 3:22)*.

(3) In the deity of our Lord Jesus Christ — that He was born of a virgin, lived a sinless life, performed miracles, died a vicarious and atoning death for our sins, rose from the dead on the third day, and was exalted to the right hand of the Father *(Matthew 1:23, Luke, 1:31-35, Hebrews 7:26, 1 Peter 2:22, Acts 2:22, 10:38, 1 Corinthians 15:3, 2 Corinthians 5:21, Matthew 28:6, Luke 24:39, 1 Corinthians 15:4, Acts 1:9-11, 2:33, Philippians 2:9-11, Hebrews 1:1-3)*.

(4) That Jesus will someday personally return — to gather His saints, and will at some future time return to the earth in power and glory to rule for a thousand years *(1 Thessalonians 4:16-17, Matthew 24:30-31, Revelations 20:1-6)*.

(5) That the only means of being saved and cleansed from sin is through repentance and faith in the precious blood of Jesus Christ — Salvation is a gift of God's grace which cannot be earned by works and comes only through faith in Jesus, the only mediator between God and man. That the Holy Spirit regenerates and indwells the heart of every true believer *(Luke 24:47, John 3:3, Romans 10:13-15, Ephesians 2:8-9, Titus 2:11, 3:5-7, 1 Timothy 2:5, Romans 8:9b).*

(6) That God hears and answers the prayers of His people — in accordance to His will *(Matthew 7:7-11, 1 John 5:14-15).*

(7) That there will someday be a resurrection of both the saved and the lost — the one to everlasting life in Heaven, and the other to everlasting damnation in the Lake of Fire *(Matthew 25:46, Mark 9:43-48, Revelations 19:20, 20:11-15, 21:8).*

(This summary does not dismiss the value of other important Biblical doctrines, taught with varying opinions, but additional teachings are not mandatory to basic Christian faith.)

Such basic beliefs are held in common agreement by thousands of Christian churches, made up of scores of denominations. If a church or minister cannot agree with the above statements, it should be assumed that they are not a Christian church, and very likely fall into the category of a cult. Don't waste your time arguing with them, but move on and find a good, Christ-centered, Bible believing church.

Because our society is peppered with cults and misguided religions, it goes without saying that persons should always thoroughly research any alleged church before getting involved with it in any way. Besides obtaining a copy of their basic beliefs or other materials (which should be thoroughly studied and compared with the Bible), ask local people in the community what they know about the group. You can seek advice from trusted Christian friends, the local ministerial association, or even a nearby Christian bookstore. And of course, there are many reliable Christian fellowships and denominations that have affiliated churches in most cities.

Many cults refer to themselves as a church, but are really not a Christian church at all. For instance, while the name "Church of Jesus Christ of Latter Day Saints" (The Mormons), sounds like a legitimate Christian group, yet it is not. Neither are the Jehovah's Witnesses, which is another group that appears to have Christian similarities. Both groups are considered cults whose beliefs are not consistent with orthodox Christianity. Most of the time, a false church will publicly promote themselves as just another church, but will usually claim to have an exclusive revelation of truth that others don't have. Beware of groups who assert that they are the only ones with the right doctrine — that's a significant danger sign.

The late Dr. Walter Martin, was probably our era's best authority on the subject of cults. He defined a cult as "any religious group which differs significantly in some or more respects as to belief or practice, from those religious groups which are regarded as the normative expressions of religion in our total culture."[2]

Author Bob Larsen says that things cults share in common are:

(1) a centralized authority which tightly structures both philosophy and lifestyle,

(2) a 'we' versus 'they' complex, pitting the supposed superior insights of the group against a hostile outside culture;

(3) a commitment for each member to intensively proselyte the unconverted; and

(4) an entrenched isolationism that divorces the devotee from the realities of the world at large.[3]

Here are a few of the more familiar cults listed in an encyclopedic fashion from Larsen's Book of Cults:

Traditional Cults	
Ananda	Mormonism
Astrology	New Age
Astara	Rosicrucianism
Bahaism	Scientology
Buddhism	Spiritism
Eckankar	Taoism

Hare Krishna	Theosophy
Hinduism	The Way
Islam	Transcendental Meditation
Jehovah's Witness	Armstrongism [4]

— 4 —
What is the mission of the church?

There may be varying opinions about the multiple tasks and functions of the church, but the following represents what would be its four highest priorities:

(1) To proclaim the Gospel throughout the world and make disciples of all kinds of people. *"Go therefore and make disciples of all the nations, baptizing them in the name of the Father and of the Son and of the Holy Spirit, teaching them to observe all things that I have commanded you; and lo, I am with you always, even to the end of the age"* (Matthew 28:19-20). *"And He said to them, Go into all the world and preach the gospel to every creature"* (Mark 16:15).

The passages above, often referred to as the Great Commission, were among Jesus' final admonitions to His disciples before He ascended to Heaven. Mark's gospel refers to Christ's command for his followers to "go preach the gospel to the world," while Matthew's reflects His emphasis for the church "to go and make disciples of all nations." The combination of these two elements, evangelism and discipleship, are generally considered as Christ's primary mission for His church. "Evangelism" is the ministry of proclaiming the good news of Jesus Christ that will bring men's souls into fellowship with God, while "discipleship" is the training of believers to become disciplined followers of Jesus and His principles.

The mission of the church is, in reality, a continuation of Christ's earthly ministry *(John 14:12)*. Jesus viewed that redeeming men's souls was His whole purpose for coming to the earth. *"For the Son of Man has come to save that which was lost"* (Matthew 18:11). And in turn, He imparted this same objective to His disciples. He said to them,

"Follow Me, and I will make you fishers of men" (Matthew 4:19). The Apostle Paul later confirmed that the ministry of bringing people to God has been imparted to all those who have been brought to Him (the church). He wrote, *"God... has reconciled us to Himself through Jesus Christ, and has given us the ministry of reconciliation" (2 Corinthians 5:18).* It is the purpose of every believer, not only pastors and clergymen, to bring souls to Jesus Christ.

Perhaps the statement which best summarizes this mission of Christ and His church, was given as Jesus read from Isaiah's prophecy in Nazareth's synagogue on the Sabbath day. He said, *"The Spirit of the LORD is upon Me, because He has anointed Me to preach the gospel to the poor. He has sent Me to heal the brokenhearted, to preach deliverance to the captives and recovery of sight to the blind, to set at liberty those who are oppressed, to preach the acceptable year of the LORD" (Luke 4:18-19).*

(2) To serve as a community of worship and fellowship — to manifest the presence and love of Jesus. *"For where two or three are gathered together in My name, I am there in the midst of them" (Matthew 18:20).*

God originally made man for His own pleasure, to enjoy his fellowship and worship *(Revelations 4:11, John 4:23).* Thus, a part of the Lord's purpose of the church, besides bringing people to God, is to gather His people together and facilitate a corporate environment of worship, to express our love toward Him and one another. Jesus described these as the two highest ideals of Christianity. *"And you shall love the LORD your God with all your heart, with all your soul, with all your mind, and with all your strength. This is the first commandment. And the second, like it, is this: You shall love your neighbor as yourself. There is no other commandment greater than these" (Mark 12:30-31).*

The Lord is greatly pleased to receive the corporate love and worship of His children who are joined together in unity and love toward one another *(Ephesians 4:1-4, 1 John 1:7).* His presence is manifested in such an environment, and authenticates our Christian witness in the eyes of the world. *"By this all will know that you are My disciples, if you have love for one another" (John 13:35).*

Sunday church services were originally modeled from Lord's Day gatherings of the early church which included the agape "love feast" *(Acts 20:7).* They would share a common meal together (Acts 2:46) and then partake in the Lord's Supper — in recognition of the Lord's sacrificial body, and in recognition of His beloved body, the church. It was a gathering of love to the Lord and toward one another.

(3) To mature believers and prepare them to perform works of ministry. *"And He Himself gave some to be apostles, some prophets, some evangelists, and some pastors and teachers, for the equipping of the saints for the work of ministry, for the edifying of the body of Christ..." (Ephesians 4:11-12).*

Another important mission of the church, by means of its ministers, is to strengthen the body of believers and equip them for works of ministry. The church should be an atmosphere of spiritual edification, where God's Word is taught, where believers are grounded, discipled and led toward maturity. This not only serves to anchor their faith in Christ, but prepares them for service. According to God's plan, each member of the body of Christ is called to serve in some aspect of ministry *(Romans 12:6, 1 Corinthians 12:14-31),* especially as it pertains toward bringing souls to Christ *(2 Corinthians 5:17).*

Even the laity is charged to encourage and spur their brethren on toward works of ministry, and according to scripture, this is one of the primary reasons of our church attendance. *"And let us consider one another in order to stir up love and good works, not forsaking the assembling of ourselves together, as is the manner of some, but exhorting one another, and so much the more as you see the Day approaching" (Hebrews 10:24-25).*

(4) To represent the interests of the Kingdom of God in the world, and to influence our society with the ideals of the Lord. *"You are the salt of the earth; but if the salt loses its flavor, how shall it be seasoned? It is then good for nothing but to be thrown out and trampled underfoot by men. You are the light of the world. A city that is set on a hill cannot be hidden" (Matthew 5:13-14).*

Jesus used salt and light as metaphors of the influential characteristics of His church in the world. Historically, salt has always been a valuable commodity used, among other things, as an antiseptic to withdraw infection. Light, of course, dispels darkness and is an essential element of life.

Likewise, the presence of the church in the world is Christ's antiseptic to sin, an influence of God's righteousness that tends to displace the infection of evil. The church is intended to represent His interests in the affairs of society. It was never intended to be passive, nor to be confined within four walls of a building, but to be involved as a catalyst of God's high ideals in the world around us.

Christ has intended for His church to let its light shine to the world — to love, to care for, and to meet needs of humanity, while upholding the redemptive truths and righteousness of Jesus Christ. *"And let our people also learn to maintain good works, to meet urgent needs, that they may not be unfruitful" (Titus 3:14).* Jesus told His church, *"Let your light so shine before men, that they may see your good works and glorify your Father in heaven" (Matthew 5:16).*

— 5 —
What are the greatest challenges for the church?

The challenges of today's church are many and it is difficult to define which are the most onerous. But from my years of working with the church, I would say that there are two dominant issues with which pastors and church leaders continually strive to overcome.

(1) Compromise with the standards of the world. Unfortunately, the modern American church seems to have been more influenced by society, rather than society being affected by the church. Recent Gallup polls show a majority of Americans profess to be Christians, but the general spiritual condition of our nation has never been worse. The fact is, although many churches have concentrated on techniques of getting people in the doors, they have not always been as successful in improving their spiritual condition. The Apostle Paul said, *"...beloved, let us cleanse ourselves from all filthiness of the flesh and spirit, perfecting holiness in the fear of God" (2 Corinthians 7:1).*

There is a widespread deficiency in the basic elements of Christian character, ethics and morality. In contrast to past generations, recent counseling statistics show that the ratio of moral dysfunctions among professing Christians closely parallel that of secular society. Domestic violence, drug abuse, alcoholism, sexual immorality and promiscuity are commonly found within the churchgoing populace.

In the 1980's, the Christian divorce rate reached the same deplorable level as that of secular marriages — today more than 50% of all marriages, including those of professing Christians, result in dissolution.

Today's pulpits are virtually silent on the issue of "sin." The church has become more and more like the world. It has sought to be popular and acceptable to society, and in doing so, it has compromised its standards of morality and holiness. The scripture warns, *"Do not love the world or the things in the world. If anyone loves the world, the love of the Father is not in him" (1 John 2:15).*

(2) Apathy toward its mission in the world. By and large, the modern church world has become mostly occupied with what God can do for them, rather than remembering their mission to reach the lost for Christ. We live in a very self-centered society, and rarely do we see churches and believers laying aside their selfish interests to serve the Lord's interests. *"But know this, that in the last days perilous times will come: For men will be lovers of themselves... lovers of pleasure rather than lovers of God" (2 Timothy 3:1,4).*

The scriptures make it very clear that it is the duty of every Christian to take on the task of helping to bring people to the saving message of Christ *(2 Corinthians 5:17-18).* But unfortunately, the statistics show that only a tiny percentage of Christians ever attempt to share their faith with others. This apathy is inexcusable and has contributed to the woes of our society, which can only be remedied by the new birth of Christ in the hearts of sinful men and women. *"...if our gospel is veiled, it is veiled to those who are perishing" (2 Corinthians 4:3).*

— 6 —
What is the most important characteristic of a church?

Without hesitation, **love** is the most significant component of the church. Jesus made it very clear that his entire teaching was hinged upon it. He said, *"You shall love the LORD your God with all your heart, with all your soul, and with all your mind. This is the first and great commandment. And the second is like it: You shall love your neighbor as* *yourself. On these two commandments hang all the Law and the Prophets"* (Matthew 22:37-40).

Jesus went as far as to say that love was the identifying mark of a Christian — that love between the brethren is what identifies us as His disciples, the church. *"By this all will know that you are My disciples, if you have love for one another"* (John 13:35).

The Apostle Peter described love as the highest priority of the church. He said *"...Above all things have fervent love for one another"* (1 Peter 4:8).

Paul also placed precedence upon love in relationship to other spiritual virtues. He wrote, *"And now abide faith, hope, love, these three; but the greatest of these is love"* (1 Corinthians 13:13).

Furthermore, John likewise described that it is not possible to know God apart from love — in fact, he made it crystal clear that any relationship with God was not possible without an extended love for our other brothers and sisters too. *"He who does not love does not know God, for God is love... If someone says, I love God, and hates his brother, he is a liar; for he who does not love his brother whom he has seen, how can he love God whom he has not seen?"* (1 John 4:8,20).

We need to, however, understand the kind of love we're talking about here. Sometimes when we discuss Christian love, there is a lack of understanding of its meaning. The Greeks used three basic words for Love:

(1) EROS - This was the name of the Greek god of love, the son of Aphrodite. The word was used in reference to sexual love, and is the root word for erotic. The characteristic of EROS refers to a self-gratifying, gimmee, gimmee type of love. Perhaps like a small baby's need or want of his parents. It is never used in the text of the New Testament.

(2) PHILEO - This is a humanitarian type of love. It's similar to a give and take, "scratch my back and I'll scratch yours," type of love — such as friendships. It is used in scripture to describe man's kind of love, his kindness or affection.

(3) AGAPE - A giving, sacrificial type of love, without expectation of anything in return. This is God's kind of love — the Christian type of love between our brethren, and between ourselves and God. This is the kind of love we're referring to in the scriptures used here.

More than any other trait, AGAPE love is the church's most important feature. It is the foundation of all of Jesus' teachings — it is the very personality of God, and is the essential proof that shows that one truly knows God. Love is the chief component of spirituality, heading the list of virtues which describe spiritual fruit: *"But the fruit of the Spirit is love [AGAPE], joy, peace, longsuffering, kindness, goodness, faithfulness, gentleness, self-control. Against such there is no law" (Galatians 5:22-23).*

Above all other things in the church, love must be demonstrated, taught and emphasized to the saints. Love will bring about the qualities of harmony, loyalty, and faithfulness that the church needs to thrive. Not only will it help to promote the stability of the fellowship and dissolve division and strife, but love produces the motivation for the church to fulfill its missions — to care about people, to reach out to the lost and needy of our world. Agape love is the spiritual fuel on which the church is powered.

— 7 —
What is the most important doctrine of the church?

The most important doctrine or teaching of the church is none other than "Jesus Christ." So many churches, in the worthy exploration of scripture sometimes begin to place their primary emphasis upon other things, or various aspects of scripture or doctrine. Obviously, every church should teach and proclaim the "whole counsel" and the broad scope of God's Word — but as it relates to Jesus. You see, Jesus is the focal point of all doctrinal teaching. He is the intersection at which all teachings converge. When anything else begins to take center-stage — that is, when anything other than Jesus Christ, such as traditions, doctrines, or interpretations become the primary focus — problems and even deception can enter in.

We are reminded of the Pharisees who held such high regard for the scriptures. They equated their intellectual knowledge of scripture as the basis for spirituality and eternal life. However, Jesus explained to them that the scriptures, themselves, were not the "end," but a

"means" to bring them to the true objective which is Himself —
Jesus Christ! He said to them, *"You search the Scriptures, for in them you
think you have eternal life; and these are they which testify of Me" (John 5:39).*

We live in an hour in which people frequently claim revelations of
so-called deeper truths, which have sometimes served as a diversion
away from the basic character and practical life application of Jesus
Christ. Some claim that they now have so much "deep spiritual
understanding," that they really cannot relate to those who are "less
spiritual" or inferior. This is ridiculous. Such persons may not realize
that although Jesus was our highest example of spirituality, yet he
was so humble, so down-to-earth and simple he could relate simple
practical truths to sinners.

Any intricate, exotic teaching, regardless of how Biblical or
spiritually deep it may seem to be, unless it lifts up Jesus Christ,
together with His character or the practical truths and principles He
taught, is probably irrelevant to you as a Christian. It may even lead
you astray into an attitude of intellectual arrogance, false spiritual
superiority, or heresy. Always remember that the doctrine of Jesus
Christ is Christ-centered, simple and practical. Paul warned believers
from being confused by complicated teachings which would lead
away from the simplicity of Jesus. *"But I fear, lest somehow, as the serpent
deceived Eve by his craftiness, so your minds may be corrupted from the simplicity
that is in Christ" (2 Corinthians 11:3).*

Although Paul was an intellectual giant, trained as a Pharisee at the
feet of the great Jewish scholar, Gamaliel *(Acts 22:3)*, he limited his
preaching to one basic thing: *"For I determined not to know anything
among you except Jesus Christ and Him crucified" (1 Corinthians 2:2).* It is
Jesus that has all the answers to life's problems. It is Jesus that
changes men's lives, if we will but proclaim Him and present Jesus
to the world. *"And I, if I am lifted up from the earth, will draw all peoples to
Myself" (John 12:32).*

In particular, the resurrection of Jesus is the foundation of the
doctrine of Jesus Christ, and is the great cornerstone of the entire
Christian faith. The Apostle Paul said that without the resurrection,
the whole concept of Christianity would be invalidated. *"And if
Christ is not risen, then our preaching is vain and your faith is also vain" (1
Corinthians 15:14)*

— 8 —
How can I select a good church?

It goes without saying that every believer should have a church home where he or she attends regularly. If you are not a part of such a fellowship, the following advice will be invaluable to your search.

(1) Look for a church prayerfully. As is the case with all other aspects of a Christian's decisions, you should begin your search for a church by seeking the Lord's direction. The Bible promises, *"In all your ways acknowledge Him, and He shall direct your paths" (Proverbs 3:6).*

(2) Look for good prospects. You might search for listings in the newspaper or in the yellow pages. Always seek the congregation which is evangelical and Bible-based. A referral from a trusted Christian friend is the most frequent way people are introduced to a church. A visit or two is helpful, but there is no way to really evaluate a church without attending most services for a month or so.

(3) Look for a fellowship of believers. A church is not a building, nor is it merely a ministry, it is the body of Christ. So seek people who love the Lord and who love each other — people that will love you and people to whom you can give your love.

(4) Look for the church that preaches the Bible. Seek the fellowship that has sound doctrine, proclaims the whole counsel of God's Word, and sincerely lifts up the Lord Jesus Christ in worship and in all they do. Much of this can be discovered by observation, but most fellowships have a printed statement of their doctrines they will provide to you upon request. For clarity, you can speak with the pastor or leadership about their beliefs or practices.

(5) Look for a church that has good character. Seek a loving, peaceful, stable church which has a pastor devoted to godliness, prayer and the word, which are more important than his eloquence, education or charisma.

(6) Look for a church that will help draw you closer to Christ. It might be nice to find a church where the music is flawless, where the seats are padded and the minister dismisses promptly at noon. But more importantly, you need a church that cares about you and will help meet your spiritual needs — that will inspire you to grow, and will motivate you toward the aspirations of God. You need a church whose preaching and teaching will not merely appease or entertain you, but will boldly challenge you to advance beyond your comfort zones to live toward God's high ideals.

(7) Look for a church where you can become committed. In many ways, your relationship with the church is similar to a marriage — what you get out of it depends on what you put into it. The only church in which you will ever grow and mature spiritually is the fellowship where you will commit yourself and get involved — where you will care about more than your own self-centered needs and reach out to minister to the needs of others — where the people submit themselves to God and to each other, and where they will both encourage you and hold you accountable.

(8) Seek that fellowship that is attempting to reach lost souls. Find the fellowship that is seeking to bring lives to Christ, both in their community and on foreign mission fields. Such a church understands its purpose on the earth and will provide a healthy environment in which to grow.

(9) Look for a church where you can contribute. I've often heard the comparison made between a church and a restaurant — a place where you get served a meal. But actually, the church is more like a "pot luck dinner". What you bring with you to church is added to the content of the meal. Your contribution to the gathering helps to make it what it is. Therefore, seek the church where you can roll up your sleeves and help them to minister to others. Don't look for a church that will only "serve you," but look for a church in which you can "serve." Always remember, a church is the combination of what its people are. So if you want your church to be the best it can be, you must be the best you can be. A church can never rise above what its individual members are.

(10) Be ready to accept the individuality of a church. Frequently people look for a church like the one in which they got saved, or like one they see on TV. But this is futile, because even though a church might have the same beliefs or similarities as another, every church is distinct and different in its personality, just like people are. Always use the Bible as the standard to measure a church — not other churches.

(11) Look for a church with reasonable expectations. Don't bother looking for a perfect church, because there aren't any. In every church you will find people who are wonderful and some who aren't. Jesus taught that it was common for weeds to be found growing together with the crops *(Matthew 13:24-30)*. Also, in every church, you'll find some things done well, and others that are not. Don't worry about finding a perfect pastor, either. Trust me, they're all human and will make mistakes. But look for a pastor who is sincere, who is trying his best to live a godly moral life, and who is proclaiming the uncompromised Word of God. In short, be content with the church that is doing the best they can.

There are probably many good churches in your community. Trust the Lord to guide you to the fellowship where he wants you, and become faithful there. Don't be a church hopper — bouncing around to one church after another each week. God wants you to be submitted to the accountability of spiritual leaders who will help you and even correct you when necessary *(Hebrews 13:17)*, and this isn't possible unless you are rooted somewhere. Don't have a neglectful attitude, going to church only when you feel like it. Attend faithfully and show up on time. Serve your church at least as diligently as you would your employer. Remember, the Lord views your attitude toward His church as your attitude toward Him *(Matthew 25:40)*, so serve the Lord in a way that if He were your employer, you wouldn't get fired.

— 9 —
Does a church's size indicate anything about its spirituality or success?

Not necessarily. There are excellent churches which have grown to great size. But there is a danger in using largeness as a standard to measure success. Size does not depend as much on spirituality as it may many other factors. There are many smaller churches which uphold the same truths as faithfully as the larger, but have never experienced the same degree of growth.

Most large churches claim that their size is a result of the ability to satisfactorily "minister" to the needs of a broad range of people. If this is so, then it would necessitate a broad range of gifts, talents, programs, and social factors to be represented in a congregation. Although their preaching, teaching, and spiritual fervor may not be any greater than many other smaller churches, they have been able to "multiply" that ministry by training others to use their gifts, and developing a network of personal interaction and care for one another. Many smaller churches have excellent preachers and ministries but may not have developed all the gifts which lend toward this type of growth. This certainly does not make them inferior.

While there are more large churches today than ever before, they still only make up a small percentage of the total number. According to a recent study by the Hartford Institute for Religion Research, a majority of churches, 59 percent, have an attendance of somewhere less than 100, another 35% have between 100 and 499, while 4% have attendances between 500 and 999. Roughly 2% of churches have attendances of more than 1000, with as many as 1,200+ "mega churches" of more than 2,000 weekly attenders.[1] Today, the largest 10% of congregations contain about half of all churchgoers,[2] however the remaining 90% of smaller churches are equally as important to the overall national church attendance.

Percentile of U.S. Church Attendance [1]	
Attendance	Percent
7 - 99	59%
100 - 499	35%
500 - 999	4%
1000+	2%

Keep in mind that if attendance alone were used to measure a church's effectiveness in its community, it would need to be balanced against the population of the community in which it resides. The church of 200 located in a population area of 10,000 has reached 2% of its citizens, while a church that runs 1,000 in a population of 500,000 has reached only one fifth of 1%. In this case, the smaller church would actually be ten times more effective than the larger.

Large numbers obviously indicate that something is being done that is appealing to people. But there are many other things, not especially based on truth or spirituality, which draw crowds. Churches may attract numbers with marketing and promotional skills, sensational entertainment or attractions, a stimulating social environment, or opportunities for participation. Or they may simply offer an appealing message that people want to hear — providing the "scratch" for those with itching ears. *"For the time will come when they will not endure sound doctrine, but according to their own desires, because they have itching ears, they will heap up for themselves teachers;" (2 Timothy 4:3).* Any organization, club or church can grow as long as they "offer something that appeals to people," and there are many ways to do this that have nothing to do with Jesus Christ or Christianity.

Popularity or growing numbers do not necessarily give credence to any religion or teaching, and in fact, can often be the mark of compromise or deception. Islam, for instance, is said to be the fastest growing religion in the world, but is a false religion. The Jehovah's Witnesses have been called one of the most rapidly growing religious groups in the United States, increasing from 373,430 members in 1950 to more than 1.2 million in 2012 — but the JW's are a cult. The Mormons are another church cult which are growing at an overwhelming pace, from 4.1 million in 1990 to nearly 6.2 million in 2012.[3] Some sociologists even classify professional football as the largest of America's religions, drawing the greatest of all Sunday congregations, but the NFL doesn't seek to lead anyone to Heaven.

We must remember that the Christian message of the cross has traditionally been unpopular, even to those quite willing to accept the other more savory aspects of the Gospel *(Philippians 3:18-19).* From the Bible, we may recall the great popularity of Jesus while he was performing miracles and distributing fish and loaves. But later, fearing reprisal for their identification with Christ, there was far less attraction at the most sacred event in history as Jesus gave his life for our sins on the cross.

If crowds alone were used as the criterion of success, then Hell would prove to be far more successful than Heaven. Jesus made it clear that the way which leads to life is not popular and relatively few will find it. *"Enter by the narrow gate; for wide is the gate and broad is the way that leads to destruction, and there are many who go in by it. Because narrow is the gate and difficult is the way which leads to life, and there are few who find it" (Matthew 7:13-14).*

— 10 —
Why do many churches place an emphasis on church growth?

There is no purer motive for a church than to want its pews filled with people who hunger for God. After all, the primary purpose of the church is to reach the masses with the saving message of Christ, *"...not desiring any to perish, but all to come to repentance" (2 Peter 3:9).*

However, a Biblical mandate for church growth is probably best associated with Jesus' commission for His church to go and *"...make disciples" (Matthew 28:19).* Not only does God want persons to be saved, but He wants them to be discipled into spiritually mature believers who will carry on His ministry — and it requires the environment of the church to do this. There, the believer is taught the word, has the guidance and correction of spiritual authority, and through worship and fellowship, will develop spiritual virtues, including a deeper love for God and others. Consequently, the Lord not only wants people to get saved, He wants them joined to a local body of believers, just as they were in the early church. *"...the Lord added to the church daily those who were being saved" (Acts 2:47).*

One of the prominent authorities on church growth, Dr. C. Peter Wagner, views this as the strongest motive for a growing congregation. He says "Evangelism is not only reaching people with the Gospel message and bringing them to a decision for Christ, it is making them disciples... To evangelize is to present Christ Jesus in the power of the Holy Spirit that men and women shall come to put their trust in God through Him, to accept Him as their Savior, and serve Him as their King in the fellowship of His church. This ties commitment to Christ with commitment to the church. God's will is clear... He wants men and women everywhere to come to Him and into the church of Jesus Christ."[1]

A desire for a growing church is one thing — but actually experiencing it is another. Despite the great emphasis of the American church growth movement, with scores of how-to books, tapes and seminars, the majority of churches are still not growing. Perhaps the reason for this lies with misdirected priorities — "getting the cart before the horse."

To illustrate this, some years ago a pastor described his prolonged struggle to get his church to grow. He tried many of the popular strategies and methods with little success. He finally withdrew from this emphasis, deciding instead to refocus his ministry toward the spiritual discipleship of his small flock. He determined that Christ would be the core of the ministry in every way possible. He personally rededicated his life to Christ's example of godliness, prayer and the Word — more than ever, Jesus became the center of his preaching — he constantly taught people to follow the love, character and example of Christ. To his surprise, the church began to do what it wouldn't previously... it started to grow. And as he continued his Christ-centered ministry, the church eventually grew to considerable size. Without realizing, he stumbled across important priorities that relate to church growth.

First, we must remember, Jesus is the one who builds His church, not us. He said, *"...I will build My church..." (Matthew 16:18).* There are numerous philosophies and methods of church growth being circulated today, but Jesus must always be at the center. Pastors and leaders need to use caution lest they find themselves trying to substitute man's wisdom and methodology in the place of the Lord. The Bible says, *"Unless the LORD builds the house, They labor in vain who build it..." (Psalms 127:1).*

Secondly, the church needs to concentrate on its main objective, to live Jesus and preach Jesus. During His earthly ministry, Christ never had a problem drawing a crowd. Therefore, if Jesus is effectively personified in the church, by being lifted up in our message and lifestyle, His presence will have the same drawing power to bring souls to His church. Growth is not really the primary goal, but is the natural derivative of lifting up Jesus Christ. *"And I, if I am lifted up from the earth, will draw all peoples to Myself"* *(John 12:32).*

With Jesus in the center stage of our philosophy, there are many concepts, authored by many outstanding leaders, which may be helpful to the church growth process. Without attempting to list them all, there are three basic issues that every church should take in consideration:

(1) The Profile of a Growing Church — It has been said that when a church begins to absorb and emulate the character of Jesus, it will exhibit the qualities and climate that naturally lend toward growth.

My personal, pastoral philosophy has always been that "the seeds for growth are in the fruit." In other words, it is a fact of nature that within the fruit of each species (such as apples, peaches or grapes), there are seeds that will yield the offspring of future harvests. Similarly, the character of spiritual fruit in the church bears spiritual seed that contributes toward the harvest of souls. *"But the fruit of the Spirit is love, joy, peace, longsuffering, kindness, goodness, faithfulness, gentleness, self-control"* *(Galatians 5:22-23).* Spiritual fruit is the loving, sweet personality of Jesus that warms the heart. Therefore, development of the spiritual character of the church contributes toward church growth.

Below are listed the frequent traits of a growing congregation, each of which can be related to spiritual fruit and a mature relationship with Christ:

   (a) Love — a genuine care for other people.

   (b) Commitment — a deep sense of direction and purpose.

   (c) Openness — to new people and new ideas.

   (d) Unity — respect for, and harmony with the team.

   (e) Flexibility — willingness to make changes when needed.

   (f) Vision — an attitude and expectancy for growth.

(2) The Primary Agent of Church Growth — There is the frequent misconception that church growth comes as a result of the wonderful preaching and warm personality of the pastor, or because of the visitation programs, or by conducting great crusades with well-known speakers. All these things have their value, however statistics show that the reason for increased numbers originates elsewhere. The Institute for American Church Growth interviewed 10,000 church attenders to learn how they came into their church.[2]

The percentage of people shown below attended for the following reasons:

Reasons People Start Attending Church	
2.0%	Due to a special Need
3.0%	Just walked in
6.0%	Because of the Pastor's influence
1.0%	In response to visitation from the church
5.0%	Due to interest in Sunday School
0.5%	In response to a special crusade
3.0%	Because of interest in a particular program
79.0%	From the influence of a friend or relative

It may come as a surprise that the most potent agent of church growth is the person in the pew — and the majority of those who will come into the church consist of their own family or friends. The church begins to grow when Christ's body identify themselves with His great commission, to "go into their world" and reach out to the persons they already know *(Mark 16:15)*.

(3) The Glue of Church Growth — It's one thing to get people to come to church, and it's quite another to get them to stay. The assimilation of individuals into the church is probably the most important element to growth. **Generally speaking, the two great reasons why persons stick in a church are:**

(a) Relationship bonds, and

(b) A task or role of service that provides a sense of purpose.[3]

Finding ways to help people develop relationships in the church, and getting them involved in its ministries will help to stop the revolving door tendency, and result in a growing adherence to the church.

It is believed that these two church adhesives are best developed in the environment of a condensed sub group, sometimes referred to as a "cell." The smaller climate better enables people to get to know each other and develop "relationship bonds," something that's not very easy in a larger setting. And in the smaller group, everyone is able to be used in their gift or a special "role of service," something not always possible when there are many gifted people in a large church. In some churches, Sunday School classes or other specific groups for youth, men or women fulfill the need for such cell groups. Other churches use a concept of home groups, where small gatherings meet for fellowship and ministry. It is a truth that for a church to grow larger, it must also grow smaller at the same time.

— 11 —
Is it necessary to be a member of a particular church to be saved?

No. Becoming a member of a good local church is great, but this in itself doesn't save a person. Salvation is based on a personal faith relationship with Jesus Christ, not whether a name is on a church membership role. The Bible says that *"Whoever calls upon the name of the LORD shall be saved" (Romans 10:13)*. As a matter of fact, there may be many persons whose names appear on a church membership roster, but who have never experienced a relationship with Christ.

At the moment that a person places their faith in Christ as their Lord and Savior, they instantly become a member of the universal church, the body of Christ *(Ephesians 5:30)*. This is not a building or an organization, but is the combination of all true believers throughout the whole world. In this sense, a person cannot be saved without being a member of Christ's church.

After a person receives Christ, and becomes a member of His body, it would be advisable to join a good local church. Every believer needs to be committed to a loving, healthy fellowship where they can receive consistent ministry, and can grow under the preaching of the Bible.

Most churches offer some form of membership, however there are those who question its premise, contending that there was no such official affiliation in the early church. But theologians cite that without local church membership, or something on this order, both the church and the individual believer are challenged from meeting their spiritual obligations.

Consider that God's word instructs every believer to "obey" and "submit" to the "authority" of spiritual leaders. In our modern culture of mavericks, these words are often met with contempt. However, we do not speak of a controlling or oppressive relationship, but one based on mutual love and respect — for the spiritual protection and progress of God's flock. *"Obey them that have the rule over you, and submit yourselves: for they watch for your souls, as they that must give account, that they may do it with joy, and not with grief: for that is unprofitable for you" (Hebrews 13:17)*. It says that our spiritual shepherds, to whom we are voluntarily submitted, "watch" (*AGRUPNEO*, remain awake) for our souls, and are even charged with the responsibility of giving an account on our behalf.

Logically, if Christians are supposed to submit to spiritual leaders, this necessitates attending a church where such leaders can be found. But how do the spiritual leaders know who are submitted to their authority? Who are the ones for whom they will give an account? Certainly not everyone who merely attends the church services. In my early days of pastoring, I quickly discovered that many who come to church wish to derive benefit from the various ministries, yet remain aloof from any sense of commitment or accountability. And by what means does the flock know if they are submitted, or to whom?

Local church membership is a way to answer these questions. It is the expression of a mutual accountability between a member and their spiritual leaders. It tells the minister that he is "your" pastor, and that "you" are his responsibility. Church membership is a commitment to be accountable, responsible, and to be a participant rather than a spectator. It's a declaration that you can be counted on to be there, to help support the church with your time, labor, and financial support.

How important it is for the church to have people who will commit themselves to its support. Noted church authority, Dr. Bruce L. Shelley, says that some people who attend the church are like a hitchhiker that wants a free ride. *"He assumes no responsibility for the money needed to purchase the car, the gas to run it or the cost of maintenance. He expects a comfortable ride and adequate safety. He assumes the driver has insurance covering him in case of an accident. He thinks nothing of requesting that he be taken to a certain place even though it means extra miles or inconvenience to his host... then consider the person who demands all the benefits and privileges of the church without feeling the slightest responsibility for its support in money, time or service. And if he does not get all he thinks is his by some natural right, he is usually demanding and critical. He too is a hitchhiker."*

Membership is also a commitment to the body of believers, an expression of your love and devotion to the people of God, something which scripture says is necessary to maintain a right relationship with God. Consistent maintenance of our love and fellowship with God's people is evidence that we're walking in His light, and will prevent us from faltering *(1 John 1:7, 1 John 2:10)*. This is the main reason why the scripture discourages absence from church meetings — "they need our love, and we need the practice" *(Hebrews 10:25-26)*.

Another issue that brings credibility to the need for local church membership, is that it may be the only way that certain acts of scriptural discipline can be carried out within the body of Christ. In the unfortunate situation where a believer would resist correction and repentance for certain immoral acts, the scripture authorizes their excommunication from the church *(1 Corinthians 5:1-13)*. However, a person could hardly be dismissed from something they were never accepted into. Dr. Shelley writes, *"Of all the practices of the apostolic churches, surely discipline argues most convincingly for church membership. How could a brother or sister be expelled from a church fellowship if there were no membership?"*

— 12 —
Why should Christians go to church?

For believers, there is no substitute for attending church. Besides something that pleases God, it is necessary for a believer's spiritual well-being. For shut-ins or invalids who aren't able to go to church, the ministries on radio or TV might be the only kind of fellowship or spiritual nourishment that they get. God certainly understands the circumstances of these people, and recognizes the sincerity of their hearts. However, it is a different matter for those who could attend church but are too lazy, or put other things such as entertainment and amusements before God, or who harbor bitterness or indifference toward other believers.

It is important to attend church for the following reasons:

(1) It is an Expression of our Love for God. *"And [they] were continually in the temple praising and blessing God" (Luke 24:53).* Going to church is a tangible expression of our love and worship toward God. It is where we can gather with other believers to bring God offerings of praise, thanks, and honor.

(2) It builds up our Spiritual Strength. *"So then faith comes by hearing, and hearing by the word of God" (Romans 10:17).* Receiving the preaching and teaching of the Word of God increases our faith and builds us up spiritually. Every believer knows what it is to face spiritual conflicts to their faith, and must realize the importance of being fed spiritually so that they can overcome the challenges. Paul states that Christians face a wrestling match with the Devil and his evil spiritual forces, and warns that the church must put on spiritual armor for protection, as it will take everything at our disposal to stand *(Ephesians 6:10-18).* How important that we take every opportunity available to receive ministry and strength from God's Word.

(3) It brings a special visitation of the Lord's Presence. *"For where two or three are gathered together in My name, I am there in the midst of them" (Matthew 18:20).* There is the promise of a special visitation of the Lord's presence whenever two or more gather specifically in the name of Jesus. By implication, this means whenever "Jesus" is the object of gathered prayer, worship, praise, preaching, etc. Even though Jesus resides within the heart of every believer, he honors a gathering in his name by coming in the "midst," with his power, awareness, and anointing. In such a gathering, Christ is able to do things in hearts that he may not at any other time. The scripture says that God inhabits the praise of His people *(Psalms 22:3),* and in such an atmosphere the Holy Spirit will often manifest spiritual gifts that minister to the body of Christ.

(4) It provides fellowship with other Christians. *"But if we walk in the light as He is in the light, we have fellowship with one another, and the blood of Jesus Christ His Son cleanses us from all sin" (1 John 1:7).* Gathering together also has compounded importance to the relationship of the Christian brethren. The Bible makes it clear that a right relationship with God requires a "vertical" and "horizontal" alignment — that is, we must have a vertical fellowship with God and a horizontal fellowship with other believers. It is not possible to love God and refuse to love the brethren. If you have a problem loving other Christians, you have a problem in your relationship with God. Scripture warns us that unforgiveness toward others will void God's forgiveness of our own sins *(Matthew 6:15).* John wrote, *"He who says he is in the light, and hates his brother, is in darkness until now. He who loves his brother abides in the light, and there is no cause for stumbling in him" (1 John 2:9-10).*

One of the most important reasons that we go to church is to practice love toward the brethren in the form of fellowship. The Bible clearly shows that if we have a right relationship with God, we have fellowship with others believers. Keeping ourselves in love and harmony with other believers keeps us humble before God so that Christ's blood can continue to cleanse us from our sins.

(5) It is an act of obedience to God. *"And let us consider one another in order to stir up love and good works, not forsaking the assembling of ourselves together, as is the manner of some, but exhorting one another, and so much the more as you see the Day approaching. For if we sin willfully after we have received the knowledge of the truth, there no longer remains a sacrifice for sins," (Hebrews 10:24-26).*

Not to be forgotten, going to church is also a matter of obedience to God's Word. The writer of the Hebrew epistle tells us not to forsake assembling together, implying that continued absence can lead to willful sin (verse 26). We're supposed to be considerate of our brethren, coming together to help motivate and encourage one another. *"Therefore, to him who knows to do good and does not do it, to him it is sin" (James 4:17).*

(6) It allows accountability to spiritual leadership. *"Obey those who rule over you, and be submissive, for they watch out for your souls, as those who must give account. Let them do so with joy and not with grief, for that would be unprofitable for you" (Hebrews 13:17).*

More strong evidence that proves that we're to be a part of a church fellowship, is that we're told to submit to the authority of spiritual leaders (within the boundaries of God's Word). God designed this system of accountability for the progress and protection of His flock. Obviously, this really isn't possible unless we are a part of an organized fellowship which has identified elders, pastors, or leaders. It is easy to see that one cannot genuinely be under submission to a TV pastor who has never met you. Nor is it possible to be under submission by visiting a different church each week. The Bible tells us to know them that are over us in the Lord *(1 Thessalonians 5:12).* Submission necessitates a commitment and relationship to a local body of believers and to their spiritual leaders.

(7) It combines our spiritual strength in prayer. *"Again I say to you that if two of you agree on earth concerning anything that they ask, it will be done for them by My Father in heaven" (Matthew 18:19).*

The Bible indicates that agreement in prayer with other believers has special favor with God. This agrees with how God has historically blessed the union of His people in battle against their enemies. *"Five of you shall chase a hundred, and a hundred of you shall put ten thousand to flight; your enemies shall fall by the sword before you" (Leviticus 26:8).*

(8) It honors the Lord's Day. *"Remember the Sabbath day, to keep it holy" (Exodus 20:8).* The fourth commandment of the law that God gave Moses was to set aside the seventh day of the week, Saturday, as a holy day to the Lord. This was, and will always remain, the official Sabbath. However, after Jesus rose from the dead on the first day of the week, Sunday, the early Christians began meeting together on this day as well as with the Jewish community in the synagogues on the Sabbath.

History indicates that due to the enmity of the orthodox Jews toward the Christian Jews in their midst, the Jewish Christians were eventually ostracized. And although they were no longer bound to a rigid code of laws *(Galatians 3:10-11, Colossians 2:16),* it is believed that they came to view Sunday as a combined observance of the

Sabbath and the resurrection day of Jesus *(Acts 20:7, 1 Corinthians 16:2)*. This day of Christian worship came to be called the Lord's Day *(Revelations 1:10)*, a day to fellowship in celebration of the resurrection, to worship, pray and study the Word together.

Today, the Christian Jew or gentile, is free from the bondage of the old law. The indwelling of God's spirit has brought a new way for Christians to fulfill the desires of God through His love *(Galatians 5:18, Romans 13:8-10)*. However, the new covenant does not invalidate the relevance of the ten commandments as they pertained to God's wishes for His people. As much as it remains God's desire for man not to kill, steal or commit adultery, God is still very much pleased for believers to honor Him on a day reserved for Him, out of their love for Him and His people.

— 13 —
Why is it so hard to find a perfect church?

Because there aren't any. Churches are made up of people like you and me, who are imperfect. As long as there are human beings involved in anything, there will always be imperfections.

Does it seem strange why there are so many sick people in a hospital? Of course not — that's what a hospital is for. Likewise, it shouldn't be strange to find people with problems in the church. The church is a spiritual hospital, treating patients with the Gospel to make them well. That's what it's for. Jesus said that He didn't come for those who were well, but those who were sick. He said, *"Those who are well have no need of a physician, but those who are sick. I did not come to call the righteous, but sinners, to repentance" (Mark 2:17)*. A church may have many patients, all in different stages of recovery. Some are in terminal or critical condition, others are nearly well, and there are those who have recovered enough to join with the hospital staff in helping to care for the other patients.

Ironically, the imperfections in other believers actually serve a helpful purpose to us. Our close-knit fellowship acts as sandpaper that will smooth out our rough edges. *"As iron sharpens iron, so a man sharpens the countenance of his friend" (Proverbs 27:17)*. Conflict is necessary to refine spiritual character. This is the same way our muscular tissue grows strong, by exercising against resistance. The church is like a spiritual gymnasium for believers to practice their love toward others, who are sometimes less than lovable. Applying spiritual virtues against resistance is what makes us grow strong. Therefore, the weak ones in our midst need our love and ministry, and we need them in order to grow mature in our love and patience. *"We then who are strong ought to bear with the scruples of the weak, and not to please ourselves" (Romans 15:1).*

It's remarkable how we are able to see our true spiritual condition through the reflection of our brethren. They are like "mirrors" in which we can see ourselves as we really are. If anyone thinks he is spiritual, just get close to your brethren, and you'll see what's really inside you. If there's hate or a lack of love, it will become obvious. Regardless of how unspiritual your brethren might be, YOUR intolerance and impatience is not their fault. It is the characteristic of your immaturity - a weakness in YOU that needs to be perfected. This is why some people choose not to fellowship with other Christians, because they see their own sins and blemishes revealed in their relationship with the brethren. If we remain an "island" to ourselves, we will never have to face up to the spiritual immaturities within us.

To illustrate this, I had a classmate in school who was very hard to get along with. He was an only child. His younger brother died as a baby, and his parents over-compensated for their sense of loss by heaping all their love upon the surviving brother. They gave him virtually anything he wanted, never made him do any chores, and nearly always let him have his way. The result was, he was a spoiled child and could never get along with anyone. All through life he had a rough time keeping friends or relationships because his parents had trained him to think that life was supposed to revolve around himself. If only he had been raised with other brothers or sisters, he could have learned to share, give-and-take, to be more patient with others of different views and preferences.

The environment of the church will always have both strengths and weaknesses. Sometimes it will encourage us, and other times, challenge us. But for the person who is truly devoted to Christ, the church will always serve to make us stronger, more mature Christians.

— 14 —
Why is there so much dishonesty and immorality among preachers and church leaders?

This view is grossly exaggerated. Due to the highly publicized sins of well-known preachers in recent times, cynicism and skepticism of all Christian leaders has risen sharply. The flood of media attention over the sins of a few created a false impression that the majority of preachers, especially those who minister on TV or who openly request financial support, must be sinister or deceptive. This is not true.

Over the years, I have known hundreds of well-known evangelical ministers, including TV preachers, and I know most to be godly, honest, and moral people. It is a great injustice to many wonderful, Christ-like spiritual leaders to stereotype them along with those of lesser integrity.

We do sadly recognize that a small percentage of preachers have been guilty of shameful practices. In such cases, it appears that most started out with sincere intentions, but somehow later fell prey to the temptations that came their way. I personally knew a world-famous evangelist who fell into sin and scandal. When he first started in the ministry, I knew him to be humble, sincere and Godly. However, fame and affluence brought temptations which corrupted his integrity. How sad it was — how devastating for the body of Christ when his sins were aired before the public.

We cannot make excuse for their sins, but at the same token, we must realize that Satan does work harder to tempt spiritual leaders to fall, knowing that if they do there will be a chain-reaction of casualties to the body of Christ.

Backsliding, sin, and hypocrisy are nothing new to the ranks of the church. Paul wrote about false brethren *(2 Corinthians 11:26)*, false apostles *(2 Corinthians 11:13)*, and specifically mentioned one of his co-workers who had backslidden. *"...for Demas has forsaken me, having loved this present world..." (2 Timothy 4:10).* There have always been, and will always be, believers, including preachers, who falter. But we can't discount all preachers because of the sins of a few.

I can remember a time or two as a kid, unwittingly biting into a wormy apple, only to quickly spit out the pieces in disgust. Those experiences left a bad taste in my mouth, but it didn't cause me to give up eating apples. I simply learned to look more closely before sticking things in my mouth.

So don't let the bad taste of a few bad apples spoil your appreciation for all ministers. Before you "bite" into anyone's ministry, you have the right to inspect their fruit *(Galatians 5:22-24)*. This is how the Bible teaches us to spot false prophets. *"Beware of false prophets, who come to you in sheep's clothing, but inwardly they are ravenous wolves. You will know them by their fruits. Do men gather grapes from thornbushes or figs from thistles? Even so, every good tree bears good fruit, but a bad tree bears bad fruit"* *(Matthew 7:15-17).*

God has chosen for godly men to be His messengers and to help point lives to our Savior *(Ephesians 4:11-12)*, but we must always remember that the basis of our faith is the Lord Jesus Christ, not preachers or anyone else. Men are still only human and are subject to failure. So keep your focus upon Jesus. He will never fail you. *"...looking unto Jesus, the author and finisher of our faith..." (Hebrews 12:2).*

— 15 —
How can I recognize a genuine man of God?

(1) Compare his message and ministry to the Bible. See if what he has to say, lines up with scripture. God's Word is the foundation upon which every true man of God will base his life, ministry and message. *"All Scripture is given by inspiration of God, and is profitable for doctrine, for reproof, for correction, for instruction in righteousness" (2 Timothy 3:16).* Jesus said *"...My doctrine is not Mine, but His who sent Me" (John 7:16).*

(2) Check to see if Jesus Christ is the center. Who does he attempt to lift up and glorify? Himself or Christ? A real man of God doesn't seek to promote himself, but seeks to glorify Christ in everything he does or says. *"He who speaks from himself seeks his own glory; but He who seeks the glory of the One who sent Him is true, and no unrighteousness is in Him" (John 7:18).* (See also 1 Corinthians 12:3)

(3) Inspect his fruit. As we have said, the Bible says that we shall know them by their fruits *(Matthew 7:16)*. Just like preachers, a lot of trees may look alike from a distance, but a close inspection of the fruit hidden among the branches will reveal their differences. Fruit is the natural product of a species which provides unmistakable identification.

If an alleged man of God is truly rooted in fellowship with Christ, he will obviously bear Christ-like fruit *(John 15:4-5)*, not corrupt, immoral qualities. In Paul's epistle to the church of Galatia, he gave a description of the kind of spiritual fruit that should be a natural product in every believer whose life is in harmony with Christ, and contrasted this with the bad fruit of the works of the flesh:

Works of the Flesh

Galatians 5:19 "Now the works of the flesh are evident, which are: adultery, fornication, uncleanness, licentiousness,
5:20 idolatry, sorcery, hatred, contentions, jealousies, outbursts of wrath, selfish ambitions, dissensions, heresies,
5:21 envy, murders, drunkenness, revelries, and the like; of which I tell you beforehand, just as I also told you in time past, that those who practice such things will not inherit the kingdom of God."

Fruit of the Spirit

Galatians 5:22 "But the fruit of the Spirit is love, joy, peace, longsuffering, kindness, goodness, faithfulness,
5:23 gentleness, self-control. Against such there is no law."

Persons who exhibit the works of the flesh are what we call "led by the flesh," and those who bear the fruit of the Spirit are "led by the Spirit." When we speak of "led," we refer to that nature which we choose to follow, whether the Spirit of Christ or the rebellious flesh.

How important it is that every Christian is genuinely led by the Spirit — but even more so for spiritual leaders, as it is the Holy Spirit which also leads us unto all truth *(John 16:13)*. If any spiritual leader does not bear spiritual fruit, he is not genuinely led by the Spirit of God, and if not led by God's Spirit, neither can we risk that his teachings, ministry, or alleged revelations are led of God's Spirit either! Jesus gave us this fruit test to protect us from deceivers. *"You will know them by their fruits..." (Matthew 7:16).*

It is clear that any preacher or purported man of God who exhibits the immoral works of the flesh is definitely not led by God's Spirit. Furthermore, this lifestyle pattern is evidence of an absence of a personal relationship with God, as it states bluntly that *"those who practice such things will not inherit the kingdom of God" (Galatians 5:21).*

It is biblical and necessary for Christians to examine the fruit of their leaders. However, exercise caution. "Fruit inspection" is not meant to be the same thing as fault finding. Examination of fruit should be confined to spiritual standards necessary for leadership, not every little personality trait, habit, or preference. Constant criticism and finding fault must be avoided, lest we discourage our godly leaders and find ourselves serving the purpose of the Devil as an "accuser of the brethren" *(Revelations 12:10).*

— 16 —
Do signs and wonders prove whether a man is of God or not?

During my years of ministry I have seen scores of genuine healings and other supernatural manifestations of the Holy Spirit. Miracles produced by the power of God indeed bear witness of Christ's reality and are still a vital part of His ministry plan for today's church *(Hebrews 13:8).* Certainly, there are men of God who have been greatly used in gifts of healings, miracles, and other such manifestations. However, signs and wonders by themselves, cannot necessarily prove whether a man is of God or not.

Signs and wonders were "among" the identifying characteristics that accompanied the ministry of Jesus and His Apostles *(2 Corinthians 12:12, Acts 2:22),* but would not have authenticated their ministry without the combination of other traits.

The Bible says that signs will inevitably follow believers *(Mark 16:17).* But again, without the other evidences of Christianity, miracles ALONE, cannot confirm the authenticity of believers. The rest of that passage says that the Lord worked with them, confirming the Word through the accompanying signs *(Mark 16:20).* You see, signs, wonders and miracles are really intended to bring confirmation to "the Word, the Lord Jesus Christ," not necessarily the believers. Whenever God truly performs miracles, it is intended to bring credibility to the Gospel and to glorify Jesus Christ.

Jesus specifically warned that the claim of performing miraculous or wonderful acts of ministry in the name of the Lord is not proof of a man's spiritual authenticity. As remarkable as it seems, in the day of judgment there will be some professed miracle workers that the Lord will say that He never knew. *"Many will say to Me in that day, Lord, Lord, have we not prophesied in Your name, cast out demons in Your name, and done many wonders in Your name? And then I will declare to them, I never knew you; depart from Me, you who practice lawlessness!" (Matthew 7:22-23)*. (See also 2 *Corinthians* 11:13-14)

It is a dangerous thing to assume that a man is of God, solely on the basis of apparent signs and wonders, for the following reasons:

(1) How can you ascertain the genuineness of a miracle? The appearance of miracles can be cleverly fabricated. Not long ago, Christian leaders were stunned when an investigator publicly exposed a respected, well-known evangelist for staging phony miracles. The evangelist had a reputation for calling people out of a congregation by the word of knowledge and would appear to supernaturally know personal details such as their disease, their name or even their address.

Shocking evidence was uncovered how the evangelist's wife would move through the audience and interview persons about personal details, and then use a miniature electronic transmitter to communicate this with her husband, who had a tiny receiver in his ear. The investigator had discovered the radio frequency used, and tape recorded the actual voice of the evangelist's wife as she described the illnesses and details to her husband on the stage. They were caught red handed. The pretense was over.

In another incident several years ago, a small-time preacher was curiously known to always ask people to take off their shoes before praying for them. It was eventually revealed that he had wired the outer casing of his microphone with a small electrical voltage and wore rubber soled shoes. When he would lay hands on people who were standing on a well-grounded concrete floor, they would receive a light electrical jolt to make them think that it was the power of

God. The preacher was protected from voltage by his insulated shoes.

But even before electronic gadgets, charlatans were exposed for hiring pretenders to throw down crutches, jump out of wheel chairs, or give false testimony of some great miracle.

Many sincere Christian people find it difficult to believe that there could be such deliberate deceptions, especially by those who use the name of Jesus. But this is exactly why deceivers are able to fool the believers. They take advantage of the sincerity of naive people who simply don't know the Biblical way to spot false prophets.

(2) Genuine miracles sometimes occur in spite of counterfeit preachers. It would seem reasonable to conclude that all alleged miracles performed by phony preachers must also be fabricated. But this is not so. One of the biggest unsolved mysteries is why genuine miracles have occurred in association with alleged preachers who have been proven to be fakes.

Many people can still remember the ministry of "Marjo," the famous Pentecostal "boy" preacher of the 1950's. He was just a child when his parents taught him to memorize and preach eloquent, Biblical sermons. Because of his youth and the claim of great miracles which followed his ministry, he was a novelty to the church world and attracted great crowds to hear him preach the Gospel. During those years, many considered him to be a rising young prophet and would drive for miles to be prayed for by the boy evangelist. Numerous people were saved and healed in his meetings.

When Marjo came of age, he shocked the world by revealing that his years as the boy preacher had only been a masquerade, a scheme invented by his parents to make money. Indeed, the attraction had raked in big profits. Marjo admitted that his participation had never been more than a scam forced upon him by his parents. He had never sincerely believed the things he had been taught to memorize or say. Ironically, Marjo eventually went to Hollywood where he remains as an actor to this day.

But left behind from this shrewd deception were scores of people who actually came to Christ through the Gospel which Marjo preached. Genuine healings were proved and documented which had occurred in Marjo's crusades. Though his ministry was fraudulent, amazingly, the Gospel messages which he memorized and preached had an unexpected effect. God genuinely "confirmed His Word with signs following," even though the messenger was a fake. The souls who were saved and miracles which occurred were never an approval of the boy preacher, but were the confirmation of the power and truth of the Gospel of Jesus Christ!

To us, it might seem better for God to withhold miracles from being connected with spurious and unholy figures, but to do this would be an injustice to the integrity and truth of His Word. Besides, if we had to wait around for preachers to become perfectly Holy, we might never see miracles. God's Word will bring faith *(Romans 10:17)*, and wherever there is faith in God's word, signs will follow. Signs and miraculous answers to prayer will follow them that believe *(Mark 11:24)*.

This point was made clear in scripture when Peter and John came across the lame man begging for alms at the beautiful gate. They had no money to give him, but they offered something else of greater value. They commanded him to rise and walk through the name of Jesus! Incredibly, the crippled man stood to his feet and began to leap, praising God for his healing. Those who witnessed this miracle were astonished, and were undoubtedly in awe of the Apostles. But Peter immediately shot down any misdirected impressions of credit. So when Peter saw it, he responded, *"Men of Israel, why do you marvel at this? Or why look so intently at us, as though by our own power or godliness we had made this man walk?" (Acts 3:12).* The Apostles disavowed that this healing had anything to do with their own power or holiness, but was due to faith in the name of Jesus *(Acts 3:16).*

But whose faith? The lame man's or the Apostles? This is another one of the mysteries. Many people may sometimes assume that the faith comes from the "anointed" preacher or the person doing the praying. But in reality, it could be the faith of the sick person, the congregation, or the combination of them all.

(3) Supernatural gifts are irrevocable. Many theologians believe that spiritual gifts are initially given only to Godly, Spirit-filled people. But later, if they become corrupt, or even deny the faith, God will not withdraw the gift. Support for this idea comes from scripture which states, *"For the gifts and the calling of God are irrevocable"* (Romans 11:29). If this interpretation is correct, this would be further explanation why signs and wonders might accompany false prophets, and further evidence why we should never use miracles, alone, as a way to identify true men of God.

Others hold the opinion that spiritual gifts are never actually given to individuals as their possession. This view is that the gifts are given only to the "body of Christ." While God uses men to display the "manifestations" of His Spirit, yet they are not the property of the man. In this case, God might use whatever vessel is available, despite its impurity, because of His love and desire to bless the body. It's not to the credit of the man, but to the credit of God who loves His people and would do anything to bless them.

— 17 —
Can real miracles and wonders be expected to occur in the church today?

Yes. Genuine miracles will occur in response to prayer and faith placed in the promises of God's Word. God's power is as potent today as it was in the days of the early apostles. *"Jesus Christ is the same yesterday, today, and forever"* (Hebrews 13:8). Indeed, God has raised up specific, anointed individuals, who have been used mightily in gifts of miracles and healings *(1 Corinthians 12:9-10)*. However, the miraculous is not confined to a select few, but will follow the sincere prayer of any Christian who will believe the Word, as James wrote, *"The effective, fervent prayer of a righteous man avails much"* (James 5:16). Any follower of Christ can believe what the Bible says, with the expectation for God to answer prayers and bring miracles in accordance to scripture. *"...these signs will follow those who believe..."* (Mark 16:17).

For many years of my early ministry, I preached the full Gospel of Jesus Christ, leading many people to Christ, praying for the sick and oppressed and seeing a great many miracles. But I regret to say that miracles have never been commonplace. I had come to accept this as a matter of fact, until the first time that I traveled overseas to minister in a third-world nation. On this missionary journey, I was startled by the spiritual hunger of the people and their eagerness to place their faith in the Gospel that I preached. But most amazing, as I prayed for the sick, nearly every person was healed. There were many other miracles. In a few days, I was teaching the new converts to lay their hands on the sick, and they began to see miracles too.

These events were so remarkable that I was in awe for days. It was as if I was living in the book of Acts! Yet I and my preaching was no different than it had been back in the states. My prayer life was not any more intense, nor did I feel that my faith was any stronger. But I saw abundant results and miracles unlike anything I had ever seen before. At first I could find no explanation for this great contrast. But I later began to realize that there was a difference in the way the people believed. These simple people had a simple faith. They didn't debate or rationalize, they simply believed what the Bible said.

Many people have a great hunger to see miracles today. But unfortunately, some tend to run after the signs and wonders more than they seek the "Lord" of the miracles. The truth is, the miraculous can happen in any church with any group of believers, if they will seek God's face and believe on His Word. Jesus said, *"And all things, whatever you ask in prayer, believing, you will receive"* (Matthew 21:22).

— 18 —
Why are preachers and ministries always after everybody's money?

This is not the case with all. Again, we must avoid the trap of stereotyping ministers. Obviously there are operating costs and expenses to maintain any ministry, and there are many Christian organizations which deal with the issue of offerings and fund raising very graciously and admirably.

We can empathize with those who may have a negative attitude. Every American already knows what it is to wade through bushels of junk mail jammed in their mailbox daily, and Christian people are especially inundated with appeals for money. Most Christian programs on TV or radio spend a lot of attention on heart-wrenching pleas for offerings, and if you subscribe to Christian periodicals or send donations to various radio or TV ministers, you're probably used to receiving their numerous monthly appeal letters. In addition, your name and address has likely been passed on to other ministries or charities, seeking eligible contributors. We then go to church and give our tithes and offerings to the Lord, but may hear more appeals for other worthwhile projects: the building program, local evangelism, the support of missionaries, the youth group, the poor, the needy, etc. Gimmee, gimmee, gimmee. It seems to never stop.

It's not surprising why people have become weary with constant appeals for money — we really can't blame them. But at the same time, we must be careful not to become critical and abandon the spreading of the Gospel because of the abuses of a few. It is crucial that the message of Jesus Christ be delivered to the world. It is a matter of their life or death! *"Let him know that he who turns a sinner from the error of his way will save a soul from death..."* (James 5:20).

Many become offended by ministries who appeal for financial support because they simply don't understand how important it is for the message of the Gospel to reach the masses, and how costly that can be. You see, the Bible says that our world is lost in sin, destined to burn for eternity in hell, and only the Gospel can avert this tragedy. The Lord is... *"not willing that any should perish but that all should come to repentance"* (2 Peter 3:9).

Out of His love for us, God sent His own son, Jesus, as a remedy for the terminal illness of sin. Persons can be spared the endless eternal suffering, and spend eternity in Heaven, only if they place their faith in Christ's substitutionary death for their own sins and make him Lord of their lives. The Bible says that Jesus Christ is the only way that anyone can ever escape the horrible judgment of the lake of fire. Jesus said, *"I am the way, the truth, and the life. No one comes to the Father except through Me"* (John 14:6).

Furthermore, the gospel of Jesus Christ is the only cure for this world's problems. The daily newspaper headlines express despair and hopelessness over the ravages of drugs, alcoholism, child abuse, crime, immorality, wars, corruption, and incurable diseases. A relationship with the Lord Jesus Christ is the only thing which will change the wicked hearts of men, give them goodness and happiness, and provide victory over the deceptions of the Devil *(John 10:10)*.

But Christ cannot save the lives of those who have never heard about Him. And just how will they hear, if ever? Will it be by a missionary which we supported to cross the ocean to tell them? Will they hear by a radio or TV broadcast which we helped to sponsor? Will it be in a church that we helped build with our contributions? Will it be by printed tracts, books, or Bibles which we donated money to help print? Souls will never be saved unless they hear about Christ, and as we can see, there are no free ways of doing that. Salvation is a free gift, but it costs money to take the message of salvation to the world.

How much value do we place on a human life? If our local fire department needs more money to obtain men and equipment to fight fires and save lives, do we gripe and complain about that? Would we criticize our hospitals who seek funds to expand emergency facilities or buy more ambulances? Do we ridicule those who raise funds to find cures for cancer or other terminal illnesses? Of course not! Because most of us realize the precious value of one life. But as important as it is to save a human life, it cannot even compare to the tremendous importance of saving a soul from eternal death!

Whatever you do, don't ever close your heart from giving to help save souls from death! Rather, be a good steward over the finances that God has given you. Always be faithful in giving your tithes to your local church, and use wisdom when selecting and supporting ministries outside your own congregation.

Here are some suggested guidelines that might help in developing good habits of giving toward God's work:

(1) Establish a "budget." Determine what you can afford to give to other ministries, after you've given tithes to your local church. Budgeting is very biblical. Jesus taught us to "count the cost," not to overextend ourselves. *(Luke 14:28-29).*

(2) Look for ministries with a proven track-record. Seek for evidence of sound beliefs, "spiritual fruit," and a primary concern to spread the Gospel of Jesus Christ.

(3) Don't be an impulsive contributor. Don't give to every touching appeal that comes your way. Be led of the Spirit in your giving — learn to know the difference between being affected emotionally, and being led spiritually. Pray first, and ask the Lord whether it's His will for you to support them. Ask your pastor for counsel or advice.

(4) Do your homework. Check up on ministries and see if they're doing what they claim. Ask them to send you financial statements and reports of their ministry progress.

(5) Make commitments carefully. Don't make promises you can't keep, and keep the ones you make.

(6) Keep your offering private between you and God. Don't give to make an impression on people, to gain influence or favor *(Matthew 6:1-4)*.

(7) Don't keep strings attached to your gift. When you give to the Lord, release the gift. Don't be possessive about your offering — it's not yours anymore.

(8) Give to God, not to man. Always be sure that, in your heart, you know that your donation is to God, not just to a preacher or a ministry. Give to God in faith, trusting Him to bring a return for your faithfulness to Him. Even if the preacher proves to be a fake, you will never lose your reward if your gifts have been given to God.

(9) Learn to say "no." Christians obviously cannot be expected to give or support every ministry or cause, regardless of how worthy they all may be. Believers must learn that "no" can be a nice Christian word. We don't have to get mad at ministries or become offended at their appeals. Just smile and say "no."

— 19 —
Why do churches teach people to give tithes of everything they earn to God?

Most Christian churches teach the Biblical principle of stewardship, which is the management over another person's affairs or possessions. When we become Christians, we come to realize that we, our possessions, and literally everything on earth comes from God. And as His heirs, we become the stewards over those things which are God's.

Tithing is an act of stewardship. The scripture says that the tithe, the first tenth (10%) of our income, is the property of the Lord and we are to always return it to Him. *"And all the tithe of the land, whether of the seed of the land or of the fruit of the tree, is the Lord's. It is holy to the LORD"* *(Leviticus 27:30).*

According to the Word, tithing is a such a serious matter with the Lord, that He calls those who do not tithe as "robbers" and pronounces a curse upon them. *"Will a man rob God? Yet you have robbed Me! But you say, In what way have we robbed You? In tithes and offerings. You are cursed with a curse, for you have robbed Me, even this whole nation"* *(Malachi 3:8-9).*

What kind of curse is this? A curse is the opposite of blessing, and the non-tither will neither have the promise of God's bountiful blessings, nor protection from the devourer of the fruit of their labors. *"Bring all the tithes into the storehouse, that there may be food in My house, and prove Me now in this, says the LORD of hosts, If I will not open for you the windows of heaven And pour out for you such blessing That there will not be room enough to receive it. And I will rebuke the devourer for your sakes, so that he will not destroy the fruit of your ground, nor shall the vine fail to bear fruit for you in the field, says the LORD of hosts"* *(Malachi 3:10-11).*

Tithing has sometimes been falsely attributed to the Law of Moses, but it actually originated long before that with Abraham's tithe to Melchizedek, who was the priest of the most high God and the king of Salem [Jerusalem] *(Genesis 14:18-20).*

Tithing is an expression of at least six important things:

(1) It is the acknowledgment of God's proprietorship. Tithing expresses our belief that everything on this earth came from God, and that He is responsible for all we earn or receive as increase *(Psalms 24:1).*

(2) It is a "believer's" expression of faith. Tithing is a statement of our faith and worship toward God. It is for believers only *(Genesis 14:19-20).*

(3) It is a test of our continued obedience to God's Word. Tithing is an expression of faithfulness to His Word and stewardship over His possessions *(1 Corinthians 4:2, Malachi 3:10).*

(4) It is an act of sowing spiritual seed. God promises the faithful tither, to continue to bless and flourish him with increased return and to meet his needs *(Malachi 3:10, 2 Corinthians 9:6)*.

(5) It is a continual memorial of God's universal laws of sowing and reaping. Virtually everything that the Lord does is based on these same divine principles *(Galatians 6:7)*.

(6) Tithing is the means which God has chosen to meet the expenses of the work of the ministry. The tithe is a sacred offering to God so that there would be spiritual meat in His house *(Malachi 3:10)*.

— 20 —
Why do churches baptize people?

Water Baptism has long been an important aspect of the Christian faith, practiced by virtually every church and denomination in some variation. Many evangelical churches consider it an ordinance — one of two given to the church, the other being the Lord's Supper.

According to the Bible, water baptism is not optional for the Christian. It is Christ's command for all those who place their faith in Christ as their Savior and Lord. To the church Jesus said, *"Go therefore and make disciples of all the nations, baptizing them in the name of the Father and of the Son and of the Holy Spirit, teaching them to observe all things that I have commanded you; and lo, I am with you always, even to the end of the age" (Matthew 28:19-20).* The matter of baptism was considered so important that even Jesus, himself, was baptized to provide an example for His followers. He said that He allowed himself to be baptized in order *"to fulfill all righteousness" (Matthew 3:15).* The Apostle Peter also stated that when persons repent of their sins, they are *"to be baptized" (Acts 2:38).*

The act of being baptized in water, in and by itself, does not wash away sins *(1 Peter 3:21)*, as is evidenced by the conversion of the thief on the cross (crucified along with Jesus), who had no chance to be baptized *(Luke 23:43)*. Salvation is not based on works, but on a relationship of faith with Christ *(Ephesians 2:8 9)*. Water baptism, however, is intended to symbolize the spiritual union *(baptism)* with Christ which "does" save us *(Galatians 3:27)*, and is the outward expression of an inward experience... "a commitment to a right relationship with God, in which we are forgiven of our sins and have a conscience of fellowship with Him."

When performed as an act of obedience based upon faith in Christ *(Acts 2:38)*, water baptism augments our faith *(James 2:17)*, and serves as a testimony of our repentance and spiritual union with Christ. As the scripture states... *"this water symbolizes baptism that now saves you also not the removal of dirt from the body but the pledge of a good conscience toward God." (1 Peter 3:21 NIV)*. Every person who accepts Jesus as his or her Savior should obey the Lord's command and be baptized in water at the earliest opportunity.

While the ceremonial submersion of a person in water may have seemed strange to the gentiles and foreigners of the first century, water baptism's symbolism was not new to the early Jewish converts to Christianity. The rite of water baptism was already a well-established procedure, performed upon those gentiles who wished to convert to Judaism. These converts, referred to as Proselyte Jews, would also be circumcised and were required to keep all other Jewish laws and observances. According to the Jewish Talmud, their baptism was symbolic of a cleansing of the past and starting over with a new life — in fact they would even be given new names.

Besides this significance, the rite of proselyte baptism may have also appeared similar to the ceremonial washing of the dead. Before burial, corpses were submerged in water and washed prior to the application of burial spices and ointments. In a visit to Israel some years ago, I viewed ancient, rock hewn troughs which archaeologists claimed were used for this purpose — which closely resemble today's baptismal tanks used in many Christian churches. Consequently, to the Jew, the rite of water baptism likely resembled the washing of a dead person for burial — that is until the person arose out of the water very much alive.

The combined symbolism of these well-known traditions, helped the New Testament people understand the meaning behind the Christian water baptism. It represented death and cleansing from the old life of sin, and a resurrection of new life in Jesus Christ. The Apostle Paul wrote, *"...buried with Him in baptism, in which you also were raised with Him through faith in the working of God, who raised Him from the dead" (Colossians 2:12)*.

Keep in mind that Water Baptism was intended to be an open, public confession of our faith in Christ *(1 Peter 3:21, Colossians 2:12)*. From the earliest days, it was usually performed in some large body of water, which was generally scarce and always a popular, public place. The Jordan River, for instance, was the main tributary through Israel from the Sea of Galilee in the north to the Dead Sea in the south, and was the main source of water for drinking, washing, or religious purposes. Consequently, people were always found near the river, gathering to socialize, to catch fish or to replenish their daily water supply. Therefore, water baptism performed in an open body of water, such as in the river, became a very public event, openly signifying one's conversion to Christianity before the curious spectators. This corresponds with Jesus' teaching, that a public confession of faith in Him is a necessary part of following him — it is not satisfactory to merely be His "secret Agent." He said, *"...whoever confesses Me before men, him I will also confess before My Father who is in heaven. But whoever denies Me before men, him I will also deny before My Father who is in heaven" (Matthew 10:32-33).*

While the method of water baptism has sometimes been a matter of different opinion by various churches and denominations, the New Testament teaches that water baptism was performed only by immersion. The Greek word *"BAPTIZO"* means "to whelm, to dip, to plunge under, or to submerge." The scriptural expressions such as "much water" *(John 3:23)*, "down both into the water" *(Acts 8:38)*, and "coming up out of the water" *(Mark 1:10)* provide proof that Bible baptism was by immersion. The Greek words which are translated "to pour," or "to sprinkle" are never found in connection with baptism.

In years past, some church denominations adopted a tradition of baptizing converts by sprinkling. Church history suggests that this tradition began when some converts were sick or bedfast and unable to undergo the physical involvement of water baptism, or when a body of water was unavailable or frozen. In an effort to obey the Lord's command, ministers would bring vessels of water and drench or sprinkle water on the convert. Later in years, for the sake of convenience, this method began to replace immersion in some Christian circles.

Remember that the printing press did not exist in those days, and copies of the scriptures were not abundant. The common people generally only knew what they heard about the Bible or what was passed down to them by the church hierarchy. Consequently, without the availability of doctrinal criticism, errors were more easily transferred into accepted church traditions.

Infant baptism was also a tradition that began without scriptural foundation, as there were no babies baptized in the New Testament. Apparently this tradition began later with the sincere attempt to secure the salvation of children. But the Bible shows that baptism is only to follow repentance, and a child does not qualify for baptism until he matures enough to "repent" of his sins and make Jesus his Savior and Lord. Since Jesus said that children are the very example of the Kingdom of Heaven *(Mark 10:14)*, it seems apparent that God holds children in a state of innocence, without sin to their charge, until they mature to an age of accountability where they recognize right from wrong. In other words, a child that dies in infancy would go to Heaven. This was the apparent view of David when his infant child died. He remarked that the child would not return to him, but he would (someday) go to be with him *(2 Samuel 12:22-23)*.

Another distinction held between some Christian groups has been the verbal "formula" or the wording of the baptism. Jesus stated clearly for his followers to baptize believers *"in the name of the Father and of the Son and of the Holy Spirit" (Matthew 28:19)*. But Peter later said to be baptized "in the name of Jesus" *(Acts 2:38)*. On the basis of this latter passage, one particular denomination contends that persons cannot be saved unless they are baptized in Jesus' name "only." This is refuted by most orthodox Christian churches, who generally baptize according to the Lord's stated terminology, "in the name of the Father, Son, and Holy Spirit."

Some churches, in an effort to satisfy both scriptures, baptize using the verbal formula which Jesus described in Matthew, and combine this with Peter's emphasis on the name of Jesus in Acts. Thus, when the minister baptizes, he says, "I baptize you in the name of God the Father, Jesus Christ the Son, and the Holy Ghost."

— 21 —
What is a fundamentalist Christian?

In recent times, the term "fundamentalist" has become commonly used by the news media to refer to any religious group whom they consider to hold radical views. We may recall frequent references to the mid-east Islamic fundamentalists who have been viewed as fanatics, and often responsible for acts of terrorism.

Similarly, liberal society uses the term fundamentalist to identify any Christian whom they consider to be an extremist. Generally, they classify a Christian as a radical fundamentalist if they merely believe in the literal interpretation of the Bible, if they hold views against sexual permissiveness, homosexuality, abortion on demand, or any views which are politically incorrect.

From the Christian perspective, fundamentalist has traditionally referred to any follower of Christ who believes that the Bible is the inspired Word of God and who believes in its literal interpretation and fundamental teachings. The fundamental Christian believes in the experience of the "new birth" which occurs when faith is placed in Christ as Savior and Lord. To the world this may be viewed as radical, but is very basic to the Christian faith.

The idea of Christian Fundamentalism first emerged as a movement in the 19th century within various Protestant bodies, who reacted against the rising tide of evolutionary theories and modernist Biblical criticism. From a Bible conference of Conservative Protestants meeting in Niagara in 1895, a statement was issued containing what came to be known as the five points of fundamentalism: The verbal inerrancy of Scripture, the divinity of Jesus Christ, the virgin birth, a substitutionary theory of the atonement, and the physical resurrection and bodily return of Christ.[1] In the first half of the 20th century, most Protestant churches in the U.S. were divided into either Fundamentalist or Modernist groups. The term has generally been applied to all those who adhere to strict, conservative (Protestant) orthodoxy in the matter of Biblical inspiration.

In the broad sense, fundamentalism may be used to describe Christians who are uncompromising, conservative and who take their beliefs to the maximum — exactly how every believer should live. But because of recent, increased activism by those identified as fundamentalists, who have promoted unethical actions such as bringing violence against abortion clinics, doctors etc., some academic circles believe that fundamentalism has been redefined by our society. They believe that the philosophy of fundamentalism (at least in the world's eyes) has evolved into a legitimate form of extremism, with views too radical for the balanced, evangelical Christian. For this reason, fundamentalism may no longer be a term which accurately conveys what orthodox Christians really believe.

— 22 —
Why are ministers referred to as "Reverend?"

Webster's dictionary defines the word, "reverend," as a title of respect for a clergyman. It comes from the idea of giving "reverence," which means "to regard with deep love and respect."

Calling a minister "reverend" did not originate in scripture. The term became accepted sometime in the seventeenth century in England as a scriptural show of respect toward men of God. *"And we urge you, brethren, to recognize those who labor among you, and are over you in the Lord and admonish you, and to esteem them very highly in love for their work's sake..." (1 Thessalonians 5:12-13).*

The prominent Bible translation of that era, the King James Version, used the word "reverence" 14 times in connection that which was holy or sacred. Those things which were to be reverenced were: the Lord's sanctuary *(Leviticus 19:30, 26:2),* the Lord Jesus Christ *(Matthew 21:37, Mark 12:6, Luke 20:13),* the Lord's anointed *(2 Samuel 9:6),* our earthly father *(Hebrews 12:9),* the husband by his wife *(Ephesians 5:33),* the way we serve the Lord *(Hebrews 12:28),* and the name of the Lord: *"He sent redemption unto his people: he hath commanded his covenant forever: holy and reverend is his name" (Psalms 111:9 KJV).*

It's obvious that the term was never actually intended to become a title, but rather, was an expression used by Christians to identify and denote respect and esteem toward their minister. To say, "The Reverend John Smith," was like saying, "The deeply loved and respected man of God, John Smith."

In later years, "reverend" began to lose its original distinction and evolved into a secular "title" of etiquette, used as a prefix in front of a clergyman's name to indicate his ministerial vocation. Some ministers don't wish to be identified by this term and may prefer to be addressed as "pastor" or "brother."

Another tradition associated with ministers, the so-called clerical collar, came from the standard style of a gentleman's dress in Europe in the middle ages. As styles changed, clergymen were slow to follow, and eventually the style became identified with formal clergy attire. Most evangelical ministers do not ascribe to the tradition of the clerical collar.

— 23 —
Why are some ministers called "Parsons?"

In the early days of America, few had access to higher education. Often in many of the small colonial towns, the only one who possessed formal education was the local minister. Besides religious matters, people would frequently consult him for information about law, science, and other secular matters. Because of his education, the local minister would often be viewed as a complete person and would be referred to as the town "person." Over the years, the evolving accent of the New Englanders distorted the pronunciation to "parson." Thus, ministers became referred to as Parsons.

— 24 —
Why do so many churches have splits and problems getting along?

The reality is, every church experiences a measure of conflict in some way or another. Churches are made up of people, and anywhere people are involved in anything, there's the potential for disagreement and conflict. Sadly, some congregations have experienced great setbacks or splits due to such unresolved discord, while other churches have learned how to head off or resolve such issues.

Church conflict frequently has to do with "power struggles" within the congregation. That is, a contention for influence or control. Sometimes this struggle for control comes from a self-serving lust for power and prominence. At other times, perhaps well-intended persons strive to gain influence to assert their own set of ideas and opinions. In any case, power struggles are unethical and cause irreparable harm to the body of Christ. God's Word tells us to pray for, respect and cooperate with those authorized spiritual leaders of our church *(Hebrews 13:17, 1 Thessalonians 5:12-13)*. Insurrection is nowhere sanctioned in scripture.

Sometimes church conflict is caused by angry, troubled people who redirect their personal unhappiness toward the church or its leaders. Those who have discontent in their marriage, their jobs or any number of problems, may lash out against other people — they may be especially quick to find fault with the church, or make mountains out of molehills. In addition, statistics say that one out of every five persons in the average church struggles with emotional/mental problems. These persons do not see reality the same way as others do. Their view of life is distorted and twisted. Exaggerations and misunderstandings are a common occurrence which can stir up turmoil and strife in the body.

One thing is dreadfully clear, those who become the source of problems of this kind will only bring trouble upon themselves. *"A worthless person, a wicked man, walks with a perverse mouth; he winks with his eyes, he shuffles his feet, he points with his fingers; perversity is in his heart, he devises evil continually, he sows discord. Therefore his calamity shall come suddenly; suddenly he shall be broken without remedy" (Proverbs 6:12-15).*

According to Apostle Paul, the general root for strife and division is spiritual immaturity and carnality. *"...for you are still carnal. For where there are envy, strife, and divisions among you, are you not carnal and behaving like mere men?" (1 Corinthians 3:3).* The cure for this is to repent for the sin of strife, and seek to grow and mature in the Lord.

— 25 —
What things contribute to the health and stability of a church congregation?

Many things can contribute to the stability of a church. Here are five of the most important features:

(1) Good Leadership — Wise, godly leadership plays a critical role in the stability of a church. Leadership can bring the best or the worst out of people. People generally become a product of what is poured into them — not in teaching only, but in the lifestyle and example of their leadership. Statistics show that a congregation which sits under the same pastor's ministry for three years will begin to emulate his character. Unfortunately, if leadership is corrupt, pretentious, domineering, or so forth, a congregation will begin to take on these traits. In order for a church to become stable it must have leadership with stability, maturity, and integrity. The pastor needs to be authoritative, but gentle. He must be a peacemaker, sound and impartial in his decision making. A pastor who earns the respect of his flock through his godly lifestyle will develop a significant influence to lead people.

(2) Balanced Doctrine — Sometimes people have "pet" doctrines which they especially like to hear or talk about. However, the healthy church needs the whole counsel of God's Word — the broad range of instruction. It needs to hear about the benefits as well as the responsibilities — the past history in addition to the future prophecies, etc. It needs to hear about God's love and encouragement, as well as His warning of judgment for sin and disobedience. A well balanced diet of practical teaching with Christ at the center will lend toward stability in a church.

(3) Proper Goals — Goals are important to the stability of a church. People must have a sense of purpose, and must be kept busy in reaching those goals. People who remain idle for very long tend to get into mischief or drift away. If a church loses its vision for its purpose and mission, it will shift focus inward, and when that happens, problems will result. A stable church must set its objectives upon Jesus and His goals — reaching the lost, evangelizing the world, and meeting the needs of people.

(4) Relational Harmony — Another of the great challenges for the church is "overcoming relational problems within the body." Today there are hundreds of thousands of persons who will not return to church because of offenses or misunderstandings which occurred there. America is a nation filled with wounded Christians — people who have been hurt in a church somewhere. And unfortunately the organized church has not been very good at healing the injured. It is no wonder that Jesus and the writers of the epistles devoted much of their teaching toward brethren loving and getting along with one another. A stable church must teach much on kindness, love, forgiveness and continually find ways of bringing people together to interact and fellowship with each other.

(5) Financial Responsibility — A church must be a wise and honest steward over the tithes and offerings of God's people. The issue of money — how it is raised or spent — is one of the most sensitive matters that many churches face. The church should keep no secrets how it spends its money. Matters should be kept out in the open, with good books and accounting records kept. Suspicion of dishonesty or unwise business decisions have split many churches — they have ruined the reputation of a church in many communities. Prudent leadership will seek to inspire a congregation's confidence of how financial matters are handled. A church is wise to avoid debt and other obligations which place an unreasonable burden on its contributors and leaders. Tithing should be taught and the church should learn to operate within its means. Constant appeals for money from the pulpit, tends to discourage the flock.

— 26 —
How should I decide if or when to change churches?

There are many things that can cause a person to consider leaving a church — some good and some not so good. Many times the Lord may reassign a person to another church so he or she can bring ministry or encouragement to another congregation — that's the best reason to leave a church. In other situations, people may discover that their church actually impedes their spiritual well-being, and may find the necessity to withdraw. Frequently, people leave a church simply because they are disinterested, dissatisfied, or feel they can find something better.

Before doing anything, it's a good idea to pray about your situation and seek the Lord's leading *(Proverbs 3:6)*. If you feel the Lord genuinely wants you to leave and go elsewhere for good reason, go to the pastor and discuss it with him. Don't just stop showing up for church. That is inconsiderate and immature. Keep in mind, leaving one church always means finding another — the Lord does not lead anyone to simply stop going to church *(Hebrews 10:25)*.

My advice to you is, if you are presently in a church that (1) is scripturally sound, (2) is reasonably stable and loving, (3) has godly, moral leadership, (4) is doing its best to exalt Jesus Christ as Savior and Lord, and (5) if they're making a reasonable effort to minister to you and your family, then hang in there and remain faithful! You don't know how blessed you are to have a healthy church like that. Many Christians would give anything to just find a church that is merely at peace!

If you're unhappy with a church which fits this fivefold description, it's very likely that the problem isn't the church, but yours. Either you're hung up on some trivial issue, your feelings have been hurt, or you struggle with discontent from other personal problems.

Seven things to consider before leaving a church:

(1) Don't leave a church out of your personal discontent. If discontent is rooted within you, it will follow you wherever you go, regardless of what church you attend. Many years ago, a certain lady who had attended our church for a few weeks came to speak with me. "Your church is so refreshing from all the other churches around here," she complimented. Curious, I asked, "Just how many other churches have you attended?" "Oh, about thirteen," was her reply. Privately, I realized that we were going to have problems with this new lady, because when it comes down to the basics, most Christian churches aren't that much different from each other. Whenever a person finds dissatisfaction with several congregations, you can be assured that the problem is their own, not the churches. And sure enough, the woman eventually became discontent and left our church too, the same as the previous thirteen.

(2) Don't leave a church because you transferred your own personal frustrations there. Avoid pushing off your feelings of disappointment from other areas of your life onto the church. Sometimes unhappiness toward the church is a derivative from other personal problems such as: Family or marital difficulties, job dissatisfaction, personal offenses, memories of childhood abuse, mental stress, emotional illness, and so forth. People who struggle with deep internal problems sometimes develop a distorted estimation of the people or situations around them, and may blame them, including the church, for their anguish. Generally speaking, the church is not your problem. Remember that it and its ministers are there because they love you and want to help you — not hurt you.

(3) Don't leave a church because your feelings got hurt. Hurt feelings are a "violation of self-interests" and are usually a result of being too self-sensitive. In any church or gathering of people there may be many offensive things said or done, mostly unintended, but you don't have to let yourself become offended. Those who are easily offended may simply be immature, too self-centered, or may retain self-sensitivities due to past, festering wounds. Hurt feelings are probably the greatest reason why people leave churches, but deepening your roots in Christ and His word can immunize you against such tenderness. *"Great peace have they which love thy law: and nothing shall offend them" (Psalm 119:165 KJV).*

(4) Don't leave a church over trivial criticisms. People sometimes have a remarkable ability of making a mountain out of molehill. I've known people to change churches merely because they didn't like the way the pastor combed his hair, the length of the services, how the bulletin was typed, or other silly reasons. Of the many excuses that persons use to leave a church, this is among the most shallow. If all you seem to do is criticize and find fault with the church, you have an attitude problem. Regardless of where you go to church, you'll find similar faults again, because the problem isn't with the church — the problem is with you.

(5) Avoid leaving a church over its style or individuality. One of the most common explanations people give for switching churches is their "disagreement with certain beliefs." However, I can recall many instances where people used this reason even though their newly selected church believed and taught the same things. In reality, it was a dislike of the personality of the church — its teaching methods, the style of worship, the structure of the services, or the pastor's preaching style, etc. Many churches actually believe and teach the same things, but each might have a slightly different method, structure, or style which makes up its unique personality. No two churches are alike in their personality or methods, any more than two people are alike, but it's not really very mature to abandon a church over such, shallow, external things. Our estimation of a church should be based on more spiritual, substantive issues, such as their beliefs, their love for one another, or their commitment to reach the lost, etc.

(6) Don't leave a church when faced with self-conflict. Many people do not understand that spiritual growth requires confronting and overcoming conflict with our self-willed nature *(James 1:3-4)*. The environment of the church provides two important features of growth producing conflict: (a) Authority who will challenge you with truth and correct you when you are wrong. And (b) an environment of believers, many of whom are imperfect and whose rough edges will serve as sandpaper to smooth out your wrinkles. *"As iron sharpens iron, so a man sharpens the countenance of his friend" (Proverbs 27:17).*

If anyone thinks he is spiritual, just get close to your brethren, and you'll find out what's really inside you. People are like "mirrors" in which we can see ourselves as we really are. If there's bitterness or a lack of love, it will become exposed. It doesn't matter how agitating, rude or unspiritual your brethren might be. This does not justify your intolerance or impatience with them. These attitudes are characteristics of your own immaturity — a weakness in YOU that needs perfecting. This is why some people run from church to church — because it exposes their bad side. They see their own sins and blemishes revealed in their relationship with the brethren, or they become outraged when their self-willed desires or sins are challenged through convicting preaching or correction.

If people remain "islands" to themselves they will never have to face the spiritual immaturity within them. But exposing themselves to the environment of the church will cause them to face conflicts that they must overcome in order to grow up. A sign of spiritually mature people is that they can be loving and patient with anyone *(1 John 2:10, Galatians 5:22-23)*, and they can humbly submit themselves to truth and the correction of authority *(Hebrews 13:17)*.

(7) Don't leave a church until you have attempted to help make it better in some way. I have always noticed that the most critical people in the church are usually the ones who do the least. Have you prayed faithfully for the church and its leaders? Have you made yourself available to serve or help in areas of ministry? Have you expressed helpful suggestions or brought your concerns to the leadership (in a non-judgmental fashion)?

Go to the leadership and share your heart, but avoid dishing out harsh criticism, verbal assaults, or nagging complaints. These will only cause a leader to become defensive and withdraw. It will not encourage him to improve or change, any more than a nagging wife can change her husband. All leaders know what it is to deal with constant criticism, and the only way they can rise above discouragement to do their job is to ignore their critics. If a leader perceives you to be a complainer, he'll immediately turn you off. He may politely listen, but inwardly will identify you as a trouble-maker. However, if he perceives you as a caring person who offers encouragement and helpful suggestions, his heart will remain open and he'll listen.

Never spread your "unhappiness," criticism or dissatisfaction to members of the body — this doesn't do anything to help, and stirs up discord in the church, a sin God hates *(Proverbs 6:19)*. If you can't keep from spreading your discontent to others, sadly, it may be in your best interest and for the peace of the congregation, for you to move on to another church. Compassionate leaders who are unable to reason with such persons would be wise, and justified by scripture, to encourage their departure from the fellowship. *"Cast out the scoffer, and contention will leave; yes, strife and reproach will cease"* (Proverbs 22:10).

— 27 —
What should I do if I'm not getting fed in my church?

If you attend a church that is not centered upon Christ, which doesn't proclaim or teach God's Word, it would be obvious why you're not receiving spiritual nourishment. In such a case, it would be a good idea to find a church that does. By all means get into a church that boldly proclaims the truths of the Bible.

However, if God's Word is being preached in your church, but you come to feel that you're not getting fed, it may mean that you're not using your own "knife and fork." Many are simply lazy and don't take responsibility to dig into God's Word and chew for themselves. They expect someone to grind up the meat and stick it in their mouth — like a helpless little baby.

Remember that "You can't suck meat from a baby bottle." That is, when you grow to a place where you need stronger meat, it's not going to come in the same fashion you used to get your milk. When a baby is fed, everything is done for him. He's held up to the bottle and all he has to do is suck. He's spoon-fed with baby food, already ground up and strained. He doesn't even have to chew. Feeding an adult is far different. The cooked meat is served on a plate with a knife and fork. The adult has to take responsibility to cut his own meat. He has his own teeth with which to chew.

Another reason for feeling unfed is that you may not be serving or ministering. Spiritual meat is not intended to be stored in a reservoir, but to be used as fuel to propel works of service. This corresponds with how Jesus described his food which sustained Him spiritually. He said that He received His nourishment from performing works of ministry. *"But He said to them, I have food to eat of which you do not know... My food is to do the will of Him who sent Me, and to finish His work"* (John 4:32,34).

There comes a time in a Christian's life that he or she must begin to minister to others and put God's Word into action, otherwise they will grow stagnant and be unable to sustain nourishment. The meat that many need is to get busy and start serving, start sharing Christ, and give the Word of God to others. Receiving the meat of God's Word nourishes us in one way — becoming a channel through which God's Word flows, nourishes us in another.

— 28 —
How can a person keep from getting hurt or injured in a church fellowship?

Statistics show that a great percentage of persons who stop going to church, do so because of some type of offense or injury to their feelings. It's unfortunate that such experiences ever occur. You may not be able to stop offensive things from happening, but by applying God's principles you can stop them from hurting you. *"Great peace have they which love thy law: and nothing shall offend them"* (Psalm 119:165 KJV).

The following are several things that people can do to protect themselves from getting hurt in the church:

(1) Avoid developing unreasonable expectations. *"My soul, wait silently for God alone, For my expectation is from Him" (Psalms 62:5).*

The definition of disappointment is "the failure to attain one's expectations." Don't expect things from the church or the minister that they can't deliver, or that the Bible doesn't teach for them to do. Many expectations have to do with preconceived "traditions" which we have come to associate with a church, perhaps from another fellowship we once attended or grew up in, etc. It's a good idea to meet with the pastor and ask what you can expect of his ministry and the church.

Occasionally people get disappointed when they find out their church can't supply all their earthly needs. Most churches attempt to help the needy during crisis and emergencies, but some expect the church to meet all their material needs or pay their bills like the early church did. Unfortunately, this just isn't possible unless everyone agrees to sell all their property and possessions and give them to the church like the early believers *(Acts 4:34-35).* Most churches would be blessed if everyone merely paid their tithes, however statistics show that only a small percentage of churchgoers give a full tithe regularly.

Neither is it realistic to expect the pastor to spend all his time with you, to attend every social function, or for him to show you constant attention. Learn to place your expectations upon God — He will always be faithful to His promises in His Word.

(2) Don't place an absolute trust in people. *"Thus says the LORD: Cursed is the man who trusts in man and makes flesh his strength, whose heart departs from the LORD" (Jer. 17:5).*

Come to terms with the fact that everyone is human and will fail you at some time or another. Even the pastor will make mistakes. The only one you can trust entirely without fail is God.

Realizing that any human can fall short, the degree of trust we place in people must be limited and will depend on their track record. The more we get to know a person's character and the history of their behavior, we'll be able to determine how trustworthy they are. This is one of the reasons why the scriptures tell us to get to know our pastors and spiritual leaders — so from their godly lifestyle, we'll be able to trust their leadership. *"And we urge you, brethren, to recognize those who labor among you, and are over you in the Lord and admonish you." (1 Thessalonians 5:12).*

There's a difference between "love" and "trust." It's possible to love and forgive someone, without placing an absolute trust in them. To illustrate this, let's say there's a school bus driver who has a drinking problem. One day while transporting a load of children he becomes intoxicated, wrecks the bus and kills all the children. As the lone survivor of the crash, he turns to the church to seek God's forgiveness for this horrible act of irresponsibility. If he repents of his sin, will God forgive him? Absolutely. Should the church love and forgive this person? Of course. And what if he would then like to volunteer to drive the church bus for us? Do we trust him? Absolutely not! It would be unthinkable to put a person in the driver's seat who has shown such recent negligence. Certainly, we love and forgive him, but because of this man's poor track record, we could not risk the lives of our passengers. Over a long period of sobriety and safe driving, this person may be able to prove that he is again reliable, capable of being trusted as a bus driver.

Remember that love and forgiveness is granted unconditionally, but trust must be "earned." Trust is the acquired confidence in a person's actions. We certainly can, and should trust persons who show trustworthy behavior, but because all men have the potential for failure, we should never put an infallible sense of trust in anyone but God.

(3) Focus on common ground. *"Now I plead with you, brethren, by the name of our Lord Jesus Christ, that you all speak the same thing, and that there be no divisions among you, but that you be perfectly joined together in the same mind and in the same judgment" (1 Corinthians 1:10).*

Avoid becoming highly opinionated. Opinions are the interpretations and ideas of men, which if constantly pressed on other people, can cause division or promote sinful debates and quarrels *(Romans 1:29).* Opinionated people are prone to get hurt when others disagree with them.

The Bible teaches for all Christians to *"speak the same thing"* so that there will be unity in the body of Christ *(1 Corinthians 1:10).* The only way such unity is possible, is for Christians to focus on the common ground of Christ and His Word. That is, we need to *"say what the Word says,"* to let the Word speak for itself and not try to promote divisive opinions about it. *In scripture, we see that Paul instructed Timothy to "Preach the Word," not his opinions (2 Timothy 4:2).* A preacher is intended be a delivery boy of God's message, not a commentator of the message. That's the Holy Spirit's job *(1 John 2:27).*

Similarly, at one time the news media was required to comply with a very strict code of ethics. They were to report the facts of the news accurately without adding their opinion or commentary. However, as time has passed, news reporting has become less factual and more opinionated — corrupted with rumors and gossip rather than real information. Reporters have evolved into commentators which manipulate what people think about the news. Like reporters, preachers need to stick with the facts.

Naturally every believer has his or her own convictions about a great many things, but if you continually try to push your opinions on others, conflict will eventually emerge. Avoid controversy over scriptures which are vague and foster many interpretations — stand fast upon those common, basic truths — Jesus, His life, death and resurrection — and don't add to what God's Word says. *"Every word of God is pure; He is a shield to those who put their trust in Him. Do not add to His words, lest He reprove you, and you be found a liar" (Proverbs 30:5-6).*

(4) Don't expect any church to be perfect. *"For I know that in me (that is, in my flesh) nothing good dwells; for to will is present with me, but how to perform what is good I do not find. For the good that I will to do, I do not do; but the evil I will not to do, that I practice." (Romans 7:18-19)*

It is remarkable to consider that the Apostle Paul confessed that he was not perfect — that is, like us, he experienced struggles in his flesh to do the right things. If one of the leading authors of scripture and apostles of the early church admitted to this, it should not seem too strange if we find other brothers and sisters in the church struggling with imperfections too.

Since churches are made up of people like you and me who have imperfections, there will never be such a thing as a perfect church. Unless people understand this, they'll have an unrealistic view of the church, and will eventually become disillusioned and hurt.

One of the jobs of the church ministry is to help perfect the saints
— like a spiritual hospital, where people go to get well. Instead of
resenting persons in the church for their flaws, be thankful they're
there trying to grow in Christ to get better. Learn to love and accept
people for what they are — they're not any more perfect than you
are.

Just as it has been said of beauty, imperfection is in the eye of the
beholder. A person with a negative attitude can find fault wherever
they wish. In contrast the person with a positive outlook can always
find the good and beauty in things. The well-adjusted person in the
church should seek out the good and encouraging things as the Bible
teaches *(Philippians 4:8)*. Those who dwell on the negative or
continually find fault with the church will eventually get hurt.

(5) Don't seek to promote yourself or your own agenda. *"Do not
lift up your horn on high; Do not speak with a stiff neck. For exaltation comes
neither from the east Nor from the west nor from the south. But God is the
Judge: He puts down one, And exalts another" (Psalms 75:5-7).*

Have a humble and meek attitude like Christ *(Matthew 11:29, Romans
12:3)*. Besides being obnoxious, pride and arrogance will set you up
for a fall *(Proverbs 16:18)*. Don't promote yourself, campaign or strive
to attain an appointed or elected position. God is the one who puts
persons in such positions, and unless He does it, stay away from it.
Lift up the Lord in all that you say and all you do. Don't boast or
talk about yourself. *"He who speaks from himself seeks his own glory; but
He who seeks the glory of the One who sent Him is true, and no unrighteousness
is in Him" (John 7:18).*

Avoid an attitude of competition which creates conflict in unity. A
competitive attitude compares self with others, and strives to rise
above that comparison *(2 Corinthians 10:12)*. The philosophy of
Christianity is not to try to outdo one another, but to submit to and
lift up one another *(Ephesians 5:21)*. We are even told to "prefer" our
brother above ourselves. *"Be kindly affectionate to one another with
brotherly love, in honor giving preference to one another" (Romans 12:10).*
Competition between churches and Christians is divisive and
contrary to the faith.

Don't expect to receive preferential treatment or to get your way
about everything. The Bible teaches that favoritism is wrong, and the

church will try to make decisions and do things in the best interest of the whole congregation, not just a certain few. *"...but if you show partiality, you commit sin, and are convicted by the law as transgressors" (James 2:9)*. If you do things for the church or give generous offerings, do it to bring glory to God, not to bring attention to yourself or to gain influence *(Colossians 3:17)*. The Bible even says that when you give charitable offerings, do it anonymously so to gain God's approval, not merely man's *(Matthew 6:1)*.

Avoid the trap of presuming that your opinions are always divinely inspired or are indisputable. Share your suggestions and ideas with church leaders, but don't press your opinions or personal agenda. Sometimes, persons feel that all their ideas come from God. They may attempt to add clout to their suggestions or complaints by saying "God told me so." Indeed, God does speak to His children, but you will not be the exclusive source through which God reveals himself in a matter. If your opinions really come from God, the Bible says that others will bear witness with it, especially His pastors and leaders *(2 Corinthians 13:1, 1 Corinthians 14:29)*. (You won't even have to invoke God's name — they'll be able to tell if your ideas came from Him. Be cautious, lest you find yourself using His name falsely, a very dangerous thing — *Exodus* 20:7). Pastors are His representatives in His ordained chain of command, and if He wants to get something across to His church, He'll bear witness with the persons in charge.

(6) Avoid blaming the church for personal problems. *"You will keep him in perfect peace, whose mind is stayed on You, because he trusts in You" (Isaiah 26:3)*.

When you go to church, you should try to dissociate the church from the other personal problems you deal with. The majority of hurt feelings in a church result from wounds and sensitivities people carry in with them. This kind of emotional distress can create "distorted perceptions" which may prevent you from seeing reality the same way others do. Such things as a low self-esteem, abuse as a child, marital problems, personal offenses, family conflict, a root of bitterness, health problems or job dissatisfaction can twist your interpretation of words and actions. You may imagine that people don't like you (paranoia), or misinterpret well-intended words as an offense. Trivial problems will seem like big problems. Blame for unhappiness may be transferred to the church, its leaders or the people. You may lash out against others or be quick to find fault with the church. Remember this: Don't jump to conclusions over anything, because things are usually not as bad as they seem.

(7) Treat others as you wish to be treated. *"Therefore, whatever you want men to do to you, do also to them, for this is the Law and the Prophets"* *(Matthew 7:12).*

Human beings tend to be "reciprocal" creatures. That is, they reflect the way they are treated. This is why Jesus gave us the Golden rule: "Do unto others as you would have them to do unto you." The way that most people interact with you is as a direct result of how you interact with them. If you have a frown on your face, you won't get many smiles. If you offer friendliness, it will usually be offered back *(Proverbs 18:24).* Be gracious, encouraging, and a blessing for others to be around. If you have a negative, critical attitude toward people it will tend to generate their critical attitude toward you. *"Judge not, and you shall not be judged. Condemn not, and you shall not be condemned. Forgive, and you will be forgiven" (Luke 6:37).*

Many hurt feelings can be avoided if we will realize that people usually react to how we deal with them. Take a close examination at the way you say things, or even how much you talk. *"...a fool's voice is known by his many words" (Ecclesiastes 5:3).* Don't be rude and impolite. Check your attitude that you're not overbearing and bossy — people will be turned off and will seek to avoid you.

(8) Have a teachable, cooperative attitude. *"Obey those who rule over you, and be submissive, for they watch out for your souls, as those who must give account. Let them do so with joy and not with grief, for that would be unprofitable for you" (Hebrews 13:17).*

The Bible teaches believers to be cooperative and submissive to their spiritual leaders — something that's not possible unless the believer is committed to a church and accountable to a local pastor. Accountability to a godly shepherd is a part of God's order for the spiritual growth of every Christian. God's Word gives the pastor authority to organize and maintain order of the church, and to teach God's truth, to correct, and to discipline when necessary to hold his flock accountable to biblical principles. In Paul's encouragement to ministers, he stated, *"Preach the word! Be ready in season and out of season.*

Convince, rebuke, exhort, with all longsuffering and teaching" (2 Timothy 4:2).
(See also 2 *Timothy* 3:16, *Titus* 2:15, 1 *Timothy* 5:20.)

A lack of proper respect toward authority is a common problem today. People don't want to be told what to do, or be corrected if they are wrong. This is one reason why the modern church is turning out so many immature believers. When some people hear something they don't like, or are corrected in some way, they simply pack up and go to another church down the street, or church-hop until they find one that says things they like to hear. *"For the time will come when they will not endure sound doctrine, but according to their own desires, because they have itching ears, they will heap up for themselves teachers"* (2 *Timothy* 4:3).

As long as you are a part of any particular church, you must come to accept that the pastor and leaders are in charge there. Regardless of how unqualified you might think they are, God recognizes them as the authority in that body and will hold them accountable to that responsibility. Consequently, God holds you accountable to respect their authority, to pray for them, and to cooperate — not to be defiant and rebellious.

Always be cooperative, willing to humble yourself. If you have a rigid, inflexible attitude in the church you will probably get hurt.

(9) Don't oppose or hinder the church. *"These six things the LORD hates, yes, seven are an abomination to Him: A proud look, a lying tongue, hands that shed innocent blood, a heart that devises wicked plans, feet that are swift in running to evil, a false witness who speaks lies, and one who sows discord among brethren"* (Proverbs 6:16-19).

One of the things that God dislikes most are those who sow discord — who create division and strife in the body of Christ. Don't be a gossip, a complainer, or stir up turmoil. If you're displeased with the church in some way, offer your help to make improvements, pray for it, or as a last resort, find another church you're happier with — but never become a source of agitation or hindrance.

Don't badmouth a man of God — if you do so, you're asking for problems. One time when Paul was punished for preaching the Gospel, he unknowingly condemned Ananias, the high priest, who had ordered the apostle slapped. However, when Paul realized who he was, he apologized for speaking against Ananias, knowing that it's forbidden to speak against God's representative — despite the fact that Ananias' treatment of Paul was in error *(Acts 23:5)*. It is a serious matter to "touch" God's anointed — either with our words or our actions. Imperfect as they may sometimes be, they are His representatives. *"He permitted no one to do them wrong; Yes, He reproved kings for their sakes, Saying, "Do not touch My anointed ones, And do My prophets no harm" (Psalms 105:14-15).*

If a minister has done you wrong in some way, don't incriminate yourself by responding in an unbiblical manner — don't lash out against him, retaliate with rumors against him, or run him down behind his back. You should go and confront him privately according to the scriptural fashion described in Matthew 18:15-17. If the first and second attempts do not bring a resolution, take the matter to the spiritual body, such as the church board, or denominational overseers to whom he is accountable — any correction or discipline should be left to them. Keep in mind, an accusation against a minister is a serious matter and will not be accepted unless the matter can be substantiated by other witnesses *(1 Timothy 5:19)*.

When things are not as they should be in the church or with its leadership, there are honorable ways to help promote improvements or resolve inequities. However, it's unethical to oppose the church or attack its leadership, and persons who do will likely end up hurt, bitter or possibly worse.

(10) Be committed to forthrightness and truth. *"Moreover if your brother sins against you, go and tell him his fault between you and him alone. If he hears you, you have gained your brother. "But if he will not hear you, take with you one or two more, that by the mouth of two or three witnesses every word may be established. And if he refuses to hear them, tell it to the church. But if he refuses even to hear the church, let him be to you like a heathen and a tax collector" (Matthew 18:15-17).*

When someone has wronged you, Jesus says that you are to first go to them and confront them privately between yourselves. Most offenses in the church result from misunderstandings, and many could be quickly resolved if offended parties would just go to the source and find out the facts. Unfortunately, some offended people will just absorb the offense silently, while growing bitter and resentful. It is important to God, and a matter of obedience to His Word, that such issues are confronted so that (1) you will not become bitter and withdraw from the church, (2) that the offender is held accountable to not repeat his offenses which could harm the faith of others, and (3) so that the offender who has perpetrated sin might be reconciled with God. If they are uncooperative with your first private effort, you are to try a second time, taking witnesses with you. Finally, if no success, turn it over to church leadership.

You should never take one side of a story and accept it as fact without verifying it with the other party. There are always two sides to a story. The scriptures address this very problem, that before we believe a rumor, we are to investigate thoroughly, to verify all the facts. *"...then you shall inquire, search out, and ask diligently... if it is indeed true and certain that such an abomination was committed among you..." (Deut. 13:14).*

Without doubt, it is not possible to have a relationship with a group of people without occasional misunderstandings and offenses. And unless you will commit yourself to confront these issues in the way Jesus described, you will become hurt in the church.

(11) Be devoted to love and forgiveness. *"He who loves his brother abides in the light, and there is no cause for stumbling in him" (1 John 2:10).*

Christians will avoid a lot of problems if they will just commit themselves to an unconditional love for their brethren. The practice of loving the brethren — all the brethren, not just the lovable ones — keeps us from stumbling. Never forget that Jesus takes personally how we entreat our Christian brothers and sisters. When we love even the "least" of our brethren, Jesus accepts that love toward Himself *(Matthew 25:40).* You cannot love the Lord any more than you love the least in the body of Christ. *"If someone says, I love God, and hates his brother, he is a liar; for he who does not love his brother whom he has seen, how can he love God whom he has not seen?" (1 John 4:20).*

Be quick to forgive and don't hold grudges. Unforgiveness and bitterness is one of the greatest reasons why people get hurt in the church and probably the greatest cause of apostasy — falling away. Remember that unforgiveness is one of your greatest enemies. If you refuse to forgive, it will prevent God's forgiveness of your sins and could keep you out of Heaven. *"For if you forgive men their trespasses, your heavenly Father will also forgive you. But if you do not forgive men their trespasses, neither will your Father forgive your trespasses" (Matthew 6:14-15).*

(12) Don't get caught up in the offenses of others. *"Lord, who may abide in Your tabernacle? Who may dwell in Your holy hill? He who walks uprightly, And works righteousness, And speaks the truth in his heart; He who does not backbite with his tongue, Nor does evil to his neighbor, Nor does he take up a reproach against his friend" (Psalms 15:1-3).*

One of the great characteristics of the body of Christ is to care about the burdens and sufferings of one another. However, as we seek to console and encourage friends that have been offended, we may be tempted to take up their offense against another. In sympathy, we may tend to take their part against the pastor, the church or whoever they blame for the offense. This is very unwise and an unscriptural thing to do, considering that your friend may be the cause of his own offense. His hurt feelings may be due to a misunderstanding, a difference of opinion, his own rebellious attitude, emotional instability — or he may be childish and immature. There are always two sides to a story, and only an idiot develops an opinion based on one side or without all the facts.

Sometimes offended persons will seek sympathy from naive, listening ears. They go about pleading their case, pouring out their bleeding-heart of injustice to those sincere, tenderhearted persons who will listen. Their goal is to seek out persons who will coddle them, support their opinion and take up their offense against the offending party. You should love and encourage a friend with hurt feelings, but reserve your opinion and avoid taking sides, lest you find yourself a partaker in other men's sins, or you also become offended and hurt with the church.

(13) Don't personalize everything that's preached. Obviously, every pastor preaches with the hope that everyone will take the message personally and apply it to his or her own life. "If the shoe fits, wear it." However, there are always a few who think the minister is pointing his sermon specifically at them. This is a common misunderstanding which causes persons to get hurt.

This feeling of personal focus from a sermon might occur if persons are (1) under conviction about a particular matter, (2) especially self-conscious, (3) under emotional distress, (4) if they spend a lot of time counseling with the pastor, or (5) if he has previously corrected them or hurt their feelings in some way. Keep in mind, a pulpit preacher doesn't focus his attention solely upon one person. His concern is for the broad range of people in attendance.

Occasionally persons think their pastor focuses on them, the same way they focus on him. When a pastor stands in front of a congregation week after week, they develop a feeling of close friendship with him — they come to know personal details of his life, his family, and other traits. However, even if the pastor knows each person in his flock, it's not really possible for him to concentrate on each with the same detail that they do on him. It's easy for dozens of people to know him well, but not realistic for him to know dozens of people in the same way. Consequently, some develop the illusion that the pastor focuses on them when he preaches — that he remembers their personal details in the same way they remember his. But the pastor has too many other people to consider. He counsels with dozens of people, hears scores of similar problems and details. It's not likely he will single someone out and preach at them, while trying to minister to the whole congregation. If there's something specific that the pastor needs to say only to you, he will deliver it to you personally, in private — not in subtle hints from his sermon.

Besides this, it is the job of the Holy Spirit to personalize God's Word to us — so that we'll examine ourselves and search our own hearts. When the Lord is dealing with us about His Word, it may seem like the pastor is speaking directly to us. Sometimes the Holy Spirit may even direct the preacher to unwittingly say things that may pertain specifically to us. The best attitude to have is to listen to each message objectively. In every sermon from the Bible, God has something to say to all of us. Be open to whatever the Lord would have to say, willing to accept His correction or guidance. Defensiveness is usually a sign of resistance to conviction.

— 29 —
How should disputes and offenses be dealt with between believers in the church fellowship?

In Matthew 18:15-17, Jesus established a procedure to be followed in the event that a brother would commit a sin or offense against another Christian. Many Christian scholars believe that this is one of the most neglected teachings of the entire Bible. It's been said that if all believers would simply obey scripture, to go and confront their offenders in the manner Jesus gave, it would solve over half of all problems which exist in the church.

It is important to confront those brethren who have trespassed against us for the following five reasons:

(1) To resolve misunderstandings. Most offenses in the church result from misunderstandings and many could be quickly resolved if offended parties would just go to the source and find out the facts. Unfortunately, some offended people will just absorb the offense silently, while growing bitter and resentful. It is important to God, and a matter of obedience to His Word, that such issues are confronted.

(2) To maintain peace in the body of Christ *(Ephesians 4:1-3).* Whenever there is friction and turmoil between believers it affects the whole body. It hinders people from entering into worship and receiving from God's Word. It creates an uninviting atmosphere for visitors in the church, it may hinder people from coming to Christ, and can even grieve the Holy Spirit *(Ephesians 4:30-32).*

(3) So Satan cannot gain advantage over us *(2 Corinthians 2:10-11).* For our own spiritual well-being, we must be quick to resolve our differences with brethren and forgive. Satan can hinder our spiritual life, and even deceive us into apostasy, through harbored bitterness or unforgiveness *(Matthew 18:35).*

(4) So that the offender is held accountable to not repeat his actions to harm the faith of others *(Matthew 18:6).* Persons who bring offense against you are likely to repeat similar acts against others. Confronting their offensive behavior may cause them to restrain their actions from causing further offenses.

(5) To restore a fallen brother *(Galatians 6:1).* Christians must make every attempt to restore brethren who fall into sin. Especially when the transgression has been committed against us, our love for our brother's spiritual well-being demands that we confront the brother so that he might be reconciled to God.

How to deal with the trespasser

The following scripture is how Jesus taught for Christians to confront those brethren who have wronged them:

Matthew 18:15 "Moreover if your brother sins against you, go and tell him his fault between you and him alone. If he hears you, you have gained your brother.
18:16 But if he will not hear you, take with you one or two more, that by the mouth of two or three witnesses every word may be established.
18:17 And if he refuses to hear them, tell it to the church. But if he refuses even to hear the church, let him be to you like a heathen and a tax collector."

First, Go to your brother privately *(Matthew 18:15).* If a fellow Christian has sinned or brought an offense against you, Jesus said for you to first go to the offending party, confront him with the offense, and keep the matter private between yourselves. Remember, the objective is to not merely to seek justice for a violation against us, but to seek "reconciliation" with our brother, and his restoration to a right relationship with God.

Why is the matter to be first kept private between you two? Because our love for our brother requires it. If we are sincerely committed to love for our brethren as Jesus commands *(John 13:34),* then even if a brother has sinned against us or has done us wrong, we will not want to maliciously injure that brother's credibility within the body — that might hinder his restoration. If this person's transgression against you is circulated within the body, but later he repents, many in the body will have already judged this brother and the accusations will have damaged their opinion of him. By spreading our accusation against an offending party, it builds a consensus against them and makes it difficult, if not nearly impossible, to restore that person to the body should they repent and desire to make things right.

Also, many alleged trespasses between brethren are a result of "misunderstandings." We need to first investigate the facts and find out for sure whether a trespass has really occurred. This is another reason why you are to first go privately to the brother or sister in question — to confront them with the alleged offense and hear their side of the story. If we disclose the offense to friends in the body, we may later discover that the matter was only a misunderstanding. But by then, their reputation will have been damaged by our allegations.

Many people foolishly allow themselves to become offended by misinterpreting other's intentions, or listening to rumors and secondhand information which always contain distortions or exaggerations. Many offenses could be immediately resolved by confronting the offending party and hearing their explanation. You'd be surprised how many people are so immature that they don't even bother to investigate the facts or hear the other side of the story. Don't ever forget, "There are always two sides to a story," and never assume you know the truth of a matter until you've heard both sides.

I can guarantee that there would be far fewer misunderstandings in the body of Christ if people would be firmly devoted to love for their brethren. Love for the brethren gives us a desire to believe the best in our brother, giving him the "benefit of the doubt," instead of jumping to conclusions and always expecting the worst. The Bible says *"If you love someone... you will always believe in him, always expect the best of him" (1 Corinthians 13:7 TLB)*.

If the trespass is proven valid, and he or she repents for their misdeed, you are to express your forgiveness *(Luke 17:3-4)*. Let the matter be forever ended, and carry no resentment toward them. Remember, if they repent, but you continue to harbor bitterness, you too become a perpetrator of sin *(Matthew 6:14-15, Acts 8:23, Ephesians 4:31-32)*.

Second, take another brother *(Matthew 18:16)*. If your private attempt fails to resolve the issue, you are then to take one other Christian and again confront the offending party. The presence of another Christian is as a witness to strengthen the serious effect of confrontation, to collaborate the exhortation of scripture, to amplify the Lord's presence in the meeting, and to verify the exchange of testimony.

Third, tell Church leadership *(Matthew 18:17).* If the first and second attempts fail, Jesus said then to "tell it to the church." This doesn't mean the "entire" church body, as this could cause unrest or damage the faith of young believers. The meaning is that the church pastors or elders are then to bear responsibility in dealing with the offending party.

Finally, if these three prescribed attempts fail, we are no longer required to entreat them with the courtesies shown to brethren. They may be dealt with in the same fashion as we would a heathen or publican *(Matthew 18:17).*

What to do if you trespass: If you are aware of any trespass you have committed against your brother, you have a responsibility to go to him and seek his forgiveness. Should you not attempt reconciliation, this will hinder your relationship with God. Your worship, your prayers and service to the Lord will not be acceptable. *"Therefore if you bring your gift to the altar, and there remember that your brother has something against you, leave your gift there before the altar, and go your way. First be reconciled to your brother, and then come and offer your gift"* *(Matthew 5:23-24).*

Note that the scripture says "if your brother has something against you." In other words, you might not feel that you have legitimately violated your brother or sister. But if you are aware that "they" harbor an offense against you, you still are obligated to go and try to resolve the issue. Be willing to be humble and submissive to others, even when you don't consider yourself to be at fault. Don't be so rigid and self-righteous that you stand in the way of a brother or sister's reconciliation with you or with God *(Romans 15:1-3).* Offer your unpretentious, sincere apology for any unintentional offense and make every effort to reconcile, so that your relationship with God will not be hindered. Whether or not they pardon you, you have done your part and released your soul from blame.

— 30 —
What is it like to be a pastor of a church?

To preface my answer to this question, I've been privileged to serve as a pastor of several congregations over the course of many years. For another decade before that, I was a guest in the homes of scores of pastors and their families as an itinerant evangelist. My opinions here come from first hand observation and personal experience.

In today's society, all too often the demands upon a pastor exceed what they really should. The pastor is traditionally considered a church's head "everything." He's the spiritual and administrative head, the sole minister, the legal corporation president — and basically the know-it-all, do-it-all, "chief cook and bottle washer." In many small churches, the pastor will conduct all the services, lead the singing, do all the preaching, handle all the visiting, counseling and spiritual matters, while he may also have to take care of the office work, bookkeeping, or even the janitorial, maintenance or building repair.

In my years of traveling to hundreds of churches, I found many pastors to be some of hardest working, most versatile, multi-skilled people I have ever met. And for the main part, they pick up all these skills out of the necessity of their circumstances — having no hired staff or few willing volunteers to do these things for them. In too many cases, the pastor has to do far more than he was ever called for or even trained to do.

This really isn't the way it should be. Ideally the pastor should be the spiritual overseer, devoting his attention to the higher priorities of prayer and ministering the word, while delegating the load of administrative tasks, details and responsibilities to other ministers, elders and deacons.

The early Apostles faced this same dilemma. They received complaints that some of the widows of the church were not being cared for as they should. So they selected qualified persons to delegate these tasks (believed to be the first deacons), so they would not be distracted away from what God had really called them to do — to be men of prayer and of the Word. *"...It is not desirable that we should leave the word of God and serve tables. Therefore, brethren, seek out from among you seven men of good reputation, full of the Holy Spirit and wisdom, whom we may appoint over this business; but we will give ourselves continually to prayer and to the ministry of the word" (Acts 6:2-4).*

The rewards of being a pastor are many. Without question, there is no other position in the world that has a higher honor, than to be called of God to be a pastor. However, it is a vocation of extreme contrasts. It can be sometimes wonderful and sometimes terrible in the same package. Despite potential blessings of leading souls to Christ, the job of pastor is one of the most difficult, agonizing tasks there is.

Some of the greatest challenges of a Pastor are:

(1) Being Misunderstood — For the most part, the life and ministry of a pastor is not understood by the average layman. A policeman once told me the same thing about law enforcement officers. He said, "The only one that really understands what a cop does is another one." I could relate to what he was trying to say. Sheep really don't have any idea what it's like to be a shepherd — only other shepherds. The average layman has little concept what a pastor is, what he really does, the hassles he deals with and so forth.

Being a pastor isn't a job, it's what a person is. When God calls a person to be a pastor, He places in him a shepherd's nature and characteristics — to love and care for his flock. He is a pastor all the time. It's what he thinks about, what he lives for, his purpose on the earth. It's not possible for him to go home at the end of a day and leave his job behind the way that most people can. His, is an all-consuming task. The pastor is on duty twenty four hours a day, seven days a week. He frequently receives phone calls at home from morning to evening, and often in the middle of the night. Most of his home activities are related to the church. Most social calls or relationships are church related. A large percentage of his conversations with his family involve the church. His home should probably be a refuge to rest or to have a life of his own, but it's usually the only place he can hide himself long enough from interruptions, to pray for the church or to study for the sermons he must preach there.

(2) Coping with Criticism — Like most other public figures, a pastor and his family live in the public eye, like a "fish bowl" where people watch them constantly, frequently viewing them with criticism and cynicism. People who enter the ministry must be prepared to face much criticism, sometimes of a brutal and cruel nature. However, all those who have risen in leadership or accomplishment know well the sting of their critics. It has been said that "the only way to avoid criticism is to 'Say nothing, Do nothing, and Be nothing.'"

People frequently find disappointment with pastors, largely due a lack of understanding of what pastors do. Rarely does a church ever have a written job description for their senior pastor, and if they do, it's usually too vague to help much. And it seems that so many have a different opinion of what they think the pastor should do. They usually hand him the keys to the church and assume that he'll take care of everything that needs to be done — without realizing the hundreds of details that it all may require.

(3) Faced with an Overwhelming Task — It's been said that 80% of the work of the church is done by 20% of the people. But when we realize that the majority of American churches have fewer than 100 people, you can imagine that the pastor and his family often make up a great portion of that 20%. As we have mentioned, in many of those churches, the pastor is often faced with having to do jobs he was never trained for — everything from plumbing to desktop publishing... and besides this, he also must be the well-studied preacher and teacher. Beyond these demands, his life will be one of constant distractions, receiving dozens of calls and letters each day, and expected always to drop anything he's doing to sympathize, counsel, or encourage those who ask his help. The pastor seldom has enough time to do everything — time is always one of his greatest needs.

I can remember being in many a pastor's home, joining with him in tearful prayers for God to send helpers, workers and finances to lift the heavy load on him and his family. Ironically, I would think back to one of my college textbooks on church administration — it was written on the lofty example of a congregation numbering 1,000 in attendance, with a staff of dozens, though to my knowledge not one of those students went on to pastor a church of that size. Many pastors will never know what it is to have a paid staff, and must pray for volunteers to train and delegate responsibilities. Unfortunately, for most churches, the pastor wears more hats than he should endure, physically and emotionally. According to researcher George Barna, among the most discouraging aspects for pastors is the extensive range of duties they must fulfill that exceed their mix of gifts and talents.[1]

Author James Rutz says that the average pastor often feels overwhelmed and lonely in his task. "He beats out his brains in the pulpit week after week to make a difference in people's lives. But sometimes he feels like he's been condemned to a lifetime of futility, trying in vain to motivate a sullen pack of foot dragging spiritual adolescents who never quite seem to see the big picture, never get excited enough to shoulder responsibilities, and never come anywhere close to a full 10% tithe."[2]

(4) Resisting Manipulation — For many, this will sound unbelievable. But the pastor is a frequent target of manipulation and control. Sometimes people unintentionally take advantage of a pastor's willing heart, and make requests and demands that begin to dominate his personal life. And then there are others who view the pastor like a politician, trying to lobby his favor or influence to attain a position, to favor their opinion, etc. But there are those who have a definite personality profile that feeds on being in control, and if they can't get the pastor to do what they want, they'll often turn on him and try to run him out. A prominent pastor once said, "There's an old saying about pastors: If they can't run God's man, they'll try to ruin him."

Because of this or other sour experiences with people, pastors will sometimes distance themselves from close personal relationships. They may even refuse favors or monetary gifts directly from persons, unless they are given anonymously, since such gifts often have strings attached — perhaps unintentionally, the giver will often expect preferred treatment, recognition, or to have a "special influence" in the pastor's decisions.

(5) Coping with Emotional Conflict — During the ministry of a pastor he will face challenges and strange conflicts in his emotions that he was never prepared for. This unique man most likely entered the ministry out of his divine calling, and his love for people. But he was probably surprised to learn that shepherding people was a life filled with wounds, hurts, and disappointment.

As the pastor faces his daily tasks, he will begin a ride an emotional roller-coaster. With each person he counsels or prays with, he will experience a momentary bond with their circumstances or burdens. During the course of a day he may console someone with a terminal illness, listen to trivial complaints, meet with a couple to discuss their marriage plans, or find it necessary to correct someone for their sinful lifestyle. He will go from one contrasting situation to another, and then within a short period, he will have to find a way to restore his composure from all these concerns to preach an encouraging, heartfelt sermon to the congregation.

Most others who deal with repeated crisis or trauma eventually learn how to develop a callousness in order to cope with the emotional upheaval of their jobs. Paramedics, police officers, or emergency room workers understand this all too well. However, when a pastor deals with a daily assortment of similar urgencies, unlike other emergency workers, he cannot distance his feelings from crisis. He cannot allow himself to become callous to protect his emotions from becoming involved. It's the nature of his calling and his job to care. His flock expects him to be sensitive, a person of genuine compassion, to feel their hurts and to share their burdens.

(6) Coping with Disappointment — Furthermore, during his ministry, he will experience many disappointments and heartaches with people. Many will fail to do what they promised and disappoint him. Others will criticize, judge, speak against him, betray him or even seek to ruin him or his family. Some will try to gain his friendship for ulterior motives — to manipulate his influence for their own agenda. Many he loves will eventually leave the church for some reason... some will move away, others may backslide, become offended, or simply reject his ministry. Dozens of times, he will experience the loss of beloved members of the flock through death. Many, many are the wounds of a shepherd, that the flock never really understands.

(7) Dealing with Satanic Attack — The pastor and his family are targets of Satan's greatest attacks. The enemy's strategy is highly intelligent. If he can overturn the shepherd with temptations or trials, he can likely scatter the sheep. According to insurance statistics, ministers experience an unusually high rate of stress related illnesses (such as ulcers and nervous conditions), depression, marital difficulties, conflict with their children or family, financial problems, and so on. To complicate matters further, if he does face such challenges, some will criticize him as a spiritual failure.

(8) Perseverance — There will be numerous temptations for the pastor to simply quit. He must be a person of tremendous faith and prayer to overcome the many challenges — to set his face as a stone, with unflinching determination and steadfastness. The average layman will never realize the price his pastor must pay to be his shepherd — the heartaches he will endure to minister to men's souls. Jesus, the Great Shepherd was a man acquainted with grief and sorrow, despised and rejected, and His under-shepherds and pastors also identify with these characteristics. How necessary it is that we pray for him, encourage him, show him love and not add to his list of wounds.

— 31 —
Should ministers receive pay for their ministry?

During the days of his missionary endeavors, we find that the Apostle Paul refused to accept wages from those churches he planted. This was a voluntary act on his part so the skeptics and unbelievers could not accuse his preaching of the Gospel as a motive for monetary gain *(1 Corinthians 9:12,15,18)*. Paul apparently financed his missions trips by working his trade as a tentmaker *(Acts 18:3)*, and from the contributions of other established churches *(Philippians 4:14-16)*.

However, Paul taught that it was a long established scriptural principle that ministers of spiritual things are entitled and ordained to receive their living from their labor of ministry. He cited from the Levitical law *(Leviticus Chapters 2 thru 7)* how the priests were to eat from the meat which were brought to the altars as sacrifices to God. *"Do you not know that those who minister the holy things eat of the things of the temple, and those who serve at the altar partake of the offerings of the altar?*

Even so the Lord has commanded that those who preach the gospel should live from the gospel" (1 Corinthians 9:13-14).

The Apostle made quite a case of reason for the provision for Gospel ministers. He asks, *"Whoever goes to war at his own expense? Who plants a vineyard and does not eat of its fruit? Or who tends a flock and does not drink of the milk of the flock?" (1 Corinthians 9:7).*

Elsewhere, Paul told Timothy that those church elders who excelled in leadership and ministry were entitled to "double honor," a reference to both respect and fiscal reward. He quoted from Moses' law *(Deut. 25:4)* which forbade the muzzling of oxen used in harvest of the cornfields — that is, in the course of their labor they were entitled to eat of the corn. Paul used this as a case to further the idea that the person who labors well in spiritual matters should be rewarded accordingly. *"Let the elders who rule well be counted worthy of double honor, especially those who labor in the word and doctrine. For the Scripture says, You shall not muzzle an ox while it treads out the grain, and, The laborer is worthy of his wages" (1 Timothy 5:17-18).*

According to scripture, a congregation should consider it a priority to care for the needs of their pastor. A pastor has a family to support, bills to pay, and is as entitled to vacations or retirement as anyone else. *"Do not withhold good from those to whom it is due, when it is in the power of your hand to do so" (Proverbs 3:27).*

If a church prospers under a pastor's ministry, that congregation should especially see that the pastor's wages reflect the fruit of his labors. If you were hired to manage a secular business, and its income doubled or tripled under your direction, wouldn't you expect to be rewarded for your efforts? If you weren't, would it tend to motivate you or discourage you in your attitude to keep working hard? God considers it a sin to suppress a laborer in his wages *(Malachi 3:5).*

Indeed, every church should recognize that the minister is entitled to receive pay for his labors. But on the other hand, the minister must always be cautious that his motives never become focused on compensation. A true pastor... a genuinely called minister of Jesus Christ is not in the ministry for money. Jesus said that a "hireling," one who watches over the sheep for the sake of pay, will selfishly abandon the sheep when attacked by the wolf, because he is not a genuine shepherd *(John 10:12-13).*

The scripture exhorts true servants of God to serve the flock willingly, out of love and obedience, not for the dishonest motive of money. *"Shepherd the flock of God which is among you, serving as overseers, not by constraint but willingly, not for dishonest gain but eagerly" (1 Peter 5:2).*

— 32 —
How come a pastor only has to work one day a week?

This has been a typical criticism of ministers, but is very far from the truth. Serving as the pastor of a church requires vastly more than one day a week, and is one of the most exhausting and time consuming jobs you could imagine. Researcher George Barna says that the average pastor works "far beyond" 40 hours a week.[1]

Because of the nature of his job, a pastor cannot escape his responsibilities when he leaves the office. He is on duty around the clock, and receives calls at home from dawn to dusk, even in the middle of the night. Most of his home activities and social relationships are church related. Even a large percentage of his family conversations involve the church in some way. If he is fortunate enough to have a day off, it will rarely be a day of leisure. It's usually the only time a pastor can find undistracted time to pray, study or do other ministry related things.

From my experience as a pastor, it is common to devote ten to twelve hours every day to ministry related activity. Sunday is obviously the longest day of the week, seldom less than fifteen hours. For many years it was my practice to arrive at the church at 5:00 a.m. to pray and finish work on my sermon or Sunday School lesson until services would begin. After lunch with my family, I would return to the church by 2:00 p.m. to pray and prepare for the evening service. Depending on the length of service, and how many people were "in line" to speak to me afterward, I might get out between 9:00 p.m. and 11:00 p.m. I can remember many occasions I was unable to leave before 1:00 a.m., making a twenty-hour day.

With that introduction, let's add up how much time it can take for a pastor to do his job. The pastor of an average church will usually preach two services on Sunday, perhaps another one on Wednesday night and maybe even teach a class for Sunday school. To prepare a fresh new sermon from scratch, he must pray and receive God's direction, research scriptures, consult commentaries for clarity, find interesting illustrations, and pray for God's anointing upon the finished product.

When I was an evangelist it was not unusual to spend dozens of hours, preparing and praying over just one sermon. According to Barna, it takes the average pastor ten hours to prepare a thirty minute sermon or teaching. If the pastor presents only three sermons or teachings a week (some do far more), this would total 30 hours of preparation. But the time demands on the pastor are so great, rarely can he devote this much time. Even at a minimum of six hours per presentation, this would come to 18 hours of preparation time a week.

If the pastor prays an hour and a half daily (10.5 hrs a week), spends a modest six hours preparing for each of his three sermons (18 hrs weekly), and works at the church on Sunday from 6:00 a.m. to 9:00 p.m. (15 hrs weekly), this would come to 43.5 hours a week devoted only toward his speaking ministry.

But for most pastors, the preparation time for their pulpit ministry is a very small percentage of their overall responsibilities. Each week there are many people who want to counsel with the pastor or speak to him by phone. In my case, I personally take an average of 20 calls a day. If only nine minutes is spent with each caller (most are much longer), this will come to 180 minutes or three hours per day. That's 21 hours per week on the telephone. I also usually counsel with about 10 people per week — either in the office or after services. Each meeting usually takes about an hour, for no less than 10 hours weekly. I usually visit with a few persons each week, either in the hospital or in their home, for a total time and travel of about five hours weekly.

So far this comes to 79.5 hours per week. But we haven't even considered the time it requires to conduct the business aspects and administration of the church. I spend no less than 2.5 hours daily

(12.5 hours weekly) in making administrative decisions, reviewing expenditures, signing checks and paperwork, dictating letters, analyzing the financial budget, directing church staff, reviewing schedules, problem solving, etc. Besides this, it takes me 12 hours a month to write my portion of the church newsletter and publications.

Then there's the attendance at midweek service each Wednesday (2 hrs), the monthly board meetings (2 hrs), evening committee meetings, the Saturday night prayer meeting (1.5 hrs). Not to mention the periodic weddings, funerals, committee meetings, business meetings, ministerial functions or social functions that the pastor is "expected" to attend. Even if the pastor doesn't conduct every meeting he attends, he is always "on duty," wherever he goes.

If you haven't a calculator handy, this all comes to more than 96.5 hours per week. Since there are only 168 hours in a seven-day week, and we hope that a pastor could sleep an average of eight hours a night (56 hours weekly), this means 95% of the pastor's 110 waking hours could be consumed with his responsibilities.

This is, of course, not the way it ought to be, but I regret to say that it is all too often, very close to the pattern of many ministers. Especially in a smaller church, where there is little or no staff to help, the load of the pastor can be overwhelming.

Needless to say, it is not true that a pastor works only one day a week.

— 33 —
What is a dysfunctional church?

This term has become used in recent years to describe a type of church which has abnormal, dysfunctional characteristics. There are scores of people who have been deeply wounded by an experience with such a church. It seems that most communities have a congregation that fits in this category. They identify themselves as Christians and may have good intentions of practicing scriptural ideals, but they seem to continually strive with combined elements of unbalanced or unorthodox doctrines, controversial government, disciplinary problems, irresponsible leadership — which result in explosive turmoil, division, wounded and confused sheep, and a derogatory reputation in their community.

A dysfunctional church has sometimes been mislabeled as a cult. The difference is, a cult is on a course of heresy based on misguided beliefs. However a dysfunctional church may theoretically be based on the right course of Christianity, but for the main part does not function the way it should. Keep in mind, every church has its share of problems — that does not make it dysfunctional. But it's when such problems dominate the church and actually cause its influence to become ineffectual or negative for the cause of Christ.

I regret to say that over my years of ministry I have come across situations in churches that seem almost unbelievable. One such church was widely reputed in the area for its continual controversy. The congregation was constantly fighting and contending with each other — the turmoil had produced several splits over a period of years. Every few months they would go on a tangent of promoting some new revelation or doctrine, which would often be refuted later as heresy. There were repeated occurrences of immorality among the leadership and congregation. Divorce within the church occurred 10 times more frequent than the rate of marriages. There were numerous financial scandals, alleged embezzlements by the pastors, and scores of church creditors left unpaid. Rumors, accusations, and slander were commonplace, causing injury and devastation to scores of individuals. The mere mention of the church name to local merchants or residents would invoke ridicule. Some might have presumed this to be some kind of weird cult, but it was not. In reality this was a dysfunctional Christian church.

A dysfunctional church will usually manifest several or all of the following symptoms:

(1) Unethical or immoral behavior tolerated in either leadership or laity.

(2) An absence of teaching or correction in matters of sin.

(3) Dictatorial or unethical church leadership or government.

(4) A failure to recognize practical spiritual priorities.

(5) Too much emphasis on esoteric thought or theory rather than practical ideals and application.

(6) Unscriptural or unbalanced preaching and teaching.

(7) Too much emphasis upon the superficial or sensational.

(8) Irresponsibility in business matters or in public relations.

(9) Isolation from the rest of the body of Christ.

(10) A sense of confusion and a lack of purpose by the congregation.

(11) An absence of spiritual fruit *(Galatians 5:22-23)*.

A dysfunctional church must be brought in order, otherwise it will cause irreparable harm for the cause of Christ in a community. If such a church has denominational affiliation, experienced ministers and officials may be sent to try to restore the fellowship back into scriptural order and stability. However, if the chaos is severe enough and resists repeated remedies, they might find it necessary to actually the close the church, temporarily or permanently.

In many cases, a church of this kind can be put in order by:

(1) Mature, godly, stable leadership — I regret to say that the problem of a dysfunctional church usually begins with a problem in the leadership. A congregation cannot rise above the level of their leaders.

(2) Scriptural, balanced preaching and teaching — The healthy church must get back on track with scriptural order. They need to hear the whole counsel of God's Word, not merely pet doctrines or narrow minded opinions *(2 Timothy 2:15)*.

(3) A patient application of love and correction — Just like parents, spiritual leaders must show the encouragement of love toward their flock. And they must be willing to confront sin with correction or discipline when necessary. *(Ephesians 4:15, 2 Timothy 3:16, 2 Timothy 4:2)*.

(4) Breaking of spiritual strongholds — A stronghold can usually be identified when the same troubling characteristics continue year after year, although the faces within the congregation change. This problem has to be dealt with through intensive prayer and spiritual authority *(2 Corinthians 10:4-5)*.

(5) Congregational repentance and revival — Some of the problems in a church cannot really be resolved until the people are willing to humble themselves before God and seek repentance and revival: *"If My people who are called by My name will humble themselves, and pray and seek My face, and turn from their wicked ways, then I will hear from heaven, and will forgive their sin and heal their land" (2 Chronicles 7:14).*

If you find yourself in a dysfunctional church, it is important for you to recognize it for what it is. If you can remain without impairing the spiritual progress of you or your family, do so that you can pray for and support the needed remedies listed above. But if your spiritual well-being begins to suffer, it may be best to cut your ties and move on to a healthy fellowship.

— 34 —
What are the qualifications of ministers and pastors?

In our society, a minister is a generic term that usually refers to a pastor, preacher or clergyman. For our purpose here, we are referring to all such ministers in general, who are officially ordained or commissioned by a church to carry out some form of spiritual leadership.

Above all things, the qualifications of a minister must first include a divine calling *(Acts 13:2)*. Someone once said that there are two kinds of people who enter the ministry: Persons called by God or fools. The meaning of this is, due to the many adversities faced in ministry, it is a great mistake to become a minister, especially a pastor, unless you have received a specific call from God. No amount of education from a Bible college or seminary can ever compensate for its absence.

A call from God is somewhat difficult to describe, and may vary in interpretation from one person to another. Some have heard audible voices or seen visions, while others have simply discerned an inner "awareness" of God's calling upon their life. A wise, elderly pastor once spoke to prospective ministerial students on the subject. He said, *"Do anything you can to stay out of the ministry, unless you can't do anything but get into it. If God has truly called you in the ministry, He'll put you there — He'll provide the opportunity and make the way. Don't seek the ministry unless it's something you can't avoid. Then you will know that it's His doing and not yours, and that He'll see you through when things get tough."*

Those who answer the call to become ministers, should be mature, Spirit-filled Christians who possess an intense love for Christ and their fellow man. They should show signs of the appropriate giftings in their inclined field of ministry, and seek to enhance these through applied study and training — by attending a Bible college or seminary if possible. But more than preaching ability or other gifts, a minister of the Gospel must be a person of exceptional character, endowed with spiritual fruit, devoted to prayer and the study of God's Word.

A minister must have a sound mind and common sense. He should possess wisdom and tact in dealing with people, and be able to communicate clearly and authoritatively. He must understand how people live, work and struggle, and be able to be empathic and compassionate to their concerns. His own financial affairs should be in good order, and he should have a strong understanding of the business aspects of a church.

A minister must be an impartial person, who will care for all the sheep of his flock equally. He must have a love for the souls of people, and a longing to lead them to a personal relationship with Christ — to contribute to their spiritual growth and development. One of the minister's greatest characteristics must be "patience," as people are very difficult to deal with, and only someone endowed with an unusual measure of patience can tolerate the ordeals of humanity. The heart of a pastor will be that of a shepherd — one who leads, feeds, cares for, and protects the flock.

A minister is a general term that refers to any of the Lord's servants or preachers, but probably more specifically relates to what the New Testament calls an "elder." Elders are an order of mature believers charged with the spiritual supervision and ministry of the church. The terms elder, bishop, and pastor were used interchangeably in scripture, and their qualifications were the same *(1 Timothy 3:1-7, Titus 1:5-9)*. (A deacon is also another type of minister, but with a separate list of qualifications in 1 *Timothy* 3:8-13.)

There are two scripture passages which specify the qualifications of
the bishop, pastor, or elder. Both were authored by Paul, first to
Timothy and then to Titus.

*1 Timothy 3:1 "This is a faithful saying: If a man desires the position of a
bishop, he desires a good work.*

*3:2 A bishop then must be blameless, the husband of one wife, temperate, sober-
minded, of good behavior, hospitable, able to teach;*

*3:3 not given to wine, not violent, not greedy for money, but gentle, not
quarrelsome, not covetous;*

*3:4 one who rules his own house well, having his children in submission with all
reverence*

*3:5 (for if a man does not know how to rule his own house, how will he take care
of the church of God?);*

*3:6 not a novice, lest being puffed up with pride he fall into the same
condemnation as the devil.*

*3:7 Moreover he must have a good testimony among those who are outside, lest he
fall into reproach and the snare of the devil."*

*Titus 1:5 "For this reason I left you in Crete, that you should set in order the
things that are lacking, and appoint elders in every city as I commanded you;*

*1:6 if a man is blameless, the husband of one wife, having faithful children not
accused of dissipation or insubordination.*

*1:7 For a bishop must be blameless, as a steward of God, not self-willed, not
quick-tempered, not given to wine, not violent, not greedy for money,*

*1:8 but hospitable, a lover of what is good, sober-minded, just, holy, self-
controlled,*

*1:9 holding fast the faithful word as he has been taught, that he may be able, by
sound doctrine, both to exhort and convict those who contradict."*

You will notice that both passages are very similar, but not identical.
By combining what he expressed in the separate epistles, we gain a
broad picture of what were considered the prerequisites of elders.

Qualifications of Elders	
Timothy	**Titus**
1. Above reproach	1. Above reproach
2. Husband of one wife	2. Husband of one wife

3. Temperate	3. Having children who believe
4. Prudent	4. Not self-willed
5. Respectable	5. Not quick tempered
6. Hospitable	6. Not addicted to wine
7. Able to teach	7. Not belligerent
8. Not addicted to wine	8. Not fond of sordid gain
9. Not belligerent	9. Hospitable
10. Gentle	10. Lover of what is good
11. Uncontentious	11. Sensible
12. Free from love of money	12. Just
13. Manages household well	13. Devout
14. Not a new convert	14. Self-controlled
15. A good reputation inside and outside the church.	15. Holding fast the word — both to exhort and refute.

In his highly respected book, Biblical Eldership, Alexander Strauch wrote the following commentary regarding these passages on church eldership:

"The elders, as Peter says, are examples to the people (1 Peter 5:3). Therefore, they must represent what God desires every member of the congregation to be in character and conduct. Those inside as well as outside the church first look to those who stand as leaders. It is understandable if a new or struggling believer falls prey to sin or hypocrisy, but when one who leads the congregation is found in reproach, the world blasphemes the teaching of the gospel, and saints within the church become disillusioned — some even turning away from the church. For these reasons, the stewards of God's household must be above reproach."

"Furthermore, local congregations tend to mold themselves according to their leaders — a tendency clearly seen throughout the Old Testament. When Israel had a bad king, for example, the people were sinful. When Israel had a good king, the people followed the Lord. Because people are like sheep, their shepherds have a profound impact on their direction and spiritual well-being. Therefore:

(1) "If an elder has a contentious spirit, the people will inevitably become contentious. So, a man with a contentious disposition is not qualified for eldership — even if he has the greatest teaching gift in the world (1 Timothy 3:3, Titus 1:7).

(2) "If an elder is not hospitable, the people will be unfriendly and cold (1 Timothy 3:2, Titus 1:8).

(3) "If an elder loves money, he will subtly use the people and work for his own ends (1 Timothy 3:3). Following his example, the people, too, will become lovers of money.

(4) "If an elder is not just and devout, he will be unable to rightly discern critical issues and problems (Titus 1:8), causing the people to become unjust and disloyal to the truth.

(5) "If an elder is not sensible, balanced, and self-controlled, his judgments will be characterized by disorganization, aimlessness, and ugly extremes — as will the judgments of the entire congregation (1 Timothy 3:1,2; Titus 1:8).

(6) "If an elder is not a faithful, one-woman husband, he will ultimately encourage others to be unfaithful (1 Timothy 3:2, Titus 1:6).

(7) "If an elder does not faithfully hold to the Word, the people will not. Such an elder will be unable to guide the church through the fierce storms of Satanic error (Titus 1:9)."

"What the churches of Jesus Christ need in the way of leadership is men of deep inner spiritual and moral character. The best systems, laws, and constitutions are impotent without men who are just, devout, lovers of what is good, sensible, self-controlled, forbearing, free from the love of money, uncontentious, and faithful keepers of God's Word. These are precisely the qualities that God requires of those who lead His people."[1]

In scripture, we will often see a common theme that is emphasized again and again. Spiritual leaders are supposed to be primarily examples to the flock. That is, the godly lifestyle of ministers, preachers, elders or pastors is critically important as it is the visual sermon that people see and emulate with their lives. Paul told Timothy, *"...be an example to the believers in word, in conduct, in love, in spirit, in faith, in purity"* (1 Timothy 4:12).

Furthermore, the lifestyle of the preacher is what brings credibility to his message. How can he hope for people to believe in a teaching that he doesn't live for himself? Someone once said, "Your life speaks so loudly, I can't hear what you're saying." It is ever so true that if we wish to influence lives for Christ, we must continually practice what we preach. *"The elders who are among you I exhort... Shepherd the flock of God which is among you, serving as overseers, not... as being lords over those entrusted to you, but being examples to the flock" (1 Peter 5:1-3).*

— 35 —
Why have some churches been accused of teaching cannibalism?

This accusation has been around even since the times of Christ, but is a misunderstanding of scriptures which use symbolic language, such as is seen here: *"Then Jesus said to them, Most assuredly, I say to you, unless you eat the flesh of the Son of Man and drink His blood, you have no life in you" (John 6:53).*

Obviously, Jesus was not inviting his followers to literally eat his body and blood, but was speaking metaphorically of Himself as the Passover lamb, describing a spiritual nourishing which would be provided from His atonement. Later, during His last supper, Jesus served bread and grape juice to his disciples as symbols of His broken body and shed blood, to show how the value of His sufferings must be consumed spiritually within and become a part of every believer.

In 1215, the Roman Catholic Church embraced the idea of "transubstantiation," which is the belief that during Holy Communion, the bread and juice actually turn into the blood and body of Jesus. However, there is no evidence to support this idea in scripture.

— 36 —
Why do churches practice the Lord's Supper?

The Lord's Supper, also referred to as Holy Communion, is one of two ordinances which Jesus gave to the church (the other being water baptism). Its practice is exercised in virtually all Christian churches in varying frequency — perhaps as often as every service or only one service a month. The origin of the practice begins with

Christ's Last Supper with his disciples, the evening before his trial and execution. The following text is taken from Paul's account of the event, and is the most frequent passage used in its association:

1 Corinthians 11:24 "...and when He had given thanks, He broke it and said, Take, eat; this is My body which is broken for you; do this in remembrance of Me.

11:25 In the same manner He also took the cup after supper, saying, This cup is the new covenant in My blood. This do, as often as you drink it, in remembrance of Me.

11:26 For as often as you eat this bread and drink this cup, you proclaim the Lord's death till He comes.

11:27 Therefore whoever eats this bread or drinks this cup of the Lord in an unworthy manner will be guilty of the body and blood of the Lord.

11:28 But let a man examine himself, and so let him eat of that bread and drink of that cup.

11:29 For he who eats and drinks in an unworthy manner eats and drinks judgment to himself, not discerning the Lord's body."

The Lord's Supper originated as a meal of fellowship between Jesus and disciples, the evening before his trial and execution. This, however, was not a typical meal, but was an event of symbolic significance. It was Thursday of the calendar week of the Passover feast in Israel, which was a commemoration of the death angel's passing over the Hebrew children in Egypt. During that historic event nearly fifteen hundred years earlier, each family obediently sacrificed a lamb for a meal and wiped its blood on their doorposts, which resulted in their national origin and deliverance from slavery *(Exodus 12:1-51)*.

The Lord's Supper was a Passover meal, in which Jesus portrayed Himself as the Lamb of the Passover. He showed that by partaking of His sacrifice by faith, with His blood wiped spiritually on the doorposts of one's heart, death will pass over, bringing deliverance from sin and everlasting life in the promised land.

During his supper with his disciples, Jesus used bread and the "fruit of the vine," as symbols of his body and blood which were soon to be rendered as an atonement for sin. He broke off portions from the unleavened bread and offered them to His disciples to eat, saying, *"This is My body which is broken for you; do this in remembrance of Me."*

Later, he shared with them a common cup, saying, "This cup is the new covenant in My blood. This do, as often as you drink it, in remembrance of Me" (1 Corinthians 11:24-25).

As the Passover feast was established as an everlasting memorial for the Jew, Jesus proclaimed his last supper as an ordinance for His followers — a memorial supper to be observed until His return. *"This do... in remembrance of me... For as often as you eat this bread and drink this cup, you proclaim the Lord's death till He comes" (1 Corinthians 11:26).*

Jesus instituted the Lord's Supper as a continual practice for His followers for several reasons, of which here are four:

(1) To remember His suffering & Covenant *(1 Corinthians 11:24-25).* Jesus did not want His followers to grow forgetful of the great sacrifice He paid for them, and the incredible testament of salvation which we received.

(2) To Proclaim His death till He returns *(1 Corinthians 11:26).* The enactment of this supper, to be repeated over and over, continually emphasized the essential fact of His death, portrayed the reasons why, and served as a reminder of His second coming.

(3) To take self-examination of our lives *(1 Corinthians 11:28).* Jesus instituted this supper as a very holy moment, for us to consider the state of our own heart before God. As we approach the sacredness of His body and blood, we weigh our heart against the awesomeness of His sacrifice. In this humble state, any faults, imperfections and sins come to realization, allowing us to confess them and obtain His forgiveness *(1 John 1:9).*

(4) To discern or recognize the Lord's body *(1 Corinthians 11:29).* Discernment of the Lord's body is one of the most remarkable truths in the Bible. Jesus served His disciples bread and wine as symbols of the divine merger which took place between Himself (His sufferings) and His followers. By becoming one with Jesus, we merge into one body, which brings about a unique effect: His body becomes ours, and our body becomes His. Christ's followers are enabled to appropriate the substitution of His body in the place of their own on the cross, while they substitute their body in the place of His on the earth.

Discernment of the Lord's body first brings recognition to how He became "our" body of sin for us, suffering and dying as the substitute for our sins. Peter wrote that Jesus *"bore our sins in His own body on the tree..." (1 Peter 2:24)*, and Paul said, God *"...made Him who knew no sin to be sin for us..." (2 Corinthians 5:21)*.

Secondly, it also takes in account how that all believers become "His" body here on the earth. Paul wrote, *"Now you are the body of Christ, and members individually" (1 Corinthians 12:27)*. Later, to the church of Ephesus he said, *"For we are members of His body, of His flesh and of His bones" (Ephesians 5:30)*. Paul also said our body is God's temple, that His Holy Spirit dwells in every believer *(1 Corinthians 3:16)*.

How important it is for believers to fully discern both elements of Christ's body. Jesus gave a solemn warning that to partake of the sacredness of the Lord's Supper in an unworthy manner, perhaps with unconfessed sin in our lives or without a proper estimation of the Lord's body, would make us guilty of the body and blood of the Lord. He also explained that some may become sickly or die prematurely, because they have not properly discerned the Lord's body *(1 Corinthians 11:29)*.

Christ's strength and blessing is connected with the value we place on this divine merger between His bodily sufferings, and His body, the church. This is consistent with other scripture, where Jesus made it clear that He combined His identity with the church. In fact, He views any actions toward His people, as actions toward Himself, saying that whatever we do for the "least" of our brethren, we have done it unto Him *(Matthew 25:40)*. Elsewhere, other passages confirm that a right relationship with Christ is not possible without a right relationship with our Christian brothers. John wrote, *"If someone says, I love God, and hates his brother, he is a liar; for he who does not love his brother whom he has seen, how can he love God whom he has not seen? And this commandment we have from Him: that he who loves God must love his brother also" (1 John 4:20-21)*.

Furthermore, how is it possible to separate Christ's sufferings from the people for which He suffered? Since "the value of anything is established by what it can be traded for," Jesus clearly expressed His value upon God's people by redeeming them with the price of His own life and sufferings. To Jesus, His people are equal to His shed blood and broken body. He views them equally as precious, and dwells in them by His Spirit, making them the body of His hands, fingers and toes through which He ministers in this world *(1 Corinthians 12:12-27)*.

Considering these facts, there may be times that Christians have lacked God's strength and healing, either because they failed to discern the atonement of Christ's bodily sufferings in their behalf, or because they did not properly love or value their brethren — the body of Christ. This may explain why the contemporary church has lacked strength, or not risen to its full potential in our world, because in many cases it has tried to value His sufferings without appreciating the whole body of Christ — including His children of different congregations or denominations.

As we partake in the Lord's Supper and consider Christ's precious sufferings, let us also examine our discernment of His body, the church. Do we love the least of our brothers in our fellowship? Do we harbor grudges or unforgiveness? Do we discern the body of Christ in our neighboring congregations? Do we esteem them and love them as a part of the family of God? Jesus said they are His body — they are the great treasure for which He traded His life, they are in whom He dwells by His Spirit. And whatever value we place upon them, is the value we place upon Christ.

"The cup of blessing which we bless, is it not the communion of the blood of Christ? The bread which we break, is it not the communion of the body of Christ? For we, being many, are one bread and one body; for we all partake of that one bread" (1 Corinthians 10:16-17).

— 37 —
Why are some churches considered nonprofit organizations?

In the United States, any legitimate group of religious people can file the appropriate documents with their secretary of state, to incorporate as a nonprofit religious organization. The state will require evidence of the religious nature of the group, articles of incorporation, a corporate constitution and bylaws, and a board of directors (usually with the assistance of an attorney).

The primary reason for this incorporation, is so that a 501(c)(3) tax exempt status from the Internal Revenue Service can be secured that will exempt the church from paying taxes on its offerings and property, and will provide a tax exemption to the organization's donors. The incorporation also serves to protect private individuals in the church from incurring personal liability in the organization's behalf. Whenever a church becomes such a corporation, it is required by law to keep detailed records of donations and financial records so to prove the nonprofit intent of the organization and to protect the intended purpose of the donor's offerings. Violations of related laws can result in revocation of a church's non-profit status.

Section 501 (c) (3) of the IRS code describes what the government considers to be an eligible nonprofit, religious group. "A tax-exempt religious organization is a legal entity or vehicle created and operated exclusively for religious purposes, no part of the net earnings of which insures to the benefit of any private individual, no substantial part of the activities of which is carrying on propaganda, or otherwise attempting to influence legislation, and which does not participate in or interfere in any political campaign on behalf of any candidate for public office."

Most churches are incorporated as nonprofit organizations, but there is no scriptural edict that requires any such status or any recognition from secular government. Some have contended that if persons regain their donation in the form of deducted taxes, it diminishes the sacrificial value of the original offering (2 Samuel 24:24). However, the tax exemption status has generally been viewed as one of God's great blessings to the American church, enabling it to direct greater sums to evangelism, benevolence, and foreign mission fields.

— 38 —
Why do many churches have a Constitution and By-laws?

A constitution and bylaws is required of any church which seeks to qualify for legal recognition as a nonprofit organization. The document, usually configured in legal terminology, is composed by the organizers of the church to describe the governing rules by which the church is organized and administrated, and to describe their beliefs and mission.

— 39 —
Why do some churches require premarital counseling?

Due to our society's deteriorated values of the sacredness of marriage, an increasing number of ministers require premarital counseling with couples before they will perform a marriage ceremony. Years past, when divorce was less frequent and children had better family role models, such counseling was not as common. Counseling will usually establish a scriptural foundation for marriage and try to prepare them for the inevitable challenges ahead.

A minister generally feels that he has been given a sacred trust by God to perform a marriage, and will be reluctant to discharge such functions for a couple who are obviously unprepared. Many ministers may refuse to perform a marriage between a Christian and an unbeliever, between persons who have been previously divorced without scriptural grounds, or for other reasons of conscience.

— 40 —
What is the difference between a Protestant church and a Catholic church?

Although both Protestants and Roman Catholics share the common ground of being founded upon faith in Jesus Christ, there are significant differences between the two groups. From general observation, one can see contrasts in everything from the way that their clergymen dress, to the way their services are conducted. Unlike most Protestant churches, Catholic masses are conducted in a liturgical fashion, with much emphasis upon symbols, rituals and ceremony.

In Addition, the Catholic church has traditionally regulated the type of Bible translation used in the church. For centuries, the only version authorized for use was the Latin Vulgate, a translation from the original languages by Jerome, in around 400 A.D. This Bible reads very similar to Protestant translations, however with a major exception. The Catholic version contains the Apocrypha, a collection of seven complete books and a few additions to others. These are considered non-inspired writings written between the period of the Old and New Testaments. Only one is actually dated. Two books, Judith and Tobit tell of the Assyrian and Babylonian invasions. Two more, 1st and 2nd Maccabees record the Jewish war of independence of around 165 B.C. Two more, Ecclesiasticus and Wisdom of Solomon, are considered books of wisdom. Another is an addendum to Jeremiah, and there are short additions to Esther and Daniel. The Protestants do not include them because they have never met the criteria for divine inspiration. Further, the writings of Jewish historian Josephus (in 90 A.D.) indicated that the Jews did not accept the books of the Apocrypha as a part of their scriptures, and although Jesus and the Apostles quoted frequently and accurately from almost every other Old Testament book, never once did they quote from the Apocrypha. Even if accepted, it would not alter the message of the New Testament, and it doesn't appear that much, if any, of the doctrines of the Catholic church had any foundation from the Apocrypha.

As we have said, there are many differences worth noting between Protestants and Catholics. However, the main distinction that sets them apart is the authority to which they look for their core beliefs. To help you understand this, let's first explain some of the detail about their origin in church history.

Catholic comes from the Greek, *KATHOLIKOS*, which means "throughout the whole, or universal," and was used as a general reference to the entire Christian church until the reformation period. However, as early as the fourth century, the Catholic church began adopting traditions and beliefs which were never a part of original Christianity as seen in the New Testament. It appears that many of these new ideas first emerged from the era of the Roman Emperor, Constantine who ruled from 313 to 337 A.D.

In contrast to his predecessor, Diocletian, who had vowed to destroy Christianity in 303, Constantine claimed a conversion to Christianity and virtually instituted it as the empire's religion by his Edict of Milan in 313 A.D. This proclamation of religious freedom brought about many positive changes for the church, and was certainly a much welcomed turnabout from the years of brutal persecution. But instead of converting completely from the old practices of paganism, this and the new Christian religion were somewhat mingled together. Since an Emperor was viewed as a god by pagan standards, and he already held the lifelong position of "Pontifex Maximus," chief priest of the pagan state religion, Constantine felt it only proper that he should also claim a high position of leadership in the church — he also authorized many of his secular officials as church leaders. This merger of a pagan, Christian and political hierarchy, produced a diluted spiritual leadership for the church, and its beliefs and doctrines thereafter became increasingly infected with a strange combination of traditions and pagan beliefs.

The Christian creed adopted at the Council of Nicaea in 325 (called for and presided over by Constantine) was theologically encouraging, but it was also in this era that the church first accepted such unscriptural ideas as praying for the dead, the veneration of angels and dead saints, the use of images, and the celebration of daily mass. This regression from scripture continued through the Council of Ephesus in 431 A.D., where the worship of Mary became an official doctrine of the church, referring to her as the "Mother of God." And only nine years later in 440, Leo, bishop of Rome was the first to declare himself the successor of St. Peter and laid claim to the role of Universal Bishop, a forerunner of papal authority. While this was widely disputed, Leo commanded that all should obey him on the false notion that he held the primacy of St. Peter.

Later, Leo's successor, Gregory I, was given the title of universal "Pope" (Latin "papas" or father) by the wicked emperor Phocas in 604. He refused the title, however his successor, Boniface III, did accept it and became the first in a long line of successors to be recognized as Pope. Under the new papal authority in the seventh century, many more new beliefs were added to the church, such as the unbiblical doctrine of purgatory (593), the required use of Latin in prayer and worship (600), and prayers said to Mary, dead saints and angels (600).

One reason many of these strange ideas gained accepted credibility was because the Bible was not readily available to the common people, either in print or in translation. They had no idea what the Bible really taught. It was restricted only to priests trained to interpret it as it pleased the church hierarchy. Further, the popes claimed the authority to speak under the unique utterance of "Ex Cathedria," which in effect meant divine inspiration. Their proclamations and decrees carried supreme authority to interpret or overrule Holy Scripture, and to invent whatever doctrines or practices they wished.

The next four hundred years saw many more new beliefs added to the church: The ritual kissing of the Pope's foot (709), temporal (political) power granted to the Pope (750), worship of the crucifix, images and relics (786), holy water mixed with a pinch of salt and blessed by a priest (850), the worship of St. Joseph (890), the establishment of the college of Cardinals to elect the popes (927), the baptism of bells (965), the canonization of dead saints (995), and prescribed fastings on Fridays and during lent (998).

A break in the church occurred in 1054 over a relatively trivial issue, when the eastern church condemned the western church for the use of unleavened bread in the Eucharist. The dispute resulted in Rome's attempt to excommunicate Michael Cerularious, the Patriarch of Constantinople, who in turn, sought to excommunicate Pope Leo IX of Rome. From that time, the western (Roman Catholic) church and the eastern (Greek Orthodox) churches developed separately — each with their distinct traditions. A classic example of a church split.

As the Roman Catholic Church continued with new independence, it added even more remarkable doctrines that were not taken from the Bible. In 1079, Pope Gregory VII declared the shocking decree of celibacy for the priesthood. Peter the Hermit invented the technique of praying with rosary beads in 1090. A few of the other beliefs and practices authorized by the church were: The inquisition of alleged heretics (1184), the sale of indulgences (1190), the doctrine of transubstantiation (1215), auricular confession of sins to a priest instead of to God (1215), adoration of the wafer (1220), the forbidding of Bible reading by laity (1229), the scapular (1251), the forbidding of sharing the communion cup with laity (1414), the establishment of purgatory as an irrefutable dogma (1439), and the composition of the "Ave Maria" (1508).

Up to this point, the somewhat similar Roman Catholic and Eastern Orthodox churches were the two main institutions representing Christianity. But in the sixteenth century, events occurred which would bring a world-shaking reformation of Christian thought. A Catholic monk and professor of theology named Martin Luther, became convinced that the Bible was the only true authority in matters of spiritual instruction, and sought to reform the church with this new insight and to expose its errant doctrines.

Born in Eisleben in 1483, Luther first pursued studies in law at Erfurt, but in 1505 he chose instead to join the Augustinian Hermits in Erfurt where he studied theology. After his ordination in 1507, he was sent by his order to the university of Wittenburg to teach moral theology, and in 1512 he became the professor of biblical studies.

Luther's ambitions of reformation emerged from his lifelong search for spiritual conclusions in his personal life. After many years of studying the scriptures, he came to reject all theology based only on tradition and embraced the idea of a personal relationship with Jesus Christ through faith. He believed that all our actions stem from God and that He chose to forgive the sinner by His sovereign grace — that we are justified not by our deeds, but by faith alone. In 1520, Luther wrote a treatise to Pope Leo X, called "The Freedom of A Christian," which outlined the conclusions of his study of scripture. In it, he made this famous statement: "The word of God cannot be received and cherished by any works whatever, but only by faith. Therefore it is clear that as the soul needs only the Word of God for its life and righteousness, so it is justified by faith alone and not by works; for if it could be justified by anything else, it would not need the Word and consequently, it would not need faith."

The move toward reformation began to emerge on the eve of All Saints Day, October 31, 1517, when Martin Luther announced a disputation regarding the indulgences of the church. He stated his argument in 95 theses which he posted on the north door of the Castle Church in Wittenburg — an act not especially unusual as the church doors were often used as a notice board.

The 95 Theses were not originally intended to promote a reformation movement. They were simply the proposal of an earnest university professor to discuss the theology of indulgences in light of the errors and abuses that had grown over the centuries. Although heavily academic in tone, news of them spread rapidly in Europe. All were amazed how one obscure monk from a new and unknown university could stir the whole of Europe.

The sale of indulgences, which Luther opposed, was based upon a common fear of purgatory, supposedly a painful place of temporal "purging" of the soul after death to make the soul pure for entrance into Heaven. The people would pay for the special indulgences of a priest to shorten their term in purgatory. Luther saw that this trade in indulgences was completely unfounded by scripture, reason or tradition. It was, in effect, directing attention away from God and His forgiveness and looking to man for the absolving of sins.

In December of 1517, the archbishop of Mainz complained to Rome about Luther. Confronted with opposition, Luther's stand became even more determined. He refused to recant his position, and fled town when summoned to Rome. In July 1519, during a disputation at Leipzig with John Eck, his fiercest opponent, Luther denied the supremacy of the Pope and the infallibility of general councils. He burned the papal bull which threatened his excommunication, but nevertheless, the decree came from the Pope in 1520, and he was subsequently outlawed by the Emperor Charles V at Worms in 1521. For his safety, Luther was seized and taken to Wartburg Castle under the protection of Frederick of Saxony. While there, he spent his time translating the New Testament into German so that everyone might have access to the Bible.

Eight months later in 1522, he returned to Wittenburg to begin the reform of worship away from the rigid forms of Rome. Over the next 25 years, Luther published many books in German, written to the common people so that they could judge for themselves, his doctrines and disputes with Rome. As a result, his followers continued to multiply.

In 1529, at the Diet of Speyer, the Emperor Charles V attempted to smother Luther's movement by force, but some of the German state princes stood up in protest. Thus, because of their protest, the movement began to be known as the "Protestants." What had originally been intended to bring reform to Catholicism from within, was now an ousted reformation, forced to split from the original body.

In 1530, Luther presented beliefs of the new movement at the Diet of Augsburg, in a peace-seeking, non-controversial attempt to explain their views. But as a result, the division between the Catholic and Protestants remained and became more distinct. New churches began to emerge referred to as "Evangelical" or "Protestant." And from this came three other branches: The Lutherans (in Germany and Scandinavia), the Zwinglian and Calvinists (in Switzerland, France, Holland and Scotland), and the Church of England.

Significant social, political and economic changes followed the reformation, and in some ways helped to shape it further before Luther's death in 1546. But besides exposing the errant beliefs of Catholicism, the reformation which produced the Protestant church was primarily a rediscovery of the authority of God's Word and the salvation which is by faith in the savior, our Lord Jesus Christ.

This is a brief explanation of the historical origin of Catholics and Protestants, and as you can see, the disparities are many. But in the simplest of terms, the basic difference between them is the authority they look to for their beliefs. The Protestant Church generally embraces the Bible as its sole source of authority and faith, while the Catholic Church views the post-biblical traditions of the church and its Popes to have more than equal authority with scripture.

— 41 —
What can I do to be a help to my church?

(1) Be faithful to attend and participate. — Obviously you can't be of much help to your church if you don't show up or take part. Some people underestimate their value of simply being present. Joining together with others adds to their encouragement, and it encourages the leaders and the pastor who have prayed and prepared all week to minister to you *(Hebrews 10:24-25)*.

I can remember back as a teenager how I "took for granted" those things my parents worked so hard to provide for me. I especially recall an incident where my mother spent her afternoon cooking something special for me for supper. However, preoccupied with something else, I didn't bother to even show up. How this hurt my mother, to feel that her labor of love was not appreciated. Pastors often feel the same way when their flock doesn't show up. I can remember times praying and fasting for the needs of our families, working into the late hours to prepare teachings that would stir their souls, only to find their empty seat on Sunday morning. This can discourage God's man from trying his best.

It helps your pastor and the whole church for you to come faithfully and on time. And don't merely sit there like a bump on a log. Be friendly, put a smile on your face, and enter into the service by singing and worshiping. You can even utter an audible Amen or two when the pastor makes a good point. Go ahead, it'll make his day!

(2) Commit yourself to love the Lord and your brethren. — The Bible teaches that all the desires of God are condensed into only two cardinal commandments that Jesus gave to His followers. He said, *"...You shall love the LORD your God with all your heart, with all your soul, with all your strength, and with all your mind, and your neighbor as yourself"* *(Luke 10:27)*. By clothing ourselves in God's love, we help the church to reinforce this objective for every believer, and we also help to eliminate the elements of conflict and division which can hinder the unity of the church. *"I... beseech you to have a walk worthy of the calling with which you were called, with all lowliness and gentleness, with longsuffering, bearing with one another in love, endeavoring to keep the unity of the Spirit in the bond of peace"* *(Ephesians 4:1-3)*.

(3) Pray for your church and its pastor and leaders. — The Apostle Paul explained that it is the duty of Christians to pray for all who are in authority, especially those in spiritual authority. *"I exhort first of all that supplications, prayers, intercessions, and giving of thanks be made for all men, for kings and all who are in authority, that we may lead a quiet and peaceable life in all godliness and reverence"* *(1 Timothy 2:1-2)*. Your church leaders are on the cutting edge of the battle with Satan, and will face temptations and spiritual conflict unlike anything you could imagine. The devil knows that if he can topple a spiritual leader or get him discouraged enough to quit, it will have a domino effect on the rest of the church. You can be a tremendous help by praying fervently for your church, and especially for the pastor and his family.

Especially helpful, attend the church prayer meetings, where you can come into agreement with others, and where the pastors and leaders can see and feel your prayer support for them and the church. God promised special strength through the combined prayer of His children. *"Again I say to you that if two of you agree on earth concerning anything that they ask, it will be done for them by My Father in heaven"* (Matthew 18:19).

(4) Help shoulder the load of responsibility. — Pastors and leaders of the church often feel much like Moses did when Israel fought with Amalek. Their arms become weary under the weight of so many responsibilities and they need brothers and sisters to stand beside them and help distribute the load. *"But Moses' hands became heavy; so they took a stone and put it under him, and he sat on it. And Aaron and Hur supported his hands, one on one side, and the other on the other side; and his hands were steady until the going down of the sun"* (Exodus 17:12).

The Lord never intended for the whole ministry of the church to be carried solely by the pastor or a mere handful of people. It's said that the majority of the work is done by the same faithful few, and sadly, this has caused the "burnout" of its many outstanding workers. If everyone would simply pitch in and do their fair share in helping, serving, giving, and so forth, all the needs would be met and no one would be overburdened.

I was once told the story of a young pastor assigned to serve as the minister of a small, rural congregation in a farming community. A part of his assignment was to try to straighten the church's severe financial problems. For years the church had struggled with its finances, unable to afford a full time pastor or to keep its bills paid.

Upon arrival the pastor examined the church income and realized it would be necessary to find additional employment to supplement his meager salary from the church. There weren't many job opportunities in the small nearby town, but he was finally hired by the local grain elevator. Most of the people in his church were farmers, and the local grain company happened to be where they all would bring their harvest to sell for market.

A year passed and the church conducted its annual business meeting. When the treasurer read the report of the finances, the congregation could hardly believe what they heard. The church income had more than doubled. All debts had been paid up and there was a surplus of savings in the bank! One church member stood and asked, "Pastor, never in our church history have we ever seen a financial miracle like this. Tell us what you did to change the situation."

The Pastor replied, "Well, when I first came and looked at the church books, I noticed that only a small portion of the church members were paying their tithes This was the problem with the finances. So, after I got hired by the grain elevator, every time you all would come and sell your grain I would just automatically deduct your tithe from your check and put it directly into the church account! You never missed the 10 percent, and all the needs of the church were more than met."

You'll be relieved to know that most pastors don't work for grain elevators, and it's not likely that your employer will secretly deduct your tithe from your wages. However, this story serves to illustrate that if everyone would just do their fair share, all the needs of the body will be met.

Be willing to volunteer for whatever needs to be done and don't be finicky about what you will or will not do — not just for strokes of attention, but do it for God's glory. *"Whatever your hand finds to do, do it with your might..." (Ecclesiastes 9:10).*

A church is like any other organization with human resources. No one ever starts out at the top. Everyone knows that we have to start at the "entry level." But if a believer continues to grow strong in Christian character and proves faithful and responsible to the basic tasks given to them in the church, he or she will likely be promoted to greater responsibility and ministry. *"He who is faithful in what is least is faithful also in much; and he who is unjust in what is least is unjust also in much" (Luke 16:10).*

(5) Get to know your spiritual leaders and cooperate with them. — The more you get to know them and their Godly lifestyle, the more you will likely come to trust their leadership. You will have a greater credibility in their teaching and counsel *(1 Thessalonians 5:12).* Show respect and cooperate with their authority. Avoid challenging their right or worthiness to serve in their position, but accept that God has seen fit to place them in this role *(Romans 13:1).* Belligerence or antagonism toward leadership may be acceptable in secular society, but there is no place for it in the Lord's church.

"Obey those who rule over you, and be submissive, for they watch out for your souls, as those who must give account..." (Hebrews 13:17).

(6) Apply the teaching and ministry to your life. — There's not much that a pastor loves more than to see his flock practicing what he has preached — living a Godly, holy life, and on their knees seeking the Lord. Learn to appreciate the spiritual values they try to instill in the congregation. *"Brethren, join in following my example, and note those who so walk, as you have us for a pattern" (Philippians 3:17).*

Each year there is a national pastor's appreciation Sunday. Upon learning about this upcoming recognition, one of my members spent time thinking about what he could do to show appreciation toward his pastor. He became inspired to do something quite amazing. Unknown to me, he took the church phone directory and called every member, urging them to come to the weekly church prayer meeting. To my pleasant surprise, the evening of the prayer was unusually packed with people. I was elated that this dear member had discovered precisely what "rings a pastor's bell." He understood my value upon spiritual things. As far as I was concerned, there could have been no greater expression of appreciation than this. A pastor doesn't enter the ministry with the goals of great earthly gain or financial rewards. He enters ministry to bring people to God, to help bring them closer to Him.

It helps your church when you live and conduct yourself in a Christ-like manner. Whether you realize it or, you're a walking billboard for your church. Whatever the people of your community see in your life, they will tend to identify with your pastor and his flock. Behave yourself and speak well of the church and your pastor. Eyes and ears are always open to the things you say and do.

(7) Seek out and use your gifts. — According to the scriptures, the Lord distributes gifts to each in the body as it pleases Him. Spiritual gifts are not provided to you merely for your own gratification, but so the church would be edified or built up. God has given you gifts that will be a help to your church — it is up to you to discover them, develop and utilize them under the direction and cooperation with your spiritual leaders. By doing so, you will glorify God and be a great help to your church. *"Even so you, since you* *are zealous for spiritual gifts, let it be for the edification of the church that you seek to excel" (1 Corinthians 14:12).*

(8) Contribute to solutions and not to problems. — Every pastor would be thrilled if each of his members got involved and helped the church in some way. However, they would rejoice if certain ones simply stopped being a "pain in the neck." It's a shame that pastors spend so much time "putting out fires," that is, squelching problems that could have a negative influence on the whole body, such as gossip, rumors, complaining, misunderstandings, hurt feelings, discontent and so forth. Regrettably, it has been said that 90% of these kinds of problems are circulated among the same 10% of the people.

Spiritually mature persons who wish to help their church don't become a part of such problems — instead, they contribute to solutions. They avoid divisive people *(Romans 16:17)* and don't get caught up in the mischief or grievances of others *(1 Timothy 5:13).* If they are aware of spreading problems in the fellowship, they will try to bring a resolution, or else they bring matters to the attention of spiritual leadership so that they can bring an end to it *(Matthew 18:15-17).* People who wish to be an asset to their church don't participate with or spread problems — they help spiritual leadership resolve them.

— 42 —
What's the difference between Elders, Bishops and Pastors?

The term Elder was originally used to denote the older men of a Jewish community which governed and made the major decisions. In the New Testament, the term evolved into a description of a mature believer charged with spiritual supervision and ministry within the church, detached from the relationship with age. The terms elder, bishop and pastor are generally used interchangeably in the New Testament, although "elder" primarily refers to the person, while "bishop or pastor" deals with their office. *"Let the elders who rule well be counted worthy of double honor, especially those who labor in the word and doctrine" (1 Timothy 5:17).*

A bishop means "an overseer," originally the principal officer or pastor of a local church, but later evolved into a position of supervision over multiple churches. *"This is a faithful saying: If a man desires the position of a bishop, he desires a good work" (1 Timothy 3:1).*

In today's society, a Pastor is generally a minister and spiritual overseer of a church congregation — the same as an elder or bishop. Pastor was probably not intended to be as much a title, as it was an adjective to describe what he does. A pastor literally means "shepherd," a metaphoric description of one who cares for and leads a flock of God's sheep. One of five office gifts described in Ephesians 4:11.

— 43 —
What are Deacons?

A Deacon is one of the ministry offices of the church and literally means a servant *(Greek, DIAKONOS)*. Besides bishops and other offices, the early church valued the ministry of the Deacon. *"Paul and Timothy, servants of Jesus Christ, To all the saints in Christ Jesus who are in Philippi, with the bishops and deacons" (Philippians 1:1).*

It is believed that the office of deacon developed out of the need for the Apostles to delegate many of the increased administrative tasks that overwhelmed the growing church. This was first seen when complaints were brought to the Apostles that some of the Greek widows of the church were being neglected in their care. So in order that they would not be distracted away from what God had really called them to do — to be men of prayer and of the Word — they selected qualified persons to look after these affairs. *"...It is not desirable that we should leave the word of God and serve tables. Therefore, brethren, seek out from among you seven men of good reputation, full of the Holy Spirit and wisdom, whom we may appoint over this business; but we will give ourselves continually to prayer and to the ministry of the word" (Acts 6:2-4).*

This follows the administrative function of how the modern church should operate. The pastor should be the spiritual overseer, devoting his attention to the higher priorities of prayer and ministering the word, while delegating the load of administrative tasks, details and responsibilities to other ministers, elders and deacons.

— 44 —
What is church government and why is it necessary?

Government is sometimes viewed negatively, seen as something that inhibits one's freedom. However, government is a necessary element of human society which serves to establish and maintain order. Anyone that doubts the need for order should think back to their school days, and remember those times when the teacher stepped out the class for a few moments. In the absence of authority and organization, the human nature lends toward mischief and chaos.

Since God is the author of government, it's easy to realize that He also desires His church to be well ordered so there will be (1) organization, order and direction of ministry, and (2) authority for leadership and correction. These are the two main functions of church government.

It is commonly agreed that Jesus is the head of the church *(Colossians 1:8)*, and has delegated His authority to be exercised through the government of the church. However the method of church government is sometimes an object of debate, and is one of the primary differences between some denominations.

The New Testament provides the grounds for government through the authority of its offices, but is silent in the specific methods of implementation. **Generally speaking, there are three prominent forms of church polity or government used in churches today. These are as follows:**

(1) Episcopal — This system of church government considers the bishop as the principal officer. Decisions are made at levels higher than the local church, usually with prayerful contemplation toward God's will and nominal consideration of the member's opinions.

(2) Presbyterian — This form of government acknowledges that Christ alone is Head of the church, and that He rules His church by His Word and Spirit. Church officials have ministerial and declarative authority, but not legislative. They declare, explain, and apply Christ's will as the Spirit clarifies the scripture to their understanding. They do not seek to make new laws for the church.

Presbyterians believe they find foundation for their form of church government in the Bible, but they readily admit that God can bless other forms as well.

(3) Congregational — This is an autonomous form of government by the church, generally by a democratic philosophy, which allows a local congregation the freedom to determine what it considers the will of Christ. The congregation governs its own affairs, however this does not suggest that it is self-governing apart from Christ's Lordship. Simply stated, the members of the congregation are given the right to determine what they consider to be Christ's will.

Many will make their case for what they believe is the preferred form of church government. However history shows that God has blessed churches who have used any of these forms.

— 45 —
What is a Pentecostal church?

A Pentecostal church takes its name from the Spirit's outpouring which occurred on the day of Pentecost in Acts 2:1-4. The primary distinction of a Pentecostal church is the belief that Christians can receive the same experience as the 120 did, of being baptized with the Holy Spirit, evidenced by speaking in other tongues. In this same vein, the Pentecostal believes in the present day operation of spiritual gifts such as miracles, healing, prophecy, and other supernatural manifestations described in 1 Corinthians 12. They generally follow a similar form of liturgy to that found in most evangelical churches, and they place high value on praise and worship.

A Pentecostal church generally identifies with the long standing history, traditions and theological views of the Pentecostal movement which began to emerge throughout the U.S. at the turn of the 20th century. The origins of the movement are usually associated with a band of believers led by minister, Charles F. Parham. In a Bible school in Topeka, Kansas, students and teachers, along with Parham, researched the book of Acts, searching for the source of the Apostle's great power and success. They all concluded that it was because of the events that began with the Day of Pentecost. After a thorough review of Acts 2,8,9,10, and 19, they concluded that the same experience was available to them. On New Year's eve 1900, the first student was filled with the spirit and spoke in tongues. Then on January 3rd, others including Parham received, igniting a rapid growing movement. The famed 1906 revival of the Azusa Street mission in Los Angeles was a derivative of the events in Topeka. From there, it spread through the U.S., Canada and abroad.

The Pentecostals have long been known and respected for their great emphasis on evangelism and foreign missions. Some of the more well-known Pentecostal fellowships are: The Assemblies of God (of Springfield, MO) with 12,362 U.S. churches (2007), The Church of God in Christ with 15,300 (2010), The Church of God (of Cleveland, TN) with 6,666 (2008), and The Foursquare Church with 1,875 (2006). In all, there are more than 51,593 U.S. churches affiliated with Pentecostal denominations, with hundreds more of independent status.[1]

Within the ranks of those who identify themselves as Pentecostals, there are small sects which are known for more extreme or even bizarre views. Some practice handling of snakes, or others of a Unitarian theology insist that only those who speak with tongues can be saved. These unorthodox beliefs are not embraced by the large body of Pentecostal churches or denominations, however the fanaticism of this small group of radicals has sometimes generated an inaccurate stereotype of all Pentecostals which has been exploited by tabloid TV news shows and so forth.

— 46 —
What is a Charismatic church?

The Charismatics derive their name from the Greek, *CHARISMATA*, which refers to the gifts of the spirit. This term and movement came into its own in the mid 1960's, as laymen and ministers in mainline churches began experiencing the manifestation of spiritual gifts. For many years the term Charismatic was used to merely identify a non-Pentecostal Christian who had such experiences. Today there are persons who attend mainline, non-Charismatic churches, yet who consider themselves Charismatics. And there are also local congregations and denominations that classify themselves as Charismatic.

In some ways a Charismatic church may be indistinguishable from a Pentecostal church in that they too embrace the belief in the modern day operation of spiritual gifts and a distinct Holy Spirit baptism which can enable persons to speak with other tongues. Their form of liturgy may vary, but with much emphasis upon a freedom of worship focused around praise. Generally a Charismatic church has a more independent, non-denominational tone, sometimes with more emphasis on spiritual exploration, and less emphasis on established tradition.

— 47 —
What is an Evangelical church?

An evangelical church is a Protestant body that emphasizes the gospel, God's redemption for man, along with the belief that salvation is obtained through faith in the grace of God, not earned by man's efforts or good works. The evangelical church promotes the basic Christian doctrines: The trinity, the deity of Christ, the personality of the Holy Spirit, the inspiration of scripture, the vicarious suffering of Christ for atonement of sin, His resurrection from death, His ascension to heaven, His personal return, the resurrection and judgment of all men, heaven and hell. The primary distinction of an evangelical church is their view of biblical authority — that scripture is the infallible, written Word of God. The form of worship may vary somewhat from church to church, but usually follows the influences of revivalistic liturgy of the 19th century.

— 48 —
Why do some churches encourage the use of offering envelopes?

Donations to a church which possesses a nonprofit organization status are tax exempt, and the church is required to retain records of donations and to issue annual receipts in order for contributors to claim these as deductions from their taxes. Most churches retain the envelopes as physical donation records to comply with IRS laws. Donations made by check alone, with the donor's name and address, will probably receive appropriate credit, but it is a help to a church's accounting to use an envelope.

Some churches take note of their members stewardship patterns as indicative of their faithfulness to scripture and the support of the church. However, it is to be noted that giving (especially to the poor) was intended to be a private matter to be kept between the contributor and God *(Matthew 6:1-4)*. Some consider the viewing of a contributor's offerings as a violation of that secrecy.

— 49 —
Why do many churches use the Bible as their sole source of teaching?

Christian churches of an evangelical base generally use the Bible as the sole authority for their beliefs and practices **because they accept the Bible as God's inspired, infallible Word**.

The foundation for this belief comes from the combination of many overwhelming facts:

(1) The Testimony of Scripture — The Bible itself, claims to be the truly inspired word of God. *"All Scripture is given by inspiration of God, and is profitable for doctrine, for reproof, for correction, for instruction in righteousness" (2 Timothy 3:16)*. The term "inspiration" comes from the Greek, *THEOPNEUSTOS*, which means "God breathed." Elsewhere, the scripture says, *"For prophecy never came by the will of man, but holy men of God spoke as they were moved by the Holy Spirit" (2 Peter 1:21)*.

(2) The Testimony of Jesus — Jesus endorsed the reliability of the scriptures by repeated claims that God was the author, that they were authoritative, and continually quoted from them *(Matthew 19:4,5, Matthew 24:37-38, Luke 4:1-13, Luke 17:28-31, John 6:49, Luke 24:27)*. If one has confidence in Christ's infallibility, one must also bring an equal weight of confidence to the credibility of the Bible from which He based His teachings.

(3) The Bible's Harmony — One of the most unique characteristics about the Bible which shows a divine origin, is its unity despite its diverse, composite structure. It was composed by dozens of different authors who lived hundreds of years apart, who spoke different languages and lived in different cultures. Yet the Bible speaks with complete harmony from Genesis to Revelation, and conveys one consistent theme throughout: God's redemption of man.

According to Christian apologist, Josh McDowell,[1] this remarkable trait of scripture is retained throughout, even though it was:

(a) Written during a span of 1,500 years.

(b) Written over 40 generations.

(c) Written by over 40 authors from every walk of life including kings, peasants, philosophers, fishermen, poets, statesmen, scholars, etc.

(d) Written in different places — everywhere from dungeons to palaces.

(e) Written at different times — sometimes in war others in peace.

(f) Written during different moods — sometimes in joy others in sadness.

(g) Written on three continents (Asia, Africa, and Europe)

(h) Written in three languages (Hebrew, Aramaic, and Greek)

To illustrate the phenomenal harmony of scripture, McDowell tells the story of his encounter with a sales representative of the "Great Books of The Western World," a series of writings by some of the great philosophers of ancient and modern times. He challenged the representative to take just ten of the authors, all from the same walk of life, the same time period, the same place, the same language and pose to them one controversial subject. Would they agree? The gentleman paused, then replied, "No! You would have a conglomeration." However the Bible is far more complex and does agree. It is a harmonious book covering many intricate and controversial issues. This fact points to an all knowing, all powerful God behind its construction and composition.

(4) The Survival of Scriptures — There is no other literature in history that has been more of a target of destruction than the Bible. Yet, it has miraculously withstood every challenge to its survival — unquestionable evidence of divine preservation. The Bible has been attacked by atheistic philosophies, higher criticism, modernists, liberal theologians, rationalists, humanists, scientific skeptics, communists and every conceivable brand of critic. And not only has it survived the determined and aggressive assaults, it has consistently triumphed over all its enemies.

The noted theologian, Bernard Ramm, writes, *"No other book has been so chopped, knifed, sifted, scrutinized, and vilified. What book on philosophy or religion or psychology or belles letters of classical or modern times has been subject to such a mass attack as the Bible? with such venom and skepticism? with such thoroughness and erudition? upon every chapter, line and tenet? ... Yet the Bible is still loved by millions, read by millions, and studied by millions."[2]*

An example of the way the Bible outlives its critics: during the 18th century, the French infidel Voltaire confidently boasted of the eventual extinction of Christianity and the Bible. However, only fifty years after his death the Geneva Bible Society actually used his own press and house to produce scores of Bibles.

In 303 A.D., Roman Emperor Diocletian issued an edict pronouncing the obliteration of Christianity. "... an imperial letter was everywhere promulgated, ordering the razing of churches to the ground and the destruction by fire of the scriptures, and proclaiming that those who held high positions would lose all civil rights, while those in households, if they persisted in their profession of Christianity, would be deprived of their liberty." And yet it was his successor, the emperor Constantine the Great, who issued the "Edict of Milan" only 10 years later, which ordered the cessation of persecution against the church (and the Bible) and legalized Christianity.

(5) Enduring Acceptance — The Bible continues to be the best-selling book in history. No other piece of literature can compare to its widespread acceptance. It has managed to survive the continual attacks of critics, and its popularity has not been eroded by time or persecution. The Latin Vulgate Bible was the first major book printed on the Gutenberg press in the 1450's, and since then more than seven billion copies have been printed. No other book comes close to its popularity and circulation. It has been translated, entirely or in part, into nearly nineteen hundred languages or dialects.

Scores of great historical figures have accepted and staked their honor upon their confidence in the Bible. The great scientist, Sir

Isaac Newton, wrote, "There are more sure marks of authenticity in the Bible than in any other profane history." The father of our nation, George Washington, wrote "It is impossible to rightly govern the world without God and the Bible." Abraham Lincoln said, "I believe the Bible is the best gift God has ever given to man. All the good from the Savior of the world is communicated to us through this book." And another notable president, Woodrow Wilson, made this profound statement: "When you have read the Bible, you will know it is the Word of God, because you will have found it the key to your own heart, your own happiness, and your own duty."[3]

The uniqueness of the Bible's long-standing acceptance by millions, both great and common, and its durability throughout the centuries attests to its divine origin and preservation.

(6) **Manuscript Accuracy** — The Bible has more manuscript evidence supporting its reliability and accuracy that any ten pieces of ancient literature combined. According to McDowell, there are over 5,300 known Greek manuscripts of the New Testament, over 10,000 of the Latin Vulgate, and at least 9,300 other early versions, and we have more than 24,000 manuscript copies of portions of the New Testament in existence today.[1]

No other document of antiquity even comes close to such numbers or attestation. In comparison, another ancient writing, Homer's Iliad, is second with only 643 manuscripts that still survive. The accuracy of translation and the massive amount of manuscripts in existence, gives tremendous credence to the divine authorship and preservation of the Bible.

(7) **Scientific Accuracy** — Despite efforts to the contrary, no fact or discovery of science has ever disproven any of the claims of the Bible. In fact, the progress of science only continues to confirm the scriptures' accuracy.

For example, long before man knew anything about bacteria, God commanded the Israelites to remove human waste and bury it outside the camp *(Deut. 23:12-13)*. This prevented the spread of deadly disease. Had this direction been followed by the people of Europe in the middle ages, the infamous black plague, which spread from the open sewers flowing freely in the city streets, would not have killed thousands.[4]

As we know from history, it was 15th century explorers that discovered that the world wasn't flat as had been thought, but the Bible had already declared that the earth was round *(Isaiah 40:22)*.

Before the invention of the telescope, gazers tried to count the number of stars that filled the skies, such as Ptolemy who established the number at 1,056. Today, we know that such estimates were futile, but as far back as 600 B.C. the prophet Jeremiah revealed that the number of stars were innumerable *(Jer. 33:22)*.

Perhaps one of science's most amazing testimonies of its interface with the Bible is contained in a document found in the Bodleian Library of Oxford, England. The following statement was signed by eight hundred of Great Britain's scientists: "We the undersigned, Students of the natural sciences, desire to express our sincere regret that researchers into scientific truth are perverted by some in our own times into occasion for casting doubt upon the truth and authenticity of the Holy scriptures. We conceive that it is impossible for the Word of God written in the book of nature, and God's Word written in Holy scripture, to contradict one another."[3]

(8) Prophetic Accuracy — The fulfillment of Bible prophecy is one of the greatest proofs of the authenticity of God's Word. There are hundreds of prophecies in the Bible which list specific detail in regard to persons, places, events and times, and history has repeatedly shown such prophecies relating to the past were fulfilled in the most exact of terms (as they will also for future events).

An example of such involves the 6th century B.C. prediction of the overthrow of the city of Tyre *(Ezek. 26:1-21)*. Seven specific things were predicted, and each were later fulfilled to the letter during the 4th century B.C. The mathematical probability of this happening by mere chance has been calculated to be 1 in 75,000,000.

Perhaps the most amazing series of prophetic fulfillments involves the numerous Messianic predictions concerning Christ. The Old Testament contains 333 specific prophecies which were fulfilled by Christ. These not only bear proof of His divine authenticity, but they also help substantiate the divine authorship of the Bible.

In the book, Science Speaks, Professor Peter Stoner used the mathematical principle called "the Law of Compound Probability,"[5] to assess some of the prophecies relating to Christ. Simply stated, this law is used to calculate the odds against a "chance" fulfillment of such predictions when compounded by a specific set of conditions, requirements, or qualifications. His findings were carefully evaluated by the American Scientific Affiliation, and were found to be sound and convincing. By this method, he was able to show evidence that would rule out coincidence, chance or human manipulation in the fulfillment of biblical prophecy.

Stoner started by calculating the probability of one individual who could precisely fulfill only eight prophecies relating to Christ. He computed the odds at 1 in 10 (17th power), the same as 1 followed by 17 zeros. This is the equivalent of covering the entire state of Texas 2 feet deep in silver dollars, specially marking one of them, and instructing a blindfolded man to pick the right silver dollar on the first try.

Dr. Stoner then computed the odds of one individual that could fulfill just 48 prophecies relating to Christ. He calculated the odds at 1 X 10 (to the 157th power) — or 1 followed by 157 zeros. This figure is astronomical and beyond human comprehension, but Christ fulfilled over 300 distinct prophecies, proving the divine authorship of scripture beyond any doubt.

(9) Archaeological Evidence — The discoveries of archaeology have consistently, and continually verified the reliability of the Bible. There has never been a discovery which has contradicted a scriptural reference, and to this day, ongoing research continues to show that the Bible was correct about its references to historical figures, civilizations and cities. Nelson Glueck, the renowned Jewish archaeologist wrote, "it may be stated categorically that no archaeological discovery has ever controverted a biblical reference."[6]

During the excavations of Jericho archaeologist John Garstang found something so starling that a statement of what was found was prepared and signed by himself and two other members of his team. In reference to these findings, Garstang said, "As to the main fact then, there remains no doubt: the walls fell outwards so completely that the attackers would be able to clamber up and over their ruins into the city." Why so unusual? Because the walls of cities do not fall outwards, they fall inwards. And yet in Joshua 6:20 we read "...the wall fell down flat, so that the people went up into the city every man straight ahead, and they took the city."[7]

(10) Sacrifice of Martyrs — Millions have laid down their lives in defense of the Bible. Foxes Book of Martyrs describes scores of believers who historically endured banishments, torture, confiscation of property, and imprisonment rather than to deny their confidence in the Holy Scripture.[8] William Tyndale was tried as a heretic, strangled and burned to death in 1536 for translating the Bible into the language of ordinary people. John Hus was burned at the stake in 1415 because he taught that the Bible was the only inspired and reliable message from God to man. If the Bible was a mere book, without the attestation of such remarkable internal and external proofs, persons would not have been willing to throw away their lives for a book of fairy tales. Among other evidence, the Bible has spoken to men's hearts and changed their lives, therefore they know it is true and have been willing to die for it.

(11) The Resurrection of Jesus — Christ's resurrection confirmed that Jesus is who He claimed to be, and that His own statements regarding scripture are reliable. The fact of the resurrection can be proven by many "infallible proofs" *(Acts 1:3)*. The appearance of Christ after the resurrection was verified by more than 500 eyewitnesses *(1 Corinthians 15:6)* who touched, spoke to, and ate with him. The number of witnesses, together with the circumstances and various appearances provide powerful proofs that the resurrection was not a hoax or plot. These witnesses were of high moral integrity and many were executed for their defense of the resurrection. Authorities claim more evidence of the resurrection than any other event in history.[1]

(12) Personal witness and Transformation — When one reads the scripture, it speaks to the heart and bears witness to our inner, spiritual man. This attests that it is a communication of God designed to speak to the heart of man — and that message changes and transforms lives. The Bible has produced the same life changing effect upon the lives of millions all over the world, despite whatever differences of sex, age, nationality, culture, social class, vocation, intellect, or religious background. Millions of born again Christians are a testimony of the transforming power of God's Word.

— 50 —
Why do many churches use different translations of the Bible?

For over three hundred years the King James Version, published in 1611, was the prominent translation used in most Protestant churches. However, as the English language continued to change, it became increasingly more difficult for people to understand it=s outdated vernacular. Faced with the obvious need for our society to understand God's Word, scholars sought to update the scriptures into more contemporary language.

Dr. Lewis Foster, one of those who helped translate the NIV and the NKJV says, "It is necessary to continue making new translations and revising old ones if people are to read the Word of God in their contemporary languages. With the passage of time, words change in meanings. For instance, in King James' day the word 'prevent' could mean 'come before' but not necessarily in a hindering way. So the translators in that day rendered 1 *Thessalonians* 4:15, 'For this we say unto you by the word of the Lord, that we which are alive and remain unto the coming of the Lord shall not prevent them which are asleep.' But today the word 'prevent' has lost that earlier meaning (come before), so it must be translated differently to convey the proper meaning: 'According to the Lord's own word, we tell you that we who are still alive, who are left till the coming of the Lord, will certainly not 'precede' those who have fallen asleep' (NIV). ...To keep the translation of God's Word living it must be kept in the living language the people are using."[1]

While new translations have generally been a welcome contribution to the comprehension of scripture, they have also received mixed reactions across the Christian spectrum. One story is told of a pastor who tried to introduce a revised version of the Bible to his rigidly conservative congregation. "So what's wrong with the King James Version?" said one woman in defense. "In my opinion, if it was good enough for Jesus, it's good enough for us!" The amusing irony is that Jesus obviously did not speak the Old English of the King

James Version — neither was the Bible originally recorded in English. Despite the sacred tradition that many revere of the KJV, it is merely a translation of the inspired Word of God, not the initial source. The Old Testament was authored in Hebrew and Aramaic, and the New Testament in Greek. While the original autographs no longer exist, translations are made from ancient manuscript copies, of which there are today at least 24,000, whole or in-part, with which to compare.[2]

An English version of the Bible did not exist until a little more than 600 years ago. Before then, a version translated into Latin by Jerome in the fourth century, called the Latin Vulgate, was the most widely-used Bible translation in the middle ages (the first major book printed on Gutenberg's press in 1456). Portions of scripture in English began to emerge in the early seventh century, but the first complete English translation was not produced until 1382 by the influence of John Wycliff. Despite fierce opposition of the Roman church, and absence of the printing press, copies of this work were widely circulated. Later in the 16th century, seven more popular English versions were produced, beginning with William Tyndale's work in 1525. This English version of the New Testament was the first to be translated directly from the Greek instead of Latin texts. Before Tyndale's completion of the Old Testament, he was tried as a heretic and executed in 1536.

After Tyndale, several other famous Bibles were produced in the 16th century. The Cloverdale Bible in 1535, Matthew's Bible in 1537, The Great Bible in 1539, The Geneva Bible in 1560 (the first to use chapters, verses, and the italicization of added words), and the Bishops Bible in 1568.

Finally in 1604, in an effort to resolve severe factions between Englishmen over Bible versions, King James I authorized the translation of another version that came to bear his name. Forty-seven scholars spent six years on the translation, with all work meticulously reviewed and refined by their combined collaboration. The four existing Massorec texts were used for the Old Testament, and a third edition of the Byzantine Greek text by Stephanus (often referred as the "Textus Receptus"), was used for the New Testament. The King James Version was finally published in 1611, and together with its four revisions (in 1629, 1638, 1762, and 1769), it remains as the most widely circulated Bible in existence.

A few other translations were produced over the centuries, but the real revolution of new Bible versions began to erupt in the 20th century, largely due to the widening language barrier. Some of the more influential, recent translations have been: The Revised Standard Version in 1952, The Amplified Bible in 1965, The New English Bible in 1970, The New American Standard Bible in 1971, The Living Bible in 1971, Today's English Version in 1976, The New International Version in 1978, the New King James Version in 1982, and the New Living Translation 1996.

Apart from these versions, there are numerous study Bible editions, such as the Scofield Reference Bible, the Open Bible, the Thompson Chain Reference Bible, or the Spirit Life Bible, etc., but these are not different translations. These volumes merely feature special study helps, commentaries or references added as a supplement to a particular translation.

Besides updating the Bible to contemporary language, another controversy with new translations arises over the issue of the original texts. The KJV New Testament (and all editions since Tyndale) was compiled primarily from the Byzantine family of manuscripts (A.D. 500 - 1000) frequently referred to as the Textus Receptus. But many of the newer translations were produced using a composite of later discoveries of other manuscripts and fragments dating from an earlier period. Among such are The "Alexandrian Family" manuscripts (A.D. 200-400) which include the three oldest: The Codex Alexandrius, the Codex Vaticanus and the Codex Sinaiticus, all which were major contributors to most Bible versions after the King James version. Other important codices come from The Western Family, (of the Western Mediterranean areas), and the Caesarean Family of manuscripts (A.D. 200). (A codex is a manuscript bound together like a book instead of rolled into a scroll. Codices is plural for codex.)

Many scholars feel that the older manuscripts have been somewhat more accurate and important to the refinement of the newer translations. However, this has been disputed by others, especially since the older copies make up a tiny portion of the large quantity of manuscripts available. At least 90% of the 5,400 existing Greek manuscripts come from the Byzantine family (the basis for the Textus Receptus), and due to the overwhelming numbers of copies with which to compare and verify for accuracy, some scholars feel that the small handful of older texts should not be used to overrule the credibility of the majority. Although textual criticism shows only slight differences between the manuscript families, in those passages where the older text differs with the newer, the modern translators usually deferred to the older, primarily from the Alexandrian Family manuscripts — Codex Sinaiticus and the Codex Vaticanus.

It should be emphasized that none of the revisions in the new era translations, such as the NIV or NASB (compiled with Alexandrian Family Manuscripts), conflict with any rule of faith or doctrinal issue, but some conservative church leaders refuse to accept any tampering with the "tried and proven" Textus Receptus translation of the King James Version. In response to such concerns, the theological community came to see the need for another version, one which would satisfy the need for updated language without venturing beyond the traditional text source. Thus, in the late 1970's, Thomas Nelson Publishers commissioned a company of scholars to produce a revision of the traditional King James Version. Relying on the familiar Textus Receptus, 130 translators made the needed revisions to modern English and corrections to minor translation errors, while making every effort to retain the traditional phraseology of the old version. This New King James Version, as it was called, was completed in 1982.

Today, most Evangelical churches will make random use of any of the various translations mentioned here. Frequently a pastor will recommend one particular version to be used exclusively by the congregation so that everyone will have an identical source to refer to during the preaching or Bible studies. This not only helps eliminate confusion, but also makes it possible to engage in corporate word-for-word readings of scripture, something that wouldn't be possible if everyone was reading from a different version.

After some research on the various versions, every believer would do well to zero in on a primary version to which they devote their study and commit passages to memory. It's inadvisable to allow the issue of translations to become a distraction. For the average layman, most of the differences between the translations are relatively insignificant. All the versions we have listed have a high degree of harmony and convey the same general message of God's Word, but will use some of their own distinctive phrases and words.

The following is a summary of the most popular versions, along with a brief evaluation:

The King James Version (KJV) — Translated in 1611 by 47 scholars using the Byzantine family of manuscripts, Textus Receptus. This remains as a good version of the Bible. It has been the most reliable translation for over three centuries, but its Shakespearian style of English is difficult for modern readers, especially youth. This is still a good translation for those who can deal with the language.

The New American Standard Bible (NASB) — Translated in 1971 by 58 scholars of the Lockman Foundation, from Kittle's Biblia Hebraica and Nestle's Greek New Testament 23rd ed., which include the Alexandrian Family codices. Though academic in tone, it is said to be the most exact English translation available. A very good version.

The New International Version (NIV) — Over 100 translators completed this work in 1978 which was composed from Kittle's, Nestle's and United Bible Society's texts, which include the Alexandrian Family codices. This is considered an "open" style translation. It is a good, easy to read version.

The New King James Version (NKJV) — 130 translators, commissioned by Thomas Nelson Publishers, produced this version from the Byzantine family (Textus Receptus) in 1982. This is a revision of the King James version, updated to modern English with minor translation corrections and retention of traditional phraseology. This is a very good version.

The New Living Translation (NLT) — Published in 1996 by the Tyndale House Foundation, this began only as a project to revise to its predecessor, The Living Bible, a 1971 paraphrased rendition of the King James Version by Kenneth Taylor. The work however, evolved into a complete new translation, involving ninety translators over seven years. Rather than a literal word-for-word rendition, this is a simpler "thought by thought" translation, based on Kittle's, Nestle's and other Hebrew, Greek and Latin texts. It is a significant improvement over the The Living Bible, easy to read and a good version for devotional study.

— 51 —
What is a liturgical church?

Most churches have some form of liturgy that guides the flow of service, but a "liturgical church" conducts its services by a strict, prescribed liturgy — a formal structure or order of worship, which has been passed down from tradition. This type of church generally places much emphasis upon ceremony and ritual, and may use various forms of religious icons.

A historical form of liturgy practiced in many such churches, is as follows:

   (1) Confession of Sins

   (2) Pronouncement of Absolution

   (3) Acknowledgment of God's Authority

   (4) The Reading of God's Word

   (5) A Hymn of Praise

   (6) A Sermon

   (7) The Offering

   (8) The Prayers of the Church

   (9) The Holy Communion

Well known liturgical churches who follow a similar form are the Roman Catholic, Lutheran, Episcopal, and Eastern Orthodox churches.

— 52 —
What is an ecumenical church?

The idea of ecumenicalism is associated with unity and universality. The word, ecumenical, *(Greek, OIKOUMENE)* is used 15 times in the New Testament as a reference to the "whole world," primarily in a geographical sense, as in Matthew 24:14.

In the post-apostolic times, various branches of the church associated with the term ecumenical in the corporate sense. The Eastern church had its ecumenical synods and theologians. The Roman church called its councils ecumenical. The creeds of the Apostles, Nicene, Athanasian and others were called ecumenical.

Today, various churches are associated with the modern ecumenical movement, primarily though affiliation with the World Council of Churches. This is a theologically liberal, leftist organization devoted to the world unification of churches and religious entities. Most theologically conservative, evangelical churches reject any association with the ecumenical movement or the World Council of Churches, as these groups are identified with compromised, pseudo-Christian philosophy, and the goal of forming a one world religion. Authorities on the subject of prophecy cite that the Antichrist will arise amid a reprobate, one world religion.

A spirit of unity between all Christian churches, across denominational boundaries, is a noble ambition that should be pursued. The body of Christ needs to be united in their love, their prayers, and their evangelistic efforts to the world. But not at the compromise of basic Christian ideals, as is embraced by modern ecumenicalism.

— 53 —
Why do churches stress the importance of authority?

We live in a time when people have a difficult time with the idea of authority, but we must understand that it's an institution of God. Authority means "the right to command and enforce obedience," and according to the Apostle Paul, all authority originates with God who has delegated it to mankind to maintain order in the world. The scripture says, *"Everyone must submit himself to the governing authorities, for there is no authority except that which God has established. The authorities that exist have been established by God. Consequently, he who rebels against the authority is rebelling against what God has instituted, and those who do so will bring judgment on themselves" (Romans 13:1-2 NIV).*

Authority is something that must be understood by every Christian, since it is the entire basis of our relationship with Christ. God has ordained at least three categories of authority that we must submit to:

(1) Christ and the Church — When we accept Jesus Christ as our Lord, this means that He becomes our "boss" and highest authority over our whole life *(Romans 10:9, Luke 6:46, Matthew 28:18).* Christians are to submit to the headship of Christ, implemented through (a) leadership of His Spirit *(Romans 8:14),* (b) the authority of His Word *(2 Timothy 3:16),* and (c) the authorities of the church *(Matthew 18:17-20, 1 Corinthians 5:4-5, Hebrews 13:7,17).*

(2) The Family — Children are to obey their parents *(Ephesians 6:10).* The wife is to cooperate with her husband, which is the head of the family *(Ephesians 5:22-24, 1 Timothy 2:12),* and the husband is to submit himself to Christ and love his wife *(Ephesians 5:23,25).* God has established these as the "delegated" extensions of His authority. If we resist cooperation, we are in effect, resisting God's own authority and Lordship. This is why Paul even told wives to submit to the authority of their husbands "as unto the Lord" *(Ephesians 5:22).*

(3) The State — We are to cooperate with those authority figures and obey the local and federal laws of the land (within the boundaries of God's laws). According to scripture, secular authority is intended to be a "minister of God for our good" *(Romans 13:1-4),* and serves God's purpose of keeping law and order on the earth *(1 Peter 2:14-15).* Again, Paul wrote, *"Submit yourselves for the Lord's sake to every authority instituted among men: whether to the King, as the supreme authority, or to governors, who are sent by him to punish those who do wrong and to commend those who do right" (1 Peter 2:13-14 NIV).*

Just as all authority is related to other authority, all rebellion is also interrelated. It does not regard any class of authority. Rebellion is "the unwillingness to be ruled by any source other than self" — it is an indiscriminate contempt toward all authority. Our attitude toward Christ as our Lord, is directly associated with our attitude toward other authority, such as the pastor, our parents, or even civil authorities. Jesus Christ cannot be fully "Lord" over the person who harbors rebellion toward authority figures. The Bible says: *"...he who rebels against the authority is rebelling against what God has instituted, and those who do so will bring judgment on themselves." (Romans 13:2 NIV)*.

Just as God is the source of all authority, Satan is author of all rebellion. We may recall that the Devil (Lucifer), a former archangel, was originally cast out of Heaven because he led an insurrection against God *(Isaiah 14:12-15)*. Rebellion is the very spirit of Satan's attitude *(Ephesians 2:2)*, and if we permit it to dominate us it will infect and taint our attitude toward all authority, including God and His Word. The prophet Samuel said that *"rebellion is as the sin of witchcraft" (1 Samuel 15:23)*. The Apostle Peter said that those who are corrupt despise authority *(2 Peter 2:10)*, and the Proverbs say, *"An evil man seeks only rebellion..." (Proverbs 17:11)*.

In the absence of Godly and moral values, sometimes there are abuses of authority and perversions in government. Such was the case when Peter and John were forbidden to preach the Gospel by the Jewish Sanhedrin. They replied, *"Whether it is right in the sight of God to listen to you more than to God, you judge" (Acts 4:19)*. The only circumstance that disobedience to authority is ever justifiable by scripture, is if it conflicts with the laws of God.

Paul tells us to pray for all those in authority *(1 Timothy 2:2)*. God can use our prayers to either change their heart or remove them from power entirely. God reserves the right of administering discipline and reproof to those who represent His authority *(Romans 14:4, Psalms 105:4-5, 1 Chronicles 16:21-22)*.

— 54 —

Why do churches teach believers to be accountable to spiritual leadership?

Because the Bible requires it. Even more important than secular authorities, Christians must be obedient and submissive toward their spiritual leaders who are charged with the responsibility to "watch for their souls." The scripture says, *"Obey those who rule over you, and be*

submissive, for they watch out for your souls, as those who must give account. Let them do so with joy and not with grief, for that would be unprofitable for you"
(Hebrews 13:17).

Not only are Christians to be accountable to the authority of a spiritual leader, but this passage also shows that believers should be a part of a local church — where such pastors and elders can be found *(Hebrews 10:25)*. One cannot really be accountable to spiritual supervision without a commitment to a church. Nor can a person be accountable if they merely drift from one church to another, week after week — making themselves inaccessible from the supervision, teaching or correction of a pastor who knows something about their personal life. Despite what some people like to think, God has no lone rangers! Accountability to a continuity of ministry and leadership is vital to God's plan of providing the necessary "checks and balances" to produce solid spiritual growth.

One common reason that some Christians "hop" from church to church, or abandon church participation, is that they foster an "independent spirit" which resists authority. They do not wish to be corrected or to confront truths they would prefer to avoid. Without accountability to authority, a believer develops "itching ears" *(2 Timothy 4:3)*. They look for teachings that agree with their own opinions, instead of "objective" instruction — the whole counsel of God's Word — that will force them to face their areas of immaturity and grow up.

Some believers with an independent attitude will contend that they don't need the church or spiritual leaders — that they have God's Spirit to teach them. Indeed, every believer has the personal indwelling of the Holy Spirit to guide them *(1 John 2:27)*, but this does not discharge them from the Biblical counsel and ministry of the church *(Hebrews 13:7,17, Proverbs 11:14-15, 2 Corinthians 13:1)*. The church is Christ's plan for His followers. He is the head *(Ephesians 5:23)*, and commissioned His church to represent Him and His authority in the world *(2 Corinthians 5:20, Matthew 18:17-20, John 14:12)*. He has ordained elders, deacons, and pastors, to supervise and manage His flock *(Acts 14:23, 1 Timothy 3:10-13)*, and additional ministries to teach, train, and spiritually equip the saints for service *(Ephesians 4:11-16)*. Ministers are not lone rangers either. They too are accountable to the authority of overseers, who may offer counsel, reproof, or discipline when necessary *(Acts 21:18-24)*.

All believers should be committed to a Bible believing, Christ-centered church. They should be accountable to a Pastor and spiritual leaders, on the condition that leadership meets basic qualifications of (1) a moral and Godly lifestyle *(Matthew 7:15-16, Galatians 5:19-25, 1 Timothy 3:1-7)*, and (2) that they proclaim the uncompromised Word of God *(2 Timothy 3:16, Romans 1:16)*. Cooperate with the man of God whose life exhibits these biblical qualities. Don't rebel or give him a hard time. The Bible warns that contempt toward God's obedient servant is equal to contempt toward God *(Exodus 16:2,8, Joshua 22:19)*.

Not only does Paul teach that all believers are to have someone over them in the Lord, he also directs that they should know their leaders *(1 Thessalonians 5:12)*. So often, the people in the church want their pastor to know all about them — however Paul says that believers should get to know their leaders. That is, know their lifestyle, their sincerity, their integrity. Knowing your pastors and leaders provides a tangible example to follow, and also enables you to have trust and respect in their ministry.

Sometimes people will balk at the authority of some pastors because they think they're too young, inexperienced, or not sufficiently spiritual. However, the Bible says we are to submit — not to those we deem qualified — but to those whom God has seen fit to give the rule. I'll never forget the rugged, old Army sergeant that lectured new recruits about the chain of authority. "As far you may see, the second lieutenant may be younger than you, inexperienced, and green behind the ears. You may not figure how in the world he got to the rank he is, but when he gives an order, you look at the bars on his uniform and say 'Yes sir!' When you obey his orders, you're obeying the one at the highest level who, for whatever reason, saw fit to grant him that authority."

God requires us to respect the authority He has placed over us, even if that authority isn't perfect. Spiritual leaders are human and will make mistakes, but the Lord still demands our respect and restraint toward them. They are His servants and He reserves the right to correct or reprove them *(Psalms 105:15)*.

We recall that even after King Saul had become disobedient to God and corrupt, he remained as the anointed King over Israel for quite some time. Saul eventually became jealous of the heir to his throne, David, and began a relentless manhunt to kill him. At one point, David and his men stumbled across Saul encamped in a cave and had the opportunity to kill their sleeping pursuer. But instead, David chose to quietly cut off a portion of Saul's robe as evidence to show his unwillingness to slay Saul when he had opportunity. However, later the Lord convicted David's heart that not only was it wrong to slay God's anointed, it was wrong to even cut his robe or lift a finger against him in any way. *"Now it happened afterward that David's heart troubled him because he had cut Saul's robe. And he said to his men, The LORD forbid that I should do this thing to my master, the Lord's anointed, to stretch out my hand against him, seeing he is the anointed of the LORD"* (1 Samuel 24:5-6).

Respect toward authority is not limited to our actions, but even relates to how we speak of them. The Bible warns against lifting our tongue against the Lord's servants, even though they might be worthy of criticism. When the Apostle Paul was unjustly punished for preaching the Gospel, he spoke defiantly until he realized that he was addressing Ananias, the High Priest. He apologized and said, *"I did not know, brethren, that he was the high priest; for it is written, You shall not speak evil of the ruler of your people"* (Acts 23:5). Just imagine. Even though this High Priest was an enemy to the Gospel, and was wrong to have Paul slapped on the mouth, yet he was still a spiritual authority whom Paul was obligated to respect. If Paul was not permitted to speak against Ananias, then you certainly don't have any right to badmouth Godly, spiritual leaders. It is an act of rebellion, for which you will answer to God.

Certainly, leaders and pastors must be held accountable for their behavior, and may even need to be corrected or disciplined. But God has ordained for this to be done in an honorable way, through an appropriate chain of authority by other spiritual overseers.

— 55 —
Why do some churches believe in washing one another's feet?

The idea of foot washings in Christian churches comes from Jesus' washing of His disciples' feet after their last supper together, prior to his trial and crucifixion. *"So when He had washed their feet, taken His garments, and sat down again, He said to them, Do you know what I have done to you? You call me Teacher and Lord, and you say well, for so I am. If I then, your Lord and Teacher, have washed your feet, you also ought to wash one another's feet. For I have given you an example, that you should do as I have done to you" (John 13:12-15).*

As we see in the passage, Jesus explained that as He washed his disciples feet, they were to do likewise to one another. Some churches take this to mean that He gave a command to literally wash the feet of our brethren, as an "ordinance," similar to observances as Water Baptism or the Lord's Supper. Other churches view Jesus' foot washing only as a metaphor of how believers need to humble themselves as servants toward each other.

In New Testament times, foot washing was a common duty for low-ranking servants. When travelers would visit an affluent home, it was the custom for the host to have their guests feet washed. It was considered a degrading task for any servant, and would be especially humbling and disgusting for the cleanliness-minded Jew to remove the sandals and wash filthy, road-stenched feet. Jesus showed that the only way to follow Him, and the only path to spiritual greatness, is to humble ourselves before our brethren with the heart of a loving servant.

Foot washing was certainly meant as an illustration of a desired attitude for every believer, but it also appears that its literal practice has beneficial results. Foot washing has often helped to inspire humility and forgiveness between dissenting brethren — it has been known to break up rigid tradition, hardness of heart and pride. And many a story has been told of church revivals which began from the contrition aroused in old fashioned foot washing services. The observance may seem strange or silly to some, but we're reminded that God routinely chooses what seem to be the foolish things of this world to confound the wise. Whether or not it is viewed as a regular ordinance, foot washing remains an accepted Biblical tradition in many churches.

— 56 —
What do churches mean by references to "traditional values?"

In recent years we've heard a lot of talk about traditional values. It seems to surface in every political campaign and has been the subject of debate and controversy by the news media.

While there may be differing interpretations, especially from secular society, traditional values generally refer to the standards and values which were embraced by most Americans from its earliest beginnings and throughout the majority of its history. It is believed by many, including myself, that these values were a great part of what made America a great and free nation — the absence of which, will likely result in the further decline of our country.

Traditional, historical American values have in the past, included a faith in God, church, prayer and the Bible, which has for a large part, been the foundation of other national traditions, such as: Respect toward authority, diligent work ethics, absolute values of right and wrong, honesty in business practices, wholesomeness in leadership, moderation rather than excess, marriage as a prerequisite before having sex or bearing children, a family which consists of both a father and mother, taking responsibility to provide for our own — such one's spouse, family and children, and so forth.

Traditional values are largely the Bible-based ethics that were a great part of our national heritage which instilled character and taught people how to grow up as human beings. People learned how to behave, to have manners, good morals, to be honest, unselfish, generous and considerate of others. They were taught the benefits of discipline, hard work, and responsibility. They were given good role models of how to be loving and kind to their spouse, encouraging and supportive to their children. This was the sort of thing which caused marriages to last, families to succeed, and which made our nation strong and free.

Many of today's political leaders are looking to a restoration of such traditional values, not especially because of such a want for faith in God. But they see that the values which were generally held by believers in the past are the cure for the sickness that plagues our nation. And on the more cynical, capitalistic side of things, politicians have come to see it as a remedy for the numerous costly government social programs. Our government has nearly gone bankrupt trying to fix the ills of society which have been produced by the absence of traditional values: Drug abuse, deadbeat dads, unwed mothers, abortion, abandoned children, abandoned elderly, the spread of AIDS and other venereal diseases, litigation abuse, welfare abuse, failure of education, lack of discipline in the schools, rampant crime, and etc.

All of these woes, and much more, are products of a society without values — and specifically, without the values which originally came from a lifestyle of faith in God. Realizing this, more and more politicians are beginning to sound like preachers in their appeal for a return to moral values.

It has been said that America is following the same historical path that led to the collapse of the Roman empire. In the famous history, "The Decline and Fall of the Roman Empire,"[1] the author gave the following reasons for Rome's fall:

(1) Excessive spending by the central government.

(2) Unwillingness of young men to bear arms in defense of their country.

(3) Overindulgence in luxuries.

(4) Widespread immorality which destroyed the integrity of family life (family values).

(5) The spread of gender confusion and homosexuality — men acting like women, and women acting like men.

(6) Disregard for religion.

Sadly, these same symptoms are the ills of our own society, and most Christian leaders believe that unless there is a revival of moral values in our nation, like Rome, it will corrupt from within and will die as a nation. It is said, "They which fail to learn from history, are destined to repeat it." We're reminded of a warning in scripture: *"The wicked shall be turned into hell, And all the nations that forget God" (Psalms 9:17).*

— 57 —
Why are there so many hypocrites in the church?

This is an age old criticism against the church that some use as an excuse to justify their lack of participation.

A hypocrite *(Greek, HUPOKRITES)* is a play-actor, a pretender, one who outwardly goes through motions which are insincere. Hypocrisy is a genuine problem that exists and often affects religious people. Jesus warned of the consequences of hypocrisy and described its symptoms to the Pharisees in His day. *"Woe to you, scribes and Pharisees, hypocrites! For you are like whitewashed tombs which indeed appear beautiful outwardly, but inside are full of dead men's bones and all uncleanness. Even so you also outwardly appear righteous to men, but inside you are full of hypocrisy and lawlessness" (Matthew 23:27-28).*

The Pharisees were a sect of the Jewish hierarchy. They made up the body of the religious leaders of that day. They went to the daily temple prayers religiously, gave their tithes and offerings, were avid students of the scriptures, kept the Sabbath day, and followed the commandments and teachings of Moses to the letter. They had the appearance of being very religious and upstanding Jews. Yet Jesus said that they were "diseased" and rotten inside, full of hypocrisy and iniquity. He described them as "whitewashed tombs," or "death covered with a coat of paint." *"For I say to you, that unless your righteousness exceeds the righteousness of the scribes and Pharisees, you will by no means enter the kingdom of heaven" (Matthew 5:20).*

Indeed there are hypocrites in the church, but maybe not as many as some think. From my experience, most people who attend a Bible preaching church, do so because they are sincerely trying to draw closer to God. However, there's another problem the church contends with that's every bit as bad, if not worse than hypocrisy. It's called judgmentalism. It's a critical "witch hunt" attitude to find fault and blame people as hypocrites.

Many sincere people, though imperfect and immature, have been falsely judged as hypocrites. To illustrate this, several years ago in the Midwest, an unknown gentleman began attending a small church on a frequent basis. He would always be seen sitting conspicuously in the rear with his hands firmly tucked in his pockets. As the months passed, people began to take note that he seemed rather unfriendly and peculiar. He declined from shaking anyone's hands, never put anything in the offering plate, and didn't participate by clapping during songs or raising his hands in worship. At the altar service, everyone came and knelt in prayer, except the same man. The rumors began to emerge. "He's probably not a Christian — certainly not a very spiritual one," remarked one critical parishioner. "He just another hypocrite who goes to church," said another prudish woman.

One day the pastor was driving through an unfamiliar neighborhood, when he noticed the same gentleman standing in front of his house, retrieving mail from his mailbox. He thought he'd stop and say hello, but as he approached the fellow, who was dressed in shorts and a T-shirt, the pastor noticed that his legs and hands were grossly disfigured. Upon recognizing the minister, the man became embarrassed and shoved his hand into his pockets. Realizing that he had already been seen, He explained, "Guess you caught me. I was badly burned in a fire years ago. I'm ashamed of my appearance and just didn't want anybody to know."

The pastor discovered that the mysterious man was a very humble, sincere believer, but feared rejection and was too embarrassed to expose his disfigured hands in church. His scarred knees were too painful to bend and kneel at the altar. As he drove away, the pastor thought to himself, "What an injustice has been served to this poor guy. He needed the encouragement and acceptance by those in our church, but instead, has been belittled and misjudged by critical people who didn't know all the facts."

This is why the Lord tells us not to judge one another. It is not possible to render an accurate judgment about anyone without knowing all the facts. Appearances don't tell us everything about a person. Jesus said, *"Do not judge according to appearance..." (John 7:24).* When a judge hears a court case, he looks carefully at all the evidence and weighs all the testimonies. Only when he has considered all the facts of evidence, can he render a fair judgment. Only God is qualified to be our judge, because only He knows what's in our hearts. He knows our true motives, our intents, and has all the facts. God told Samuel, *"...the Lord does not see as man sees; for man looks at the outward appearance, but the LORD looks at the heart" (1 Samuel 16:7).* Judgment is something that God has reserved exclusively for Himself. Whenever a person judges another, he is attempting to sit on God's throne. He is presuming himself to be God — both judge and jury *(James 4:11).*

When I was a new Christian I noticed a fellow in our church who wore a button on his lapel that displayed the letters: PBPWMGINFWMY. Curious, I asked him what they meant, and he said, they stand for "Please Be Patient With Me. God Is Not Finished With Me Yet." This was a clever way to remind people to not be judgmental of a Christian "under construction."

Unfortunately, many believers have fallen to the judgmentalism of others. Without knowing the contents of their heart, some have sharply criticized the faults and weakness of their brethren, or ridiculed them with rumors and gossip. We are warned against causing such stumbling-blocks of judgmentalism. *"Therefore let us not judge one another anymore, but rather resolve this, not to put a stumbling block or a cause to fall in our brother's way" (Romans 14:13).* Those who oppress their brethren this way, who cause their departure from the faith, will face the stern recompense of almighty God. *"Then He said to the disciples, It is impossible that no offenses should come, but woe to him through whom they do come! It would be better for him if a millstone were hung around his neck, and he were thrown into the sea, than that he should offend one of these little ones" (Luke 17:1-2).*

Every organization, including the church, will have some who are insincere or who are there for ulterior motives, as Jesus suggested with his reference to the tares found in the wheat *(Matthew 13:14-30).* But don't ever let that hold you back from your enthusiasm for the church. My pastor once told me, "Never let a hypocrite stand between you and God, otherwise they'll be standing closer to God than you are." The person who has flaws but is humbly trying to serve God, is far better off than the person who shakes their finger in judgment and does nothing.

— 58 —
Why have some churches turned persons over to Satan?

This idea may sound contradictory to the church's purpose, however this comes from the Apostle Paul's instruction to the church of Corinth regarding an internal disciplinary matter. It seems that there was a person in the church who was persisting in a matter of sexual immorality, and Paul told the leaders that such continued sin by a professing believer was not to be tolerated within the church fellowship. He told them, *"In the name of our Lord Jesus Christ, when you are gathered together, along with my spirit, with the power of our Lord Jesus Christ, deliver such a one to Satan for the destruction of the flesh, that his spirit may be saved in the day of the Lord Jesus" (1 Corinthians 5:4-5).*

To implement this action, it appears that the church did little more than to excommunicate this person from the fellowship of the saints. *"...Therefore put away from yourselves that wicked person" (1 Corinthians 5:13).* Such expulsion obviously removed them from the church's comforting influence and exposed them to the harsh reality of the Holy Spirit's absence — thus turning them over to Satan's world of darkness and torments. Some suggest that "destruction of the flesh" may mean a direct visitation of some type of physical affliction or even death.

Today, Bible believing churches still utilize this type of disciplinary action when such circumstances warrant. The purpose of turning a person over to Satan is not merely punitive, but for a twofold objective:

(1) To reconcile the person back to God. *"...that his spirit may be saved in the day of the Lord Jesus..."* The hope was that when abandoned to the wages of sin — the inevitable loss of peace and Satan's torments, they would seek repentance and restoration.

(2) To protect the church from further infection by such sinful behavior. Paul reminded them that it was one thing to be among immoral people in the world, but it is not acceptable to fellowship with immoral people who profess to be Christian brethren. *"But now I have written to you not to keep company with anyone named a brother, who is a fornicator, or covetous, or an idolater, or a reviler, or a drunkard, or an*

extortioner; not even to eat with such a person" (1 Corinthians 5:11). Persons
in the church fellowship who resist correction in any of the immoral
behavior mentioned, are eligible for expulsion.

Excommunication is never the first choice for the church. The
Lord is a reconciler and wants His church to restore people
whenever possible. Paul wrote, *"Brethren, if a man is overtaken in any
trespass, you who are spiritual restore such a one in a spirit of gentleness,
considering yourself lest you also be tempted" (Galatians 6:1).* Our Lord is the
Father of the prodigal, whom He so much wants to repent and to
receive His forgiveness *(1 John 1:9).* But despite our best efforts,
there are times when loving correction is not accepted and fails to
alter communicable sinful behavior. In those cases, God requires
that such persons be removed from the fellowship so to prevent sin
from spreading, and to impress upon them their need for
repentance.

Jesus used the metaphor of a spreading infection to warn us from
withholding personal sin in any area of our life. Similarly, if the
infection of sin is allowed to spread unabated within the body of
Christ, it will bring gangrene that will destroy the whole body.
Obviously, to expel anyone from Christ's body is a dreaded and
painful task, no more desirable than to amputate one of our own
limbs or organs, but there will be times where there is no other
choice. Jesus said, *"...if your hand or foot causes you to sin, cut it off and cast
it from you. It is better for you to enter into life lame or maimed, rather than
having two hands or two feet, to be cast into the everlasting fire. And if your eye
causes you to sin, pluck it out and cast it from you. It is better for you to enter
into life with one eye, rather than having two eyes, to be cast into hell fire"
(Matthew 18:8-9).*

According to the Victor Bible Source Book,[1] **the Bible indicates at
least seven specific sins for which excommunication is
prescribed if repentance is not secured** (See *Proverbs* 22:10, 1
Corinthians 5:1-13, Titus 3:10-11, *Matthew* 18:15-20):

(1) Immorality (homosexuality, lesbianism, incest, sexual impurity)

(2) Greed — The desire to get gains by base methods.

(3) Idolatry — Participation in occult practices.

(4) Drunkenness — Intoxication with alcohol.

(5) Extortion — Robbery.

(6) Foul tongue — A railer, verbally abusive, reviling, slandering, insulting, contentious, using speech to injure or damage.

(7) Heretic — One who causes divisions by a party spirit, factions, and a self-willed opinion which is substituted for submission to the power of truth and leads to division (An expository Dictionary of New Testament Words, by W.E. Vine). The procedure to seek either restoration, or grounds for excommunication, is usually based from Jesus' teaching in *Matthew* 18:15-20.

— 59 —
Why do some churches forbid women to be preachers?

This issue remains a controversial one in many churches and denominations. It stems from two scripture passages written by the Apostle Paul, which are frequently interpreted differently. In the first, Paul writes, *"Let your women keep silent in the churches, for they are not permitted to speak; but they are to be submissive, as the law also says. And if they want to learn something, let them ask their own husbands at home; for it is shameful for women to speak in church" (1 Corinthians 14:34-35)*. Some churches interpret this to mean that Paul forbade women to speak publicly or preach in the church. However, others contend that he used the Greek verb that described "talk or chatter," and was only discouraging conversational interruptions in the assembly. The tradition of the early church (synagogue) was that the men and women sat on opposite sides, divided by a waist-high partition. There's speculation that during the teaching, there was disruptive chatting between the women or perhaps they asked questions of their husbands across the partition.

The other passage written to Timothy is even more controversial. Paul wrote, *"I do not permit a woman to teach or to have authority over a man, but to be in silence [submission]" (1 Timothy 2:12)*. This is seen by some as an indisputable restriction against women holding church positions of teaching or authority, but others believe that Paul was speaking to a wife's domestic submission to the authority of her husband. Whatever Paul meant, it apparently was not intended to be a sexist bias against women, as he explained elsewhere that gender held no distinction to those in Christ. *"...there is neither male nor female; for you are all one in Christ Jesus" (Galatians 3:28).*

What is clear is that the broad context of the New Testament shows that women did have a significant role in the early church. Besides continuing with the Apostles in prayer, there were women, such as Phebe, whom Paul described as a deaconess *(Greek, DIAKONOS)*, a term which referred to an office of ministry *(Romans 16:1)*. And there were other women, such as Philip's four daughters, who prophesied, proclaiming public messages from God *(Acts 21:8-9)*.

Throughout church history, women have played a vital role in its success. Many a pioneer church, while in short supply of men, has relied upon the faithfulness of women to carry the load of prayer, ministry and other responsibilities. Today, women continue to play a great part in the success of church ministries. Many churches authorize women to teach, preach or even pastor churches, but there are others which still restrict their participation to non-authoritative positions.

— 60 —
How did followers of Jesus come to be called Christians?

Apparently, Antioch, the capital of the Roman province of Syria (now within the region of Antakya, Turkey), was the location where "Christian" was first associated with early believers. *"And the disciples were first called Christians in Antioch" (Acts 11:26).*

Obviously, the term is identified with the idea of being a follower of Jesus Christ. In classical times the followers of a leader would identify themselves by a descriptive extension to their leader's name (ianus). Pompey's troops were called Pompeiani, and Caesar's were referred to as, Caesariani. The Christianus (of Latin origin, and hellenized), was similarly viewed as the descriptive term of the followers of Christ.[1]

However, Theophilus of Antioch, writing about 170 A.D. claimed that the term "Christian" was used, not as much because of association with Jesus, but because it was derived from the Greek word for oil, *CHRISM*, which means anointed — and "the followers of Jesus appeared to be anointed with the Spirit."[2] Chrism is also the Greek word used for Christ, and means anointed one.

— 61 —
Why do many churches have such different ways of worship?

In our society, one church may conduct worship in a highly structured, formal fashion with prescribed liturgies, ritual or ceremony. On the other hand, another church may worship very informally, with little structure, spontaneous expressions of praise to God, lively, hand clapping music or even manifestations of spiritual gifts. Such differences are largely a matter of whether a church follows post apostolic traditions handed down through the historic church, or subscribes to various conventions of reform which have sought to return to more authentic, New Testament patterns.

Worship is the fundamental objective of a church service, whose basic idea is simply stated as "worthship," the act of ascribing a value of high worth to something. Worship is the esteemed value in one's heart toward God, with honor and reverence expressed through acts of devotion, obedience and service. In the broad sense, worship can be displayed to God through such things as attending church, reading scripture, singing hymns, giving tithes and offerings, prayer, public testimonies of thanksgiving, receiving communion, offering oral praise, clapping or lifting hands. But in the strictest sense, worship is pure adoration, lifting up the redeemed spirit toward God in contemplation of His holy perfection.[1] *"God is a Spirit; and they that worship Him must worship Him in Spirit and in truth" (John 4:24).*

In the beginning of the church, it is believed that early Christian worship was a continuation of the traditional Jewish order, combined with the Apostles' teachings and fervor of the Holy Spirit. According to scripture, the services consisted of: Preaching or Exhortation *(Acts 20:7)*, Reading the Scriptures *(Acts 2:42, 17:2,11)*, Personal and Corporate Prayer *(Acts 2:42, 4:31, 12:5, 20:36)*, Singing *(Acts 16:25, Ephesians 5:19, Colossians 3:16)*, Water Baptism *(Acts*

2:41), Communion *(Acts 2:42, 1 Corinthians 11:18-34)*, Stewardship *(1 Corinthians 16:2)*, and Charismatic Gifts *(1 Corinthians 14:26)*.

Many of these observances were described of a typical Sunday service in the year A.D. 140, by Justin Martyr: "On the Lord's Day, a meeting of all, who live in the cities and villages, is held, and a section from the Memoirs of the Apostles (the Gospels) and the writings of the Prophets (the Old Testament) is read, as long as the time permits. When the reader has finished, the president, in a discourse, gives an exhortation to the imitation of these noble things. After this we all rise in common prayer. At the close of the prayer, as we have before described, bread and wine with water are brought. The president offers prayer and thanks for them, according to the power given him, and the congregation responds the Amen. Then the consecrated elements are distributed to each one, and partaken, and are carried by the deacons to the houses of the absent. The wealthy and the willing then give contributions according to their free will, and this collection is deposited with the president, who therewith supplies orphans and widows, poor and needy, prisoners and strangers, and takes care of all who are in want."[2] (Songs were not mentioned here, but were elsewhere in his writings — Charismatic gifts are mentioned by Iraneus in 150).

Both the scriptures and later historical writings suggest that gatherings of early Christian worship were organized with some measure of liturgy (formal order). But the book of Acts shows that the believers also possessed a spontaneous freedom of worship, not confined to formality or structure. There was remarkable intimacy with God, with an inclination to worship God any time, any place. For example, while Paul and Silas were jailed in Philippi, in the middle of the night, they were heard throughout the prison, singing and worshiping the Lord. They had no song books, no worship leader, nor padded pews. Their feet were fastened in stocks, and were likely in pain from the earlier beating — but in the unlighted, stench-filled dungeon, the sounds of their spontaneous, heartfelt praise were heard. *"But at midnight Paul and Silas were praying and singing hymns to God, and the prisoners were listening to them"* (Acts 16:25).

In the New Testament church, oral expressions of giving thanks and praise to God were never intended to be restricted to a formal ritual — they were meant to be personal, continual and spontaneous.

"Therefore by Him let us continually offer the sacrifice of praise to God, that is, the fruit of our lips, giving thanks to His name" (Hebrews 13:15). The services were not confined to rigid structure, but there was sensitivity to the promptings of the Holy Spirit who might redirect the order on the spur of the moment *(Acts 13:2).* And unlike today's well-polished, twenty minute sermons, the preaching was extemporaneous and the length of services were flexible. *"Now on the first day of the week, when the disciples came together to break bread, Paul, ready to depart the next day, spoke to them and continued his message until midnight" (Acts 20:7).*

Furthermore, another unique characteristic of the early church was that its ministry was not confined to clergymen. The meetings were mainly in homes, and the laity were not mere spectators — all were participants to what was happening. They were *"...teaching and admonishing one another in psalms and hymns and spiritual songs, singing with grace in their hearts to the Lord" (Colossians 3:16).* James even exhorted the believers to confess their trespasses to each other and to pray for one another *(James 5:16).* The trend of whole-body ministry apparently continued through later centuries, as one of the third-century church fathers, Tertullian, described his church services: "In our Christian meetings we have plenty of songs, verses, sentences and proverbs. After hand-washing and bringing in the lights, each Christian is asked to stand forth and sing, as best he can, a hymn to God, either of his own composing, or one from the Holy Scriptures."[3]

The original New Testament form of worship is the format that every modern church should seek to emulate. However, it seems to be a great contrast to today's conventional service which is sometimes more comparable to the setting of a "theater." The platform is viewed as the "stage." The ministers on the stage are the "performers." The congregation is the "audience" — spectators to the performance on the stage. The order of service or liturgy, is the formal "script" which directs the performance.

These concepts and other perfunctory trends of worship evolved throughout a millennium of formalism that first began to emerge in the fourth century. For over three hundred years, the church had structure and order *(1 Corinthians 14:40),* combined with a liberty that fostered body participation and spontaneity to the Holy Spirit. But now its focus would shift toward a formal replication of ceremony, ritual and symbolic icons, largely from the influence of the newly converted Emperor of Rome, Constantine (A.D. 312), who sought to integrate Christianity with the grandiose paradigms of the empire. It was during this era, that the first cathedrals for Christian worship were constructed and prescribed liturgies were imposed upon the churches. Today, liturgical churches such as the Roman Catholic church, still subscribe to such formalistic views of worship.

The progression of formalism, liturgy, and ritual continued for over a thousand years under the two formal Christian institutions, the Roman Catholic and Eastern Orthodox churches. But the era of reformation in the 16th century brought reformed concepts to worship. Two of the principal reformers, Martin Luther and John Calvin, made significant contributions that would influence liturgical thought for many generations. Luther's liturgical reform was guided by the principle that if the scriptures did not expressly reject a particular practice, the church was free to keep it. Consequently, Lutheran worship retained much of the ceremonial practice of Catholic worship. Calvin however, argued that only practices explicitly taught in Scripture could be used in worship. For this reason, churches influenced by Calvin have been less inclined to restore pre-Reformation practices of worship perceived as unbiblical or Catholic.[4]

The famed spiritual awakenings of the 18th and 19th centuries brought about further reforms to worship, developed in the revival movements of the American frontier. Many leaders and groups were instrumental in integrating these influences into the local churches. One such key figure was the legendary evangelist of the early 19th century, Charles Finney. When Finney settled down to a pastorate in the mid 1830's, the methods used in his revival campaigns became the basis for a revised approach to liturgy (called the new measures) which increasingly became adapted by churches on the eastern seaboard.

Finney viewed evangelism as the primary focus in church life, and integrated the concepts of the camp meeting into Sunday worship. He tried to do away with what he described as "dead orthodoxy" — prepared and lengthy prayers, written sermons, ominous psalm-singing — in favor of sprightly songs directed to the needs of the sinner, emotionally stirring sermons designed to promote repentant response on the part of the souls for the lost. The focus and content of sermons changed to imitate the revival pattern as well. With conversion rather than corporate worship as the focus, the sermon became the most direct means of persuading the unconverted in the congregation to give their lives to Christ. Altar calls, previously unheard of in a worship service, became frequent elements of a standard service. This "revivalistic" approach to worship continued as the dominant tradition of free churches and is today the general order within the fundamentalist and evangelical churches.[4]

In the twentieth century, attitudes of worship were again greatly influenced by spiritual awakenings. The Pentecostal movement of the early 1900's, and the Charismatic renewal of the 1960's, both emphasized the operation of spiritual gifts and a return to New Testament practices of worship freedom. The influence of these movements upon celebrated ministers, Gospel music artists, and media personalities, combined with a widespread hunger for spiritual renewal, effectuated the birth of what became called the "praise and worship" movement. This describes a growing, popular worship style that draws on contemporary choruses, usually in a flowing or connected sequence, and often features the lifting of hands in praise, ministry through the laying on of hands, and an inviting and informal worship climate.[4] More than all other liturgical reforms, these more recent renewals have brought worshipers closer to the authentic New Testament patterns of worship.

— 62 —
Is it true that some churches believe in handling snakes and drinking poison?

As shocking as this sounds, there are indeed such churches. Years ago I conducted revival meetings in a small church, located in a remote, mountainous community called "Snake Holler." The name was derived from the fact that virtually all churches in the area (except the one I was preaching in!) believed in snake handling.

Such churches are few in number, and are mainly concentrated in the southern U.S. They believe and teach that handling venomous snakes (such as rattlers) and drinking poison is a part of their

Christian faith. They get this idea from a misinterpretation of a passage in the 16th chapter of Mark, where Jesus expressed His great commission to take the Gospel to the world. He remarked, *"And these signs will follow those who believe: In My name they will cast out demons; they will speak with new tongues; they will take up serpents; and if they drink anything deadly, it will by no means hurt them; they will lay hands on the sick, and they will recover"* (Mark 16:17-18).

"Snake handling churches," as they are called, generally identify themselves of Pentecostal origin, although they are disassociated from other mainstream Pentecostal groups and are viewed as a "Christian cult." They believe snake handling to be consistent with other supernatural gifts such as speaking in tongues or healing the sick. They interpret that they are supposed to literally "take up" or handle deadly snakes and drink poison to prove the anointing and power of God at work in their lives.

This belief, of course, is erroneous and would not be consistent with God's Word that warns us against testing Him by deliberately placing ourselves in danger *(Matthew 4:7)*. However, it is possible Jesus was describing special powers of protection from the natural conditions of that period, as they went forth to preach the Gospel. Deadly snakes were abundant and a very real natural danger to those who would travel, and it was the custom for a stranger to accept the hospitality of food and drink offered to him, regardless of its purity.

Also, while we usually seek to interpret God's Word literally, there are those exceptions where it is obviously symbolic, as may be the case here. The scriptures frequently describe Satan as a serpent, who masqueraded in this form to appear to Adam and Eve. Therefore, it's likely that Jesus' reference to serpents here, as it was elsewhere *(Luke 10:19)*, was only symbolic of the subtle, creeping nature of the devil — perhaps referring to those wicked things which Satan hides behind or uses as weapons against us. Furthermore, in the Greek, the term "take up" can as easily be translated "put away," and it is believed that since Jesus had already referred to casting out demons, He was possibly saying His believers would have power to "put away" those instruments or forms used by Satan (perhaps such things in our society like drugs, alcohol, or so forth).

Still, another controversy surrounds these verses in Mark. Some of the newer Bible versions suggest that verses 9-20 of Mark 16 should be omitted because of a dispute about their inclusion in the original. It seems that a few of the oldest manuscripts do not contain these verses.

However, such an omission would be presumptuous since there remains much evidence to support the genuineness of these verses. Even the "codices Vaticanus and Sinaiticus," most often cited for leaving out the passage, have a blank space between Mark 16:8 and the book of Luke, as if the scribe was not sure whether he should include it in his copy or not.

With few exceptions, all of the Unical manuscripts retain these twelve verses, and the Cursive manuscripts unanimously recognize the passage as genuine. Besides inclusion in the Textus Receptus, the Vulgate version which was translated from the original by Jerome in the fourth century, also includes the disputed verses, and many of the early church fathers, such as Iraneus in the second century, quote from the verses in writings, giving further weight to their authenticity.

Although Jesus' reference to tongues, healing, and demon exorcism may be troubling to those who oppose supernatural gifts, and His reference to serpents and poison may be an issue of controversy and misunderstanding, yet the verses in Mark 16:9-20 cannot be excluded from the text of God's Word without more conclusive evidence than what has been suggested.

— 63 —
Why do many churches believe in speaking in tongues?

Pentecostals and Charismatics make up the main body of churches who embrace speaking in tongues as a part of their official doctrine. They represent about 10% of all American congregations.

Speaking in tongues has long been considered a controversial issue among many churches. Often blamed for creating division, or attributed to heresy or fanaticism, the practice has been banned entirely by many churches. This seems somewhat ironic since the primary author of the New Testament, the Apostle Paul, possessed an abundant gift of tongues *(1 Corinthians 14:18)*, encouraged all believers to have the same experience *(1 Corinthians 14:5)*, and warned the church to not forbid persons from speaking with tongues *(1 Corinthians 14:39)*.

Some have sought to discredit the modern day validity of speaking in tongues, claiming that it vanished with the other Charismatic gifts at the close of the apostolic era. However, any good student of church history realizes this theory is baseless, as numerous references to tongues and other gifts are consistently seen in the writings of church leaders for twenty centuries. The History of the Christian Church, by Philip Schaff records that speaking in tongues occurred among the Camisards, the Cevennes in France, among the early Quakers and Methodists in the Irish revival of 1859, and among the Irvingites in 1831. The Encyclopedia Britannica states that glossolalia (speaking in tongues) has recurred in Christian revivals of every age — among the mendicant friars of the thirteenth century, among the Jasenists and early Quakers, the persecuted Protestants of the Cevennes, and the Irvingites.

The idea of speaking in tongues originates in the New Testament book of Acts. At the height of the Jewish festival, Pentecost, the post ascension disciples of Jesus were filled with the Holy Spirit and manifested this unique phenomena of speaking in other languages (glossolalia).

Acts 2:1 "Now when the Day of Pentecost had fully come, they were all with one accord in one place.
2:2 And suddenly there came a sound from heaven, as of a rushing mighty wind, and it filled the whole house where they were sitting.
2:3 Then there appeared to them divided tongues, as of fire, and one sat upon each of them.
2:4 And they were all filled with the Holy Spirit and began to speak with other tongues, as the Spirit gave them utterance."

Prior to His departure to Heaven, Jesus had instructed his followers to wait in Jerusalem until they received this promised blessing *(Acts 1:4)*. The baptism with the Holy Spirit, as He described it *(Acts 1:5)*, would give them special power *(Greek, DUNAMIS, miraculous, dynamic power)*, enabling them to proclaim the Gospel everywhere.

"But you shall receive power when the Holy Spirit has come upon you; and you shall be witnesses to Me in Jerusalem, and in all Judea and Samaria, and to the end of the earth" (Acts 1:8).

The day of Pentecost marked the beginning of the Holy Spirit's outpouring upon the church, but it was not the conclusion. Other followers also experienced this infilling of the Holy Spirit, accompanied by the same manifestation of speaking in other tongues. In fact, it appears that speaking in tongues became viewed as the initial, physical evidence which proved the infilling of the Holy Spirit. This was first seen by the events which occurred at the house of Cornelius, a gentile, to whom God sent Peter to minister. Until this time, most believers (who were mainly Jewish) thought the baptism with the Holy Spirit was exclusive to the Jews. However, Peter was amazed to see Holy Spirit given to Cornelius and his family. How was he able to recognize this? He cited, *"For they heard them speak with tongues and magnify God..." (Acts 10:46).*

This pattern was repeated again when Paul ministered at Ephesus. Once more tongues accompanied the gift of the Holy Spirit. *"And when Paul had laid hands on them, the Holy Spirit came upon them, and they spoke with tongues and prophesied" (Acts 19:6).* However, when Peter and John ministered at Samaria, the Holy Spirit was given again, but this time nothing is mentioned about tongues. *"Then they laid hands on them, and they received the Holy Spirit" (Acts 8:17).* Verses 18 and 19 say that an observer, Simon the Sorcerer, "saw" the reception of the Spirit by the Samaritans, and whatever he witnessed motivated him to offer money to purchase the same ability to bestow the Spirit. It's speculated that he probably saw them speaking in tongues.

The fifth century church father, Augustine of Hippo, was very insightful about the beliefs held by the early church regarding speaking in tongues and supported this view. From his comments about Acts 8:17-19, it was his assumption, due to his own experience in such matters, that Simon must have seen the Samaritans speaking in tongues. Augustine wrote, "We still do what the apostles did when they laid hands on the Samaritans and called down the Holy Spirit on them by laying on of hands. It is expected that new converts should speak with new tongues."[1]

Most Pentecostals and Charismatics generally agree that the baptism with the Holy Spirit is evidenced by speaking in tongues, and is separate and distinct from the birth of the Spirit *(John 3:7)*, which occurs when faith is placed in Christ for salvation.

Furthermore, they believe that speaking in tongues is involved in three distinct functions: (1) As the initial, physical evidence of the baptism with the Holy Spirit *(Acts 10:46)*, (2) as a spiritual prayer language which is used for personal edification *(1 Corinthians 14:4, Romans 8:26-27)*, and (3) as a special utterance gift to the church, which when interpreted, serves to edify the body *(1 Corinthians 12:10, 14:6)*. Paul indicated that not all persons would have the latter "gift of tongues" used to edify the church *(1 Corinthians 12:30)*, but desired for all believers to be able to speak in tongues for personal edification. *"I wish you all spoke with tongues..." (1 Corinthians 14:5)*.

— 64 —
Why do churches hold revivals?

In the strictest sense, a revival is really a spiritual awakening — a stirring of repentance among God's people to a fresh obedience to God. However, in the casual sense, a revival has often been used to refer to a special series of evangelistic church meetings, conducted by an evangelist or minister, hoping to arouse renewed spiritual fervor. In recent years, it was an annual tradition for many evangelical churches to conduct one or more such meetings, which would extend nightly for a week or longer. In years past I conducted hundreds of these type meetings, however, due to the trends of our present society, prolonged revival meetings have (sadly) become unpopular and nearly obsolete in some circles.

The idea of revivalism, and special meetings devoted toward revival, emerged from the evangelistic preaching and prayer meetings of the Great Awakening of the early to mid-1700's, with such famed preachers as John Wesley, George Whitefield and Jonathan Edwards. This was later combined with the tradition of the camp style meetings of the early 1800's, popularized by pioneer preachers such as Presbyterian, James McGready, Methodist Circuit Rider, Peter Cartwright, and evangelist Charles Finney.[1]

It's possible to conduct a series of revival meetings anytime we wish. Such meetings would be advisable and a good idea for every church, as has been the tradition of many evangelical churches at least a couple times a year. But real revival — that is a spiritual awakening, occurs only under certain conditions. Charles Finney (1792-1875) was one of our nation's greatest revivalists, and taught on the subject later in his life. In his "Lectures on Revival," Finney wrote that there are several things that suggest when a revival is imminent: "First, when the providence of God indicates that a revival is at hand... Second, where the wickedness of the wicked grieves, humbles and distresses Christians... Third, when Christians have a spirit of prayer for revival... And lastly, when believers have a desire and anxiety to a call of repentance and to a new or fresh obedience to God."[2]

History shows that the great revivals of times past turned the tide of our nation's morality, yielded hundreds of thousands of converts to Christ, reversed religious apathy and rekindled the spiritual fervor of churchgoers.

Jonathan Edwards (1703-1764), one of God's choice instruments of the Great Awakening of the eighteenth century, described his observations of the effect that revival has upon the hearts of people:[3]

(1) "Revival brings an extraordinary sense of the awful majesty, greatness and holiness of God so as sometimes to overwhelm soul and body, a sense of the piercing, all-seeing eye of God so as to sometimes take away the bodily strength; and an extraordinary view of the infinite terribleness of the wrath of God, together with a sense of the ineffable misery of sinners exposed to this wrath."

(2) "Revival especially brings a longing after these two things; to be more perfect in humility and adoration. The flesh and the heart seem often to cry out, lying low before God and adoring Him with greater love and humility... The person felt a great delight in singing praises to God and Jesus Christ, and longing that this present life may be as it were one continued song of praise to God. There was a longing as one person expressed it, 'to sit and sing this life away;' and an overcoming pleasure in the thought of spending an eternity in that exercise. Together with living by faith to a great degree, there was a constant and extraordinary distrust of our own strength and wisdom;

a great dependence on God for His help in order to the performance of anything to God's acceptance and being retrained from the most horrid sins."

By all means, a spiritual awakening is something desperately needed again in our nation — an objective that every Christ-devoted church should be praying for. Without exaggeration, America's widespread sin and rebellion toward God has brought our nation to the precipice of judgment and disaster.

The verse of scripture that probably best summarizes the cause and effect of revival is found in 2 Chronicles. *"If My people who are called by My name will humble themselves, and pray and seek My face, and turn from their wicked ways, then I will hear from heaven, and will forgive their sin and heal their land" (2 Chronicles 7:14).*

— 65 —
Why do many churches have conflicting views about spiritual gifts?

Most churches have far more in agreement than people ever realize. However, the matter of spiritual gifts is one of those particular issues that remains controversial and divisive to some, with varying degrees of opinions.

The New Testament describes 21 gifts to the church that are sometimes categorized under the heading of (1) Ministry (office) gifts, (2) Motivational (practical) gifts, and (3) Charismatic (spiritual) gifts. These are found in *Ephesians* 4:11, *Romans* 12:3-7, 1 *Corinthians* 12:1-12, and are listed below:

Spiritual Gifts to the Church		
Ministry	**Motivational**	**Charismatic**
Apostle	Service	Wisdom
Prophet	Exhortation	Knowledge
Evangelist	Giving	Discernment
Pastor	Leadership	Prophecy
Teacher	Mercy	Tongues

	Helps	Interpretation
	Administration	Faith
		Healing
		Miracles

Among various churches and denominations there's not too much squabble over the acceptance of the more subtle, "Motivational" and "Ministry" gifts (although the modern day offices of apostle and prophet are frequently disputed).

However most of the controversy usually lies with the nine spiritual gifts *(Greek, CHARISMATA)* listed in 1 *Corinthians* 12:1-12. On the farthest extreme, some churches do not believe in any modern day operation of such gifts. In brief, their view is that these were only intended as a limited supernatural empowerment to help the early church get started, and that they vanished after the last Apostles of Jesus died — the scriptures taking their place. Their estimation of those who embrace these supernatural gifts, such as the Pentecostals or Charismatics, may vary — that they are either fanatical extremists or possibly even demonic and cultish. This view, however, is not as prominent as it once was and has been diminishing since the emergence of the Charismatic renewal in the late 1960's, which affected many of the historic, mainline churches — believed to be a part of a latter day outpouring of the Holy Spirit as described in Acts 2:17 and James 5:7.

Historical records indicate that the abundant exercise of the Charismatic gifts may have diminished somewhat after the post New Testament era — especially in the dark ages, due to the years of inaccessibility of scripture to the common people in their own language. But there is much history to substantiate that the supernatural gifts were never absent from the church. Scores of statements to this effect were recorded by church leaders such as Irenaeus, who wrote around A.D. 150 "...we hear many of the brethren in the church who have prophetic gifts, and who speak in tongues through the spirit, and who also bring to light the secret things of men for their benefit [word of knowledge]..." Elsewhere he said, "When God saw it necessary, and the church prayed and fasted much, they did miraculous things, even of bringing back the spirit to a dead man."[1] Near the close of the second century, Tertullian cited similar incidents, describing the operation of prophecies, healings and tongues,[2] and in 210, Origen reported many healings and other Charismatic gifts, as did later writers such as Eusebius, Firmilian, Chrysostom and others through many centuries.[3]

The Encyclopedia Britannica says that Charismatic gifts such as glossolalia (speaking in tongues) have occurred in Christian revivals of every age.[4] In the same vein, Souer's History of the Christian Church cites a reference to the famed leader of the Protestant reformation of the 16th century, stating, "Dr. Martin Luther was a prophet, evangelist, speaker in tongues, and interpreter, in one person, endowed with all the gifts of the Spirit."[5]

Today, Charismatic gifts are increasingly being manifested in all kinds of Christian fellowships and denominations throughout the world. Although the Pentecostal and Charismatic churches are especially known for this, the gifts seem to emerge wherever believers or congregations are receptive to their existence and open themselves to the inner workings of the Holy Spirit.

It is obvious that the Charismatic gifts never vanished and remain as a part of God's plan for His church. These gifts are sometimes called God's "power tools," given to the body of Christ as valuable helps to accomplish ministry objectives. As the scripture describes, they are distributed through persons within the body at the Holy Spirit's discretion.

1 Corinthians 12:7 "But the manifestation of the Spirit is given to each one for the profit of all:
12:8 for to one is given the word of wisdom through the Spirit, to another the word of knowledge through the same Spirit,
12:9 to another faith by the same Spirit, to another gifts of healings by the same Spirit,
12:10 to another the working of miracles, to another prophecy, to another discerning of spirits, to another different kinds of tongues, to another the interpretation of tongues.
12:11 But one and the same Spirit works all these things, distributing to each one individually as He wills."

Among those fellowships which embrace the operation of Charismatic gifts, as with most other doctrines, there continue to be moderate differences in opinion as to their value, application, order, and so forth. But most will generally agree that each of the nine gifts are a supernatural intervention of natural laws, bestowed by the Holy Spirit where His presence is invited and accommodated.

A definition of the 9 Charismatic gifts:

(1) Word of Wisdom — A Word means "a supernaturally imparted fragment." Wisdom generally means a practical skill in the affairs of life, such as prudence, decision making.

(2) Word of Knowledge — Supernaturally inspired utterance of facts.

(3) Faith — Supernatural impartation of assurance in God.

(4) Gifts of Healings — Supernaturally ministering health to the sick.

(5) Working of Miracles — Supernatural intervention of natural laws. The Greek describes it as "works of power" and implies instantaneous results.

(6) Prophecy — A supernaturally inspired utterance from God. A genuine prophetic utterance never contradicts, neither is equal to, the written Word of God. To forthtell or foretell. To speak from the mind of God. (Prophecies are to be judged according to 1 *Corinthians* 14:29, 1 *Thessalonians* 5:20-21).

(7) Discerning of Spirits — This gift enables one to discern a person's spiritual character and the source of his actions and messages, such as the Holy Spirit, demon spirits, the human spirit or the flesh.

(8) Different Kinds of Tongues — Supernaturally imparted utterance in an unlearned language. The purpose is to edify the body. This is distinguished from "praying" in tongues, which is intended to edify one's own spirit *(1 Corinthians 14:14)*. A message in tongues to the body is always to be interpreted (by another gift), and is limited to three within a gathering *(1 Corinthians 14:27)*.

(9) Interpretation of Tongues — To interpret a message in tongues into the understandable language of the hearers. It is not a "translation" but an interpretation.

The scriptures show that the purpose of the charismatic gifts is to edify the church, and their delegation within the body relies upon the volition of the Holy Spirit *(1 Corinthians 12:11)*. The Apostle Paul intimated that it's appropriate to seek particular gifts, however, one's motive must be for the building up of the church, not for self-gratification. *"...since you are zealous for spiritual gifts, let it be for the edification of the church that you seek to excel" (1 Corinthians 14:12)*.

There is a difference between spiritual gifts and fruit. Gifts are the Spirit's manifestation through a vessel, but fruit is the offspring of one's spiritual character. Spirituality cannot be measured by gifts, but by fruit *(Galatians 5:22-24)*. Love is the predominate feature of spirituality *(1 Corinthians 13:13)*, without which, charismatic gifts cannot function effectively *(1 Corinthians 13:1-2)*. Paul expressed that the church should have a desire for spiritual gifts, but it should follow the foremost pursuit of love. *"Pursue love, and desire spiritual gifts," (1 Corinthians 14:1)*.

Churches who allow such gifts to operate within their services are sometimes criticized for promoting confusion or mayhem. Without doubt, the service where these gifts function will take on a less structured, more spontaneous environment that may seem peculiar to some. But in 1 Corinthians 14, the Apostle Paul established specific guidelines for their use so to remove the potential for confusion and disorder. Rather than banishing the operation of these gifts entirely as some churches have done, they should seek to understand and implement the order Paul instituted. Concerned that churches might "throw the baby out with the bath water," the Apostle addressed this issue with his closing words of that chapter: *"Therefore, brethren, desire earnestly to prophesy, and do not forbid to speak with tongues. Let all things be done decently and in order" (1 Corinthians 14:39-40)*.

Generally speaking, the various gifts to the church have several beneficial effects: (1) They manifest Christ's body on the earth *(1 Corinthians 12:12-14,27)*, (2) They assist in world evangelization *(Mark 16:15-18)*, (3) They demonstrate God's power and bring Him glory *(1 Corinthians 2:4-5, 1 Corinthians 12:7)*, (4) They edify the church *(1 Corinthians 14:3,12,26)*, (5) They provide ministry help and deliverance of God's people *(Romans 12:6-8)*, and (6) They contribute toward the maturing and equipping of the church *(Ephesians 4:11-14)*.

— 66 —
How can I help the spiritual climate of my church?

Despite what people sometimes think, the spiritual environment of the church does not rest solely on the shoulders of the minister. We may remember the extraordinary miracles performed by Jesus throughout his earthly ministry. However, when he returned to Nazareth, his hometown, he was unable to do many great miracles there. Imagine, Jesus Christ himself, the son of God, could not bring revival to Nazareth — He could not produce many great results there. But it was not due to a lack of anointing upon his ministry, but because of their unbelief. *"And He did not do many mighty works there because of their unbelief"* (Matthew 13:58).

If we want to improve the spiritual climate of our church, the congregation must work together with their spiritual leaders as a team, becoming a people of prayer, faith and spiritual commitment. We must learn to add our faith to the preachers', to lift up Christ together to promote an environment that will invite the moving of the Holy Spirit.

In the services, the preacher and worship leaders seek to encourage an "atmosphere" of worship to the Lord, along with faith, expectancy, unity, and enthusiasm. Those in the congregation need to cooperate in this endeavor, to help lift the atmosphere of the service into a spiritual climate. By participating in worship, we help to create a corporate environment of God's presence that will accommodate faith and the richness of the Holy Spirit. This attitude tends to subdue unbelief, a lack of expectancy, and other negatives represented there that will hinder the effectiveness of the ministry.

The word "atmosphere" is an important word as it relates to the disposition and climate of a church service. The atmosphere is the impression or the "awareness" that is perceived by the people in the congregational setting. Any gathering of people has a collective personality or "spirit," in the same way individuals do. When we assemble with a group, we sense the overall spirit and attitude of that group. Since human beings are reflectional creatures, we tend to reflect the attitude of that group's personality. When people laugh, we tend to laugh. If people are friendly, we are inclined to be friendly.

In effect, when people come into a group atmosphere charged with praise and worship, they will likely react by joining in. An atmosphere of excitement and expectancy breeds excitement and expectancy. If the atmosphere tends to be disinterested, unresponsive, and unbelieving, people tend to reflect this attitude.

Christians should learn to help be catalysts of worship. By faith, we should try to help encourage praise to God within the body, by leading out with our own attitude of worship. Our enthusiastic participation helps to influence the atmosphere of the whole gathering. As more people participate in such attitudes, the service takes on an enhanced personality. Perhaps this is one reason why David saw the importance of expressing his worship boldly before his brethren. *"I will declare Your name to My brethren; In the midst of the congregation I will praise You" (Psalms 22:22)*. The psalmist also said, *"I will give You thanks in the great congregation; I will praise You among many people" (Psalms 35:18)*.

Since "we" are the temple of the Holy Spirit, it makes sense for believers to let the Holy Spirit's presence flow out of their temple and into the environment of the service *(1 Corinthians 6:9)*. The Word says the Lord "inhabits" the praises of His people *(Psalms 22:3)*. That means He brings His presence to wherever He is praised and lifted up — that His presence resides in the praises of His children. When we lift praise and worship to Christ out of our spirit, His presence is made real and flows in the atmosphere of the service. This is what Jesus was referring to when He said, *"For where two or three are gathered together in My name, I am there in the midst of them" (Matthew 18:20)*. We should always gather with the goal to lift up Christ and allow the Spirit of God to fill the climate of the service — the atmosphere of the meeting.

Every believer can help lift the spiritual climate of their church, if they will be people of participation, prayer and spiritual commitment. Intercede regularly and fervently for your church — pray for your pastor and leaders. And when you gather with the church to worship the Lord, contribute to the positive impact of the gathering. By faith — that is without relying on feelings — enter into the service enthusiastically. Participate eagerly with the songs of worship. Respond to the preaching with an audible "Amen" once in a while (guaranteed to be noticed by the pastor). Make the joyful noise of praise and help overcome any climate of lethargy, spiritual coldness, or unbelief. This will help elevate the service into an awareness of the Lord's presence and will help to improve the spiritual climate of your church. *"Shout joyfully to the LORD, all the earth; Break forth in song, rejoice, and sing praises" (Psalms 98:4).*

— 67 —
Why is the celebration of Christmas considered to be controversial in some churches?

Historically, Christmas has been an object of debate and controversy by church leaders, largely because its celebration did not originate in the Bible, and because many of its customs contain a mixture of non-Christian ideas which evolved from various secular and pagan cultures over a period of centuries. In fact, Christmas was actually outlawed in colonial New England, from 1649 to 1658, by the influence of Oliver Cromwell and the Puritans, who cited the "heathenistic traditions" involved in the celebration. It took two centuries for the celebration to gradually gain acceptance in the New World. Massachusetts was the first American state to recognize Christmas as a legal holiday in 1856.

Christmas was never mentioned in the New Testament, and we have no evidence that it was ever celebrated by the earliest believers. However, this fact alone does not invalidate its place in Christian worship. Since the birth of Christ is a Biblical truth, we are at liberty to celebrate His birth anytime we wish, especially once a year set aside for this purpose.

The annual celebration of Christ's birth can be traced back to at least 336 A.D., when it was observed by western churches on December 25th. Since the event was honored in the form of a religious service, the term "Christmas" came from the Old English term Cristes Maesse, meaning "Christ's Mass."

The original date of Jesus' birth was never known for certain, as it remains today. But toward the end of the second century, Clement of Alexandria was known to have cited various opinions of concerning Christ's birth date, the two most prominent of which were January 6th and December 25th. Later in the fifth century, Augustine commented: "For He is believed to have been conceived on the 25th of March, upon which day He also suffered... but He was born according to tradition upon December 25th."[1]

It's strongly speculated that December 25th was selected for the Christmas celebration as an effort to bridge the gap between Christian and pagan traditions. Such mergers became common practice for Constantine, Emperor of Rome (306-337), after his controversial conversion to Christ. He legalized Christianity, and by decree, combined numerous pagan customs with state Christianity — which provided many of the traditions observed by the church of that era. In Rome, the supposed birthday of the pagan sun god was on December 25th, and the pagan winter feast of Saturnalia was celebrated for seven days from December 17th to the 24th, marked by a spirit of merriment, gift giving to children, and various forms of entertainment. It seems likely the latter was the basis for modern day Christmas gift traditions. Later, the cultures of such nations as the Germans, French, English, Scandinavians and others, eventually influenced the celebration by their added traditions.

The Christmas tree has especially been a major source of controversy, as it has sometimes been associated with an idol, described in Jeremiah: *"Thus says the LORD: Do not learn the way of the Gentiles; do not be dismayed at the signs of heaven, for the Gentiles are dismayed at them. For the customs of the peoples are futile; for one cuts a tree from the forest, the work of the hands of the workman, with the ax. They decorate it with silver and gold; they fasten it with nails and hammers so that it will not topple. They are upright, like a palm tree, and they cannot speak; they must be carried, because they cannot go by themselves. Do not be afraid of them, for they cannot do evil, nor can they do any good"* (Jer. 10:2-5). Indeed, this rendering does sound much like a Christmas tree. But the original Hebrew makes it clearer, *"They cut a tree out of the forest, and a craftsman shapes it with a chisel."* This would indicate that the tree itself was not the idol, but its wood was carved into an idol which was overlaid with silver and gold. While a Christmas tree is admittedly secular in its origin, it's not likely that it came from the idol described by Jeremiah.

The traditional Christmas tree, an evergreen trimmed with decorations, only dates back a few centuries. There are several unverified traditions which claim its origin — even one which says that it began with Martin Luther, the famed reformist of the church, who used candles to decorate it as symbols of the light of the world. However, historical references seem to show that it was probably derived from the so-called "paradise tree" that symbolized the Garden of Eden portrayed in German mystery plays in the 16th century.

The widespread use of the Christmas tree in connection with the holiday gained popularity in the early 17th century, spreading throughout Germany, France and northern Europe. In 1841, Albert, prince consort of Queen Victoria, introduced the Christmas tree custom to Great Britain.

The custom had apparently accompanied immigrants to the U.S. where it gained acceptance in the early 19th century. From a family diary, the earliest evidence of an American Christmas tree was recorded on December 20, 1821 in Lancaster, Pennsylvania — where a tree was displayed in the German settlement home of Matthew Zahn.[2]

Santa Claus has been criticized as a counterfeit persona which diverts attention away from the real central figure of Christmas, which is Christ. In reality, Santa is a fictional character, a combination of the Germanic legend of Kriss Kringle, derived from Christkindle, meaning "Christ child," intermingled with the inspiring history of Saint Nicholas in the fourth century.

Nicholas was orphaned in his youth by the sudden death of his wealthy Christian parents, and eventually rose to become the bishop of Myra, a coastal town of Lycia (now in Turkey). He was legendary for his generosity and giving of gifts, especially to children. The term, Santa, is another spelling for saint, and Claus was a Dutch pronunciation of the last part of his name, Cholas. Over the years, these interwoven legends of "Santa Cholas" were handed down from one European generation to another.

Eventually Dutch immigrants to America brought their custom of celebrating St. Nicholas Day on December 6th, and especially on St. Nicholas eve, when gifts were given to children. British settlers to America later incorporated the tradition as part of their Christmas eve celebration, and Santa Cholas gradually evolved into the embellished image of Santa Claus, who was assimilated into our common Christmas customs.

These secular traditions and others, combined with a very commercialized, materialistic emphasis makes Christmas somewhat less than a pure Christian celebration. However, we realize that our society is filled with many other secular customs in which we all participate. For instance, many of the traditions surrounding a wedding ceremony are based upon non-biblical ideas. Dozens of other social customs, which are common to most Americans, also had their roots in secular beliefs. Merely because a custom is not biblical in origin, doesn't make it evil. It would, however, be inappropriate for a Christian to "substitute" these customs in the place of what Christmas is supposed to represent to us — the birthday of our Lord and Savior Jesus Christ.

Regardless of whether Christmas began in New Testament times or not, its origin seems ordained of God. It is the one day of the year when Jesus is spoken of more than any other. It perhaps is the single greatest opportunity to speak about Christ during an entire year, giving an open door to explain his birth — His reason for coming into this world. In my opinion, Christians need not be concerned about secular Christmas customs as long as they don't "secularize Christmas" into the commercial, pagan holiday it has become to the world.

— 68 —
Why do many churches oppose Halloween?

Churches frequently disapprove of Halloween because it is really a modern version of ancient, satanic traditions which were originated by the pagan Celtic religion, and their druid priests, long before Christianity. It is assumed that the traditions of Halloween were carried to America by the early European settlers, some who viewed the traditions as mere "folklore," and others who held these rituals as sacred to their cultic beliefs. Halloween was eventually trivialized as intriguing folklore for the amusement of children and young adults. Today, it is highly commercialized, bringing great profits from the sale of candy, pumpkins, costumes, and other "ghoulish" items.

The World Book Encyclopedia says, "Halloween is a festival that takes place on October 31st. In the United States, children wear costumes on Halloween and go trick-or-treating. Many carry jack-o-lanterns carved out of pumpkins. At Halloween parties, people enjoy such activities as fortune-telling, hearing stories about ghosts and witches, and bobbing for apples."[1]

However, the Dictionary of the Occult and Paranormal,[2] states "Halloween was originally a pagan festival of darkness, fire, and death. All Hallows Eve was celebrated by the Celts of northern Europe... Halloween was also an important date for the witches' calendar."

According to witchcraft organizations, witches have eight major festivals throughout the year. Four are the solar festivals: one at both equinoxes, and one at both solstices. The other four occur almost midpoint between the Solar festivals; the most famous of these are Samhain (Halloween to non-witches) and Beltane (May day). Samhain, or Halloween, is the beginning of their new year, and is the time when they claim that they can most effectively communicate with the dead.

Author, Richard Cavendish, in the encyclopedia Man, Myth, and Magic,[3] states *"All Hallows Eve, or Halloween, was originally a festival of fire, the dead, and the powers of darkness. It's the evening of 31 October, the night before the Christian festival of All Hallows Day. All Hallows Day commemorates the saints and martyrs, and was first introduced in the seventh century. Its date was changed from 13 May to 1 November in the following century, probably to make it coincide with and Christianize a pagan festival of the dead. All Souls Day in the Roman Catholic calendar is 2 November. It is marked by prayers for the souls of the dead. It is only in recent times that Halloween was reduced to a minor jollification for the children."*

Cavendish continues, *"The Druids were pagan priests of an early Celtic religion. Druids are mentioned by name in thirty references in Greek and Roman writers between the second century B.C. and the fourth century A.D. They were a barbaric order, dreaded for their power and blood-thirstiness. They certainly appear as lawgivers, and as being directly concerned with animal and human sacrifices..."*

"They were, of course, the sole interpreters of religion. They determined all disputes by a final and unalterable decision, and had the power of inflicting the punishment of death. And, indeed, their altars streamed with the blood of human victims. Men, women, and children were often given as human sacrifices."

Irene Park, a former witch and authority on the history of Halloween says, *"The Druids in Ireland would go through the neighborhoods and countryside on the eve of October 31 to collect offerings for Satan. They would carry lanterns, bags for money, and canes with very sharp points on their ends (known as leprechaun staffs, good luck horns, or fairies' wands). At each house they would demand a specified amount. If the household would not, or could not, give the offering (Penance or treat), the Druid would use his cane to castrate the male human or one of their prize animals."*[3]

Park says, *"The guisers went from house to house, singing and dancing. Their blood-curdling masks and grotesque costumes may have been meant to keep evil at bay, or more likely, were a visible representation of the ghosts and goblins that lurked in the night. These masks have now been transferred to the children, who in the United States, visit neighbors for the food offering which once belonged to the dead - or play tricks akin to the legendary destructiveness of witches and imps abroad on the night."*

Most of the original folklore of Halloween has been preserved in the modern traditions: the goblins, jack-o-lanterns, Halloween parties, begging for gifts, etc., which all had their origin in the ancient celebration of All Hallows Eve.

Most people and children who participate with modern Halloween festivities, usually do so innocently, without any intention of associating themselves with the occult or other satanic traditions. However, the great tragedy is that it domesticates the occult and the powers of darkness. It creates a "tongue-in-cheek" attitude that the forces of evil are not to be taken seriously — that devils, witches, and goblins are considered merely make-believe, plastic masks, with child-like impotence. It also tends to promote an acceptance and friendliness toward dark traditions and occult beliefs; that Satan is not really so bad, witches are really not evil, demons are not really dangerous.

Members of the occult and devotees to the true satanic traditions of Halloween are ecstatic by the widespread acceptance and participation in their sacred festival. They view society's celebration of Halloween as an enormous public relations victory, and believe it's a time when their dark powers are greatly intensified, due to the unity of the masses which magnify and exalt the forces of evil. With thousands focusing their energies upon traditions of Satan, they feel this strengthens his influence in the affairs of the world.

For these reasons, many churches oppose any participation with Halloween on the basis that its relationship to evil is contrary to our relationship with Christ. The scriptures mention nothing about Halloween, but they do warn that a believer cannot mingle a relationship with God and the Devil *(1 Corinthians 10:21)*, and that we should even *"Abstain from every form [appearance] of evil" (1 Thessalonians 5:22)*.

— 69 —
What does a church look for in the selection of lay leaders and workers?

A pastor is always encouraged whenever anyone says they feel the calling to serve in some aspect of ministry or leadership in the church. There is always a great need of qualified laypersons to serve in such roles. But before believers seek such avenues of Christian service, they should understand four common principles that apply to all Christian leadership:

(1) Faithfulness is the chief qualification for leadership. — Persons considered for leadership roles in the church should first show spiritual character, maturity, and faithfulness. Generally speaking, a pastor will select his leaders on the merits that they are consistent and cooperative to the basic expectations that are preached and presented to the whole congregation — that they are outstanding Christians.

Faithfulness in basic things is the cornerstone of leadership, and is the scriptural method to discern leadership potential. Jesus said, *"He who is faithful in what is least is faithful also in much; and he who is unjust in what is least is unjust also in much" (Luke 16:10)*.

WhatPeopleAskAboutTheChurch

Paul shared these same views and instructed Timothy to commission men of faithfulness to carry on the ministry of the Gospel. *"And the things that you have heard from me among many witnesses, commit these to faithful men who will be able to teach others also" (2 Timothy 2:2).*

Regardless of their skills or talents, if a person does not have some degree of mastery in the basic fundamentals of Christian faith, morals, and character, they do not yet have qualifications for leadership and should not be considered.

Besides the previous issues mentioned, many churches or pastors will not consider persons for leadership (a) if they do not attend church and its functions faithfully, (b) if they do not have an uplifting attitude, (c) if they do not demonstrate loyalty to the pastor and other leadership, (d) if they do not show voluntary eagerness and cooperation, (e) if they do not manifest patterns of scriptural stewardship, (f) if they don't share the same doctrinal views or ministry goals, and (g) if they don't show some evidence of appropriate giftings or leadership traits.

(2) Leaders will be held to higher standards than non-leaders.
— To some it may seem unfair to expect more from leadership than the average believer, especially if they do not understand that leadership is supposed to be a role-model. But the Bible makes clear that those with higher responsibilities also have higher accountability. *"For everyone to whom much is given, from him much will be required; and to whom much has been committed, of him they will ask the more" (Luke 12:48).*

The life of any leader, especially a pastor, will always be under a magnifying glass, being scrutinized and criticized for flaws or imperfections. Whether we think this is just or unfair, it's a fact — and a matter of necessity, as the perceived godliness of a leader helps bring credibility to his message.

However, keep in mind that the success of leadership does not depend on the total absence of flaws. There are, of course, prescribed standards of morality and character that every leader must possess, but if it were possible for a leader to be completely perfect without any faults, he might fall short as a role model for believers who are destined to make many mistakes in their lives. It is because leaders are human, still subject to mistakes and even sin, they provide an attainable role-model for the average believer. Flawlessness is not the realistic goal that leadership hopes to demonstrate. Rather, they must show the wholehearted effort of following the Lord, the example of a humble, repentant heart if they fail, and the determination to rise above their failures to keep going on for God.

Since a leader's Godly lifestyle contributes to the credibility of his message or teaching, he must make himself accessible to people. As persons observe the Christ-likeness and genuineness of their leader in a casual environment, they will grow in their trust and respect of his guidance and counsel. *"And we urge you, brethren, to recognize those who labor among you, and are over you in the Lord and admonish you" (1 Thess. 5:12).*

To illustrate this, one church member was a staunch opponent of many of the pastor's sermons. He would often write letters of rebuttal and openly criticize the pastor. Finally, in an effort to resolve this discontent, the pastor invited the member to his home to fellowship on several occasions. As a result, the member began to know the pastor better and began to trust the content of his messages. It may seem odd to many of us, but people sometimes view church meetings and services as a "staged," superficial environment, where ministers and people act religious only because they're supposed to. These people have the greatest need to know their leaders outside of the church meeting environment.

Even if persons are not seeking to be leaders, but are given significant roles of visibility or influence in the church, they are usually also held to a similar standard expected for leadership. This is because anyone who stands in front of people performs a role of leadership whether they intend to or not. In times past, I've known some in the church to be extremely gifted as musicians, singers, or teachers who could have been a great blessing to the fellowship, but they showed such immaturity, unfaithfulness, or impure character, that I could not use them, as it would put them forth to the congregation as an example. Gifts and talents are obviously important, but sincerity and integrity is far more critical than how talented they are.

(3) Leaders lead by example. — The basic definition of a leader is "one who stands in front of." And of course, what they stand in front of is people. A leader stands in front of people in order to be seen, because a leader is one who demonstrates a visual example. A leader is a role model who leads the way, who shows how it's done. *"...in all things showing yourself to be a pattern of good works; in doctrine showing integrity, reverence, incorruptibility" (Titus 2:7).*

Leaders must be good followers in order to be good role models. Usually a pastor will not have a problem encouraging the congregation to do what he's been able to get his leaders to do. When the pastor encourages the people to worship, the leaders should be the first to worship. When the congregation is invited to the altars to pray, the leaders should be the first to respond. When the congregation is asked to sacrifice and give, the leaders should be the first to give. When the people are asked to go shake hands and be friendly, the leaders should "lead" the way in going to people introducing themselves and being friendly. When the people are asked to make church attendance a priority, the leaders should be the first to cooperate. If the people are challenged to pray, the leaders should lead the way. *"...be an example to the believers in word, in conduct, in love, in spirit, in faith, in purity" (1 Timothy 4:12).*

(4) Spiritual leaders inspire cooperation from the heart. — The objective of Christian ministry is not merely to influence behavior. Rather, it is to inspire the attitude of the heart, which affects behavior. While it might be possible to demand and enforce outward obedience to certain rules or laws, it is not possible to change inner "spiritual" desires or attitudes by such demands.

For instance, one could demand a kiss from one's spouse, and might get compliance, but it doesn't mean they did so willingly. And what real value was the kiss if it was only compliance to orders — and not from the heart? Love is something that comes from the heart and cannot be bought, forced, demanded or manipulated. So it is with spiritual virtues. You can't order someone to be joyful or peaceful. These virtues must be birthed in the "want to" of a person's spirit. They can be inspired, coaxed, courted or motivated, but they cannot be forced, coerced, or pressured.

If the church was only concerned with outward results, or in maintaining a regimented organization, it might be possible to coerce the cooperation of most people with tough rules and methods of enforcement. Even the unruly nature of criminals can be contained by the controlled environment of a prison. However, everyone knows that prisoners are not voluntarily cooperative. In their hearts, they resent their harsh environment of shackles and chains. And if a gate was left open, or a guard's back turned long enough, any one of them would willingly escape.

The only way a church can accomplish its mission of changing people's lives, is when there is a "want to" born in the heart — a desire to serve God and to do His will. The objective of leadership and the ministry is not to "coerce" people into obeying God, but to "inspire and motivate" faith that will bring about obedience. Our tools for this are God's Word and the person of the Holy Spirit, who invites, convicts, and persuades the heart of men. A hunger for God, peace, love, unity, or joy cannot be forced upon a church. These, and all other spiritual things can only come when there is a desire birthed in the heart of the believer. This is a basic rudiment of spiritual leadership. There is no pastor or leader that will succeed until they understand this.

— 70 —
What is meant by the Church Fathers?

Fathers of the Church was a term given by the Christian church to many of the outstanding theologians of at least the first six centuries. It is used in an ecclesiastical sense, to refer to those who have preceded us in the faith, and thus able to instruct us in it. Their patristic writings and commentaries have been invaluable to an understanding of the early, historic church and its doctrines.[1]

The church established four qualifications for bestowing the honorary title of Church Father on an early writer. In addition to belonging to the early period of the church, a Father of the church must have led a holy life. His writings must be generally free from doctrinal error and must contain an outstanding defense or explanation of Christian doctrine. Finally, his writings must have received the approval of the church.

A roster of all the post apostolic Church Fathers would not be feasible here, however some of the most notable of the first century were Polycarp, Ignatius, Papias, and Justin Martyr. Of the second and third centuries were Clement, Origen, Irenaeus, Tertullian and Hippolytus. It has been said that the fourth century produced many of the more prominent scholars, such as Athanasius, Hilary, Basil, Gregory of Nyssa, Gregory of Nazianzus, Ambrose, Augustine, Chrysostom and Jerome.

The use of the term "father," both in regard to the historic church leaders, or priests of the Catholic church, has been considered controversial, as it appears to contradict Jesus' disapproval of such titles, *"Do not call anyone on earth your father; for One is your Father, He who is in heaven" (Matthew 23:9)*. However, the context of this passage *(Matthew 23:1-39)* deals with one of Jesus' most scathing censures of the self-righteousness and hypocrisy of the Pharisees. He repudiated their ostentatious use of titles such as "Father, Rabbi, or Teacher," which they used to posture themselves as superior to others. His objection was actually targeted at "arrogance and self-exaltation," not the humble use as adjectives. The scriptures later validate descriptive titles such as Pastors and Teachers *(Ephesians 4:11)*, and even Paul described himself as a father to his young understudy, Timothy. *"...as a son with his father he served with me in the gospel" (Philippians 2:22)*.

— 71 —
Why is the term Easter considered to be controversial in some churches?

Easter is the annual commemoration of the resurrection of Jesus Christ, and is considered the principal festival of the Christian church. It is celebrated on the first Sunday following the full moon that occurs on or after March 21st — or one week later if the full moon falls on Sunday. Because of this, it is referred to as a movable feast, since it might be observed on varying dates between March 22 and April 25.

Some Christian leaders have objected to the use of Easter in association with Christ's resurrection because of two particular reasons: First, the one and only Biblical reference to the word

"Easter" appears in the 1611 King James Version, and was a mistranslation of *"PASCHA,"* the ordinary Greek word for Passover. Secondly, Easter was never used in association to Christ's resurrection until the eighth century, when it is believed that the pagan term was used as another effort to paganize Christian traditions.

According to 8th-century English scholar, Bede, the term, Easter, came from Eastre, the Anglo-Saxon name of a Teutonic goddess of spring and fertility, to whom was dedicated a month corresponding to April. Her festival was celebrated on the day of the vernal equinox. Traditions associated with the festival are embodied in the Easter rabbit, a symbol of fertility, and in colored Easter eggs, originally painted with bright colors to represent the sunlight of spring, and used in Easter-egg rolling contests or given as gifts.

In an effort to be more scriptural or to abstain from the association with pagan philosophies connected with Easter, churches sometimes prefer to use "The Resurrection Day" or other terminology that highlights the true Christian meaning of the observance. To use the term Easter or its traditions does not constitute any sin or violation of scripture, and should not be viewed as an issue of contention. However as with other pagan-influenced Christian traditions (such as Christmas), it is helpful for churches to educate people of the differences between historical fact and myths of antiquity.

— 72 —
Why do most Christian churches meet on Sunday instead of the Sabbath?

Up until the beginning of the church, God's people were used to going to synagogue on the seventh day of the week (Saturday) which was called the Sabbath. This was a holy day to the Lord, the fourth of Ten Commandments God gave Moses. *"Remember the Sabbath day, to keep it holy" (Exodus 20:8).* This was, and will always remain, the official Sabbath. However, after Jesus rose from the dead on the first day of the week, Sunday, the New Testament shows that the early Christians began meeting together on this new day as a weekly commemoration of their new life in Christ. *"Now on the first day of the week, when the disciples came together to break bread, Paul, ready to depart the next day, spoke to them and continued his message until midnight" (Acts 20:7).* (See also 1 *Corinthians* 16:2)

Historians indicate that the earliest Christians not only met together on Sunday, but also came together regularly with their Jewish community in the synagogues on the Sabbath. This was their traditional heritage and where most of their neighbors, friends and family would congregate — a great place to witness. However it seems about A.D. 135, there was great upheaval in the synagogues. The influential Rabbi, Akiba, proclaimed the leader of the Jewish rebellion in Palestine, Bar Cochba, as the Messiah,[1] and the Jewish Christians were quick to refute this. Such hostility arose against the believers that a curse against "sectarians" (which referred to the Christians) was introduced into the synagogue services. Thus, anyone who would not pronounce the curse with other worshipers would be ejected. This effectively ostracized the Christians from participation in the synagogues on Saturday, but they continued with their meetings on Sunday.

Although they were no longer bound to a rigid code of laws or Sabbath keeping *(Galatians 3:10-11, Colossians 2:16)*, it is believed that the early church probably came to view Sunday as a combined observance of the Sabbath and the resurrection day of Jesus *(Acts 20:7, 1 Corinthians 16:2)*. This day of Christian worship came to be called the Lord's Day *(Revelations 1:10)*, a day to fellowship in celebration of the resurrection, to worship, pray and study the Word together.

There are several early, historical references which confirm the continued Sunday tradition by the early Christians. One of these is the "Didache," a compilation of teachings of the first century church, thought by some to be a copy of teachings by the first disciples (possibly A.D. 100-130), and clearly describes the church meeting on the Lord's day. "On the Lord's day of the Lord, come together, break bread and hold Eucharist, after confessing your transgressions that your offering may be pure; but let none who has a quarrel with another join in your meeting until they be reconciled, that your sacrifice be not defiled..."[2]

Another such reference is found in the writings of Justin Martyr (Approx. A.D. 140). Not only did he affirm the churches' meeting day, but also gave one of the best explanations of the meaning behind it, as viewed by the early believers. "We assemble in common on Sunday [the Lord's day], because this is the first day, on which God created the world and the light, and because Jesus Christ our Saviour on the same day rose from the dead and appeared to his disciples."[3]

Sunday worship took on new dimensions in the fourth century as the Christian Emperor of Rome, Constantine, proclaimed the believers' day of worship (the first weekday) to be a holiday (A.D. 321). However, instead of using the term that Christians used, the Lord's Day, he continued with a term, "Dies Solis" (The Day of the Sun) which the Romans had already used for a couple centuries in homage to their worship of the sun god. Prior to his Christian profession in 312, Constantine was a pagan worshiper, his favorite deity being the Unconquered Sun, and throughout the remainder of his life, his understanding of the Christian faith was less than perfect and never did fully extract himself from pagan philosophy.[4] He was apparently unable to clearly distinguish between the Father of Jesus Christ and the sun deity, and while he sanctioned the Christian's day of worship, his title for it left a lasting legacy to the pagan sun god, what is known on our calendar as Sunday.

— 73 —
What does it mean to call for the elders of the church?

Calling for the elders of the church refers to the request by one who is ill, for the church ministers to come anoint them with oil, and pray for them. *"Is anyone among you sick? Let him call for the elders of the church, and let them pray over him, anointing him with oil in the name of the Lord. And the prayer of faith will save the sick, and the Lord will raise him up. And if he has committed sins, he will be forgiven"* (James 5:14-15).

It should be noted that the sick person is the one who initiates the invitation to the elders. This suggests that while the afflicted party certainly needs the added strength of the elders prayer and faith, yet the afflicted must also have faith — at least enough to call for the church leaders to come and pray. The technology of the telephone has made it much easier to "call" for the elders than it once was.

Usually the elders will also lay their hands on the sick during the anointing and prayer. This was a very common act by Jesus and his Apostles when they prayed for people *(Luke 4:40, Acts 14:3)*, and He especially exhorted His followers to emulate this procedure when administering healing. *"...they will lay hands on the sick, and they will recover" (Mark 16:18)*.

The oil referred to by James has no medicinal effect or mystical powers, but is only used as a symbol of the Holy Spirit. Neither must we necessarily assume that a conductive power flows out from the elders' hands into the sick body. There are no definite, scientific reasons for any of these acts, except they are matters of obedience to God's Word — expressions of faith to which God promises to respond. *"...the prayer of faith will save the sick, and the Lord will raise him up."*

The passage in James' epistle also makes another interesting reference. Besides providing a strong assurance of healing, he says, *"...And if he has committed sins, he will be forgiven" (James 5:15)*. Throughout the Bible, this unique relationship between "healing" and "forgiveness" is frequently repeated. Such as with the Psalmist, who refers to healing as one of the believer's benefits, as well as the forgiveness of sins. *"Bless the LORD, O my soul, And forget not all His benefits: Who forgives all your iniquities, Who heals all your diseases" (Psalms 103:2-3)*.

Healing has an interwoven relationship with forgiveness. The word "salvation" so frequently used in the New Testament, comes from the Greek, *SOTERIA*, which literally means "wholeness and healing, both in the physical and spiritual." Furthermore, on one occasion, Jesus explained that this was one of the great reasons why he cured the sick — so they would know He also has power to save them. *"For which is easier, to say, Your sins are forgiven you, or to say, Arise and walk? But that you may know that the Son of Man has power on earth to forgive sins; then He said to the paralytic, Arise, take up your bed, and go to your house" (Matthew 9:5-6)*.

Healing is considered one of the many attributes which were appropriated by the atonement of our suffering savior. Jesus not only purchased the salvation of our soul, but His sufferings also procured our physical healing. *"Surely He has borne our griefs and carried our sorrows; yet we esteemed Him stricken, smitten by God, and afflicted. But He was wounded for our transgressions, He was bruised for our iniquities; the chastisement for our peace was upon Him, and by His stripes we are healed"* *(Isaiah 53:4-5).* Healing is a gift which was paid for by Christ's substitutionary act, and is also listed as one of nine spiritual gifts given to the church *(1 Corinthians 12:9).*

Sometimes people question whether healing is really God's will. However, a noted physician once said: "I've become convinced that no one seriously doubts God's will to heal. If they really believed He wanted them sick, why would they try to evade His will by coming to see me? And what do you suppose I could do for them if it wasn't His will for them to get well?"

Perhaps God's will is best revealed by Jesus' earthly ministry, of which the New Testament records eleven occasions where Jesus was approached for healing. Not once did He turn anyone away or express that it was not His will. This is significant since the Bible is designed to show God's will, and gave us our foundation for faith *(Romans 10:17).* In one instance, a leper came to Jesus inquiring whether it was His will to heal him. *"Lord, if it is your will you can heal me, he said. In response, Jesus extended his hand and said, it's my will; be healed! And the man's leprosy vanished"* *(Matthew 8:2-3).*

Finally, one of the most remarkable endorsements of healing is expressed through God's very name. Historically, the names of many people were derived from their trade, occupation or descriptive characteristics. For instance, those named "Smith" came from generations of blacksmiths. It was also a good way for a person to advertise his trade, "I'm Walter the Smith." Similarly, God identifies His own name by what He does. In the Old Testament, He says that His name is JEHOVAH RAHPA, or, *"I am the LORD who heals you"* *(Exodus 15:26).* This is a convincing testimony of God's will and nature regarding healing. How could He express His desire more clearly than to identify himself by the name, "I'm The Lord that heals you?" Not only does it convey His will — It's His very name. "Healing" is who He is and what He does.

— 74 —
Why is a church building sometimes referred to as a "House of Prayer?"

This comes from a scripture passage where Jesus rebuked moneychangers and vendors who were selling sacrifices in the outer court of Herod's Temple in Jerusalem. Besides a violation of the Sabbath laws, Jesus considered this as exploitation of the sacredness of God's house. Quoting from Isaiah 56:7, He scolded them, *"It is written, My house shall be called a house of prayer, but you have made it a den of thieves." (Matthew 21:13).*

The old covenant temple was, indeed, intended to be a house of prayer, a place that was holy and sacred, where God correlated with His people. However, technically speaking, this really cannot correspond to a church facility, because under the new covenant of Christ, the believer becomes God's temple. While every church facility should be dedicated for prayer, in today's era God's people are the house or "household" of prayer, the tabernacle in whom the Holy Spirit dwells. *"Do you not know that you are the temple of God and that the Spirit of God dwells in you?" (1 Corinthians 3:16).*

Needless to say, Christians should be a people of prayer, dedicated to a life of spiritual devotion to God. Prayer is indispensable to the Christian life and is the key that will open the door to God's provisions, divine guidance, and solutions to every problem. The scriptures say, *"Rejoice always, pray without ceasing, in everything give thanks; for this is the will of God in Christ Jesus for you" (1 Thessalonians 5:16-18).*

— 75 —
Why are most church services based around preaching?

Preaching means to orally "proclaim" something, and is usually used to describe the act of bringing forth a sermon or message. It is viewed as an important ingredient of a church service, largely because the whole foundation of the Christian faith, and the very reason for the church's existence, is derived from the Word of God, the object of preaching.

Scripture has a prominent place in Christian worship, just as it did in the Jewish Synagogue on the Sabbath. It was in this setting that Matthew's Gospel recounts a reading in Nazareth's synagogue by the local, rising young prophet, Jesus. Remarkably, it was on this occasion that He revealed His Messianic identity, that He was the fulfillment of the prophesy of Isaiah 61:1, from which He read. *"The Spirit of the LORD is upon Me, because He has anointed Me to preach the gospel to the poor. He has sent Me to heal the brokenhearted, to preach deliverance to the captives and recovery of sight to the blind, to set at liberty those who are oppressed, to preach the acceptable year of the LORD" (Luke 4:18-19).*

Preaching was considered a primary thrust of Christ's mission on earth — a task that He passed on to the church to continue. He commissioned His followers to evangelize the world with Gospel preaching *(Mark 16:15)*, and later when the church came together on Sundays, the course of worship would also include ample preaching or teaching, sometimes of a lengthy nature. *"Now on the first day of the week, when the disciples came together to break bread, Paul, ready to depart the next day, spoke to them and continued his message until midnight" (Acts 20:7).* (Now doesn't this make you feel better about the length of your pastor's sermons?)

Preaching is always intended to bring about some desired result. To the unsaved, hopefully the preaching will inspire a decision for Christ. For the believers, the objective is to edify them spiritually. Dr. Jay Adams, a widely respected professor of homiletics, says "the purpose of preaching is to effect changes among the members of God's church that build them up individually and that build up the body as a whole. Individually, good pastoral preaching helps each person in the congregation to grow in his faith, conforming his life more and more to biblical standards. Corporately, such preaching builds up the church as a body in the relationship of the parts to the whole, and the whole to God and to the world."[1]

Customarily, preachers will organize their message into the form of a sermon, which is "a speech with an organized collection of thoughts." It is usually constructed around an outline of key points, combined with an array of scripture references, metaphors, or illustrative stories to help convey the point. A sermon may also be referred to as a "homily," derived from the Greek *HOMILIA*, a mutual talk or set discourse.

There are a variety of sermon formats used by Bible preachers today:

(1) A Textual sermon is one that limits itself to one certain thought or topic suggested by a particular scripture text.

(2) An Expository sermon deals with the explanation and exegesis of a scripture passage.

(3) A Manuscript sermon is one that is written and read to the congregation.

(4) An Illustrated sermon is one that uses some means, such as props or drama, to visually depict the theme or point of the sermon.

(5) An Evangelistic sermon is one focused on the appeal to unsaved persons to accept Christ — sometimes used to describe the fervent delivery of the preacher.

(6) An Extemporaneous sermon is one that is brought forth on the spot without any deliberate preparation. Most of the preaching of the early church was on this fashion.

Many of the philosophies surrounding sermon rhetoric (the style and structure of oratory) were handed down from John Chrysostom, the fourth century preacher of Antioch and Bishop of Constantinople (A.D. 350-407). His preaching gift was enhanced by his childhood studies of Greek oratory. From the 6th century, he was referred to as Chrysostom, which means "Golden Mouth," due to the eloquent structure of his written homilies. Hundreds of these were preserved and upheld as model sermon outlines for generations of preachers.

Besides sermon structure, there are other great diversities in the styles of preaching, mainly due to the different personalities of preachers. The 19th century theologian, Phillips Brooks said, "Preaching is the communication of truth by man to men. It has two essential elements, truth and personality. Neither of these can it spare... Preaching is the bringing of truth through personality."[2] Personality refers to the distinctive traits of a preacher — his speaking ability, his disposition, manners and enthusiasm — which deliver the message to the hearers.

It is generally not encouraged, but preaching styles are frequently influenced by the styles of admired peers and well known ministers. Billy Graham is one of the most emulated preachers in history — primarily due to his wide exposure through broadcasting. It is not uncommon to hear a preacher who sounds very similar. I know of several pastors who (perhaps unconsciously) use similar phrases, mannerisms, and the same rhythm of speech, which makes them sound very much like Graham.

One might assume that preaching is always based on scripture, but this is not always the case. Ministers in some contemporary churches rarely refer to scripture, if at all. Unfortunately, such sermons become nothing more than secular speeches or lectures, contrary to the pattern of New Testament preaching. More than anything else, people need to hear the unadulterated proclamation of God's Word that has power to transform their lives. The Apostle Paul's instruction to his young understudy, Timothy, was not to make speeches or sermons — he said to *"Preach the word..." (2 Tim 4:2)*.

A Godly lifestyle, combined with the calling of God are the most important qualifications for a preacher. One doesn't have to possess a formal education to preach, any more than did the earliest disciples, many of whom were common fishermen and tradesmen. But it's to the preacher's advantage if he can attend a Bible college or seminary. Besides a need for mentoring and Biblical instruction, there are two preparatory studies especially helpful to the preparation of preaching. (1) Hermeneutics, "the science and art of Biblical interpretation," (derived from the Greek, *HERMES*, mythical herald of the gods and interpreter of Jupiter), and (2) Homiletics, "the art and science of preaching," (from the Greek *"HOMILIA,"* a mutual talk or set discourse).

Glossary of Church Terms

Frequently asked questions about the church often include the many clichés, theological terms, and vernacular used by ministers and laymen. Many of these terms originated from scripture or tradition, perhaps taken from Greek or Latin words, or from the old vernacular of the King James Version. The following are many of such terms and their meaning:

Anathema — The Greek word for cursed or condemned, as used in the King James Version. *"If any man love not the Lord Jesus Christ, let him be Anathema Maranatha" (1 Corinthians 16:22 KJV).*

Anointing — A biblical term to describe the application of oil (a symbol of the Holy Spirit) in an act of consecrating sacred objects or persons, such as a priest or King. It also refers to an endowment of God's Spirit, blessing, or approval upon a servant of God. The Messiah literally means "anointed one." *"But the anointing which you have received from Him abides in you, and you do not need that anyone teach you..." (1 John 2:27).*

Anointing the sick — From the New Testament, this refers to elders of the church, applying oil (a symbol of the Holy Spirit) upon the body of one who is sick, to be followed by prayer. Olive oil is believed to be the original type used. *"Is anyone among you sick? Let him call for the elders of the church, and let them pray over him, anointing him with oil in the name of the Lord" (James 5:14).*

Apocalypse — From the Greek, *APOKALYPSIS*, meaning "revelation or unveiling," as used in *Revelations* 1:1. The New Testament book of Revelation is frequently referred to as the Apocalypse.

Apostle — A person sent by God. One of five office gifts described in Ephesians 4:11.

Arminian — Generally used as a reference to subscribers of a theological view held by Arminius, A Dutch Protestant theologian (1560 - 1609). Arminius refuted Calvin's doctrine of unconditional predestination, limited atonement and unresistable grace, and stood for universal salvation for all.

Atonement — Literally, "a covering," as in covering our sins from God's sight. It is used in reference to a sinner's reconciliation with God through the sufferings of Christ. *"Help us, O God of our salvation, For the glory of Your name; And deliver us, and provide atonement for our sins, For Your name's sake!" (Psalms 79:9).*

Apology — A theological term to describe a contention made in defense of the Christian faith. It is derived from the Greek, *APOLOGIA*, meaning "a defense in conduct or procedure." Apologetics is the study of this explanation or defense.

Baptism in water — The act of being immersed in water in obedience to scripture, as a statement of faith in Christ. *"Go therefore and make disciples of all the nations, baptizing them in the name of the Father and of the Son and of the Holy Spirit" (Matthew 28:19).*

Baptism in Holy Spirit — The experience of being immersed and filled with the Holy Spirit. *"...for John truly baptized with water, but you shall be baptized with the Holy Spirit not many days from now" (Acts 1:5).*

Baptismal — A term describing the event of baptizing or the place where baptisms are performed.

Bishop — An overseer, originally the principle officer of a local church, but evolved into a position of supervision over multiple churches. Elder or presbyter usually referred to the same person. *"This is a faithful saying: If a man desires the position of a bishop, he desires a good work" (1 Timothy 3:1).*

Body of Christ — The universal assembly of all believers. *"Now you are the body of Christ, and members individually" (1 Corinthians 12:27).*

Born-again — The state of being born in the Spirit, resulting from placing faith in Jesus Christ. *"Jesus answered and said to him, Most assuredly, I say to you, unless one is born again, he cannot see the kingdom of God" (John 3:3).*

Brethren — A plural term for brothers, either as siblings or Christian brothers. *"Who is My mother and who are My brothers? And He stretched out His hand toward His disciples and said, Here are My mother and My brothers!" (Matthew 12:48-49).*

Bride of Christ — The church, or the body of Christ. *"...Blessed are those who are called to the marriage supper of the Lamb!" (Revelations 19:9). "Come, I will show you the bride, the Lamb's wife" (Revelations 21:9).*

Called — To be chosen of God for a particular purpose. *"Paul, called to be an apostle of Jesus Christ through the will of God..." (1 Corinthians 1:1).*

Calvinist — A reference to those who subscribe to the doctrines of John Calvin (1509-64), who taught the concept of unconditional predestination, limited atonement, and irresistible grace, sometimes referred to as eternal security.

Canon — A Greek reference to a "reed" or measuring rule. This pertains to those writings which are considered to be sacred or divinely inspired.

Canticles — From Latin, CANTICUM which means a "song." Often interchanged as the title of the Old Testament book, Song of Solomon.

Catholic — A Latin term taken from the Greek, *KATHOLIKOS*, meaning "universal," referring to all believers.

Charismatic — Comes from the Greek word *CHARISMATA* which means gifted. A Christian who believes in or practices speaking in tongues and the present-day operation of the spiritual gifts.

Church Hopper — A person who attends different churches without a commitment to any one in particular, or one who changes churches frequently.

Communion — A memorial supper of bread and wine, symbolizing the broken body and shed blood of Jesus. *"The cup of blessing which we bless, is it not the communion of the blood of Christ? The bread which we break, is it not the communion of the body of Christ?" (1 Corinthians 10:16).*

Contrition — An expression of humility, sorrow or repentance for sin. *"The LORD is near to those who have a broken heart, And saves such as have a contrite spirit" (Psalms 34:18).*

Convert — One who has been "converted" as a Christian by placing faith in Jesus Christ. *"Assuredly, I say to you, unless you are converted and become as little children, you will by no means enter the kingdom of heaven" (Matthew 18:3).*

Covenant — A sacred, irrevocable promise between God and man. *"You are sons of the prophets, and of the covenant which God made with our fathers, saying to Abraham, And in your seed all the families of the earth shall be blessed" (Acts 3:25).*

Conviction — An inner awareness of truth. *"Then those who heard it, being convicted by their conscience, went out one by one, beginning with the oldest even to the last. And Jesus was left alone, and the woman standing in the midst" (John 8:9).*

Creed — A statement of beliefs which include the fundamentals considered necessary to salvation.

Deacon — Literally a servant. An office of servant ministry within the church. *"But let these also first be proved; then let them serve as deacons, being found blameless" (1 Timothy 3:10).*

Decalogue — A reference to the ten commandments.

Demon — A devil, an agent of Satan.

Demon possessed — To have a demon or demons. Sometimes interpreted as being possessed by demons. *"When evening had come, they brought to Him many who were demon-possessed. And He cast out the spirits with a word, and healed all who were sick" (Matthew 8:16).*

Denomination — A cluster of individual churches, which have unified together due to their agreement on certain issues, and perhaps due to their disagreement with the viewpoints of other churches or denominations.

Devil — A reference to Satan, or one of his demon agents. *"Put on the whole armor of God, that you may be able to stand against the wiles of the devil" (Ephesians 6:11).*

Disciple — One who is taught or trained. *"And whoever does not bear his cross and come after Me cannot be My disciple" (Luke 14:27).*

Dispensation — A determined period of time. *"...that in the dispensation of the fullness of the times He might gather together in one all things in Christ, both which are in heaven and which are on earth; in Him" (Ephesians 1:10).*

Doctrine — A teaching; That which is taught as the belief of a church. *"All Scripture is given by inspiration of God, and is profitable for* *doctrine, for reproof, for correction, for instruction in righteousness" (2 Timothy 3:16).*

Dogma — A belief which is held as authoritative and indisputable by a religious body.

Ecclesiastical — A term from the Greek, *EKKLESIA*, pertaining to the church or used in association with clergymen.

Edification — To build up and strengthen. *"He who speaks in a tongue edifies himself, but he who prophesies edifies the church" (1 Corinthians 14:4).*

Elder — A mature believer charged with spiritual supervision and ministry within the church. Elder and bishop are generally used interchangeably in the New Testament. *"Let the elders who rule well be counted worthy of double honor, especially those who labor in the word and doctrine" (1 Timothy 5:17).*

Election — A term which means the process by which God selects someone to be saved. *"...knowing, beloved brethren, your election by God" (1 Thessalonians 1:4).*

Enemy — A synonym for Satan. *"Behold, I give you the authority to trample on serpents and scorpions, and over all the power of the enemy, and nothing shall by any means hurt you" (Luke 10:19).*

Epistles — Letters written under inspiration of the Holy Spirit, to be read as instruction to the churches. *"I charge you by the Lord that this epistle be read to all the holy brethren" (1 Thessalonians 5:27).*

Eschatology — A theological term to describe the study of last events.

Esoteric — A term based upon customs in mysterious Greek religions to explain advanced doctrines only to the fully enlightened, as was probably inferred by this passage: *"For all the Athenians and the foreigners who were there spent their time in nothing else but either to tell or to hear some new thing" (Acts 17:21).*

Eternal Security — A term which generally refers to the doctrine of Calvinism and predestination. Stated simply, it suggests that once a person is saved, they cannot lose that salvation — they are eternally secure.

Eucharist — The Lord's supper, communion.

Evangelical — A term to describe those with devotion to the Gospel of Jesus instead of the ecclesiastical or rationalistic forms of Christianity — Spiritual mindedness and zeal for Christ rather than ritualism.

Evangelist — A proclaimer or preacher of the good news. One of five office gifts described in Ephesians 4:11.

Fall of Man — Mankind's estranged condition from God through sin, as originated with the disobedience of Adam and Eve in the garden.

Fasting — Abstaining from eating food for specified periods of time. *"So when they had appointed elders in every church, and prayed with fasting, they commended them to the Lord in whom they had believed" (Acts 14:23).*

Fellowship — The spiritual relationship between believers and the Lord, and the gathering together of Christians in the name of Jesus. *"If we say that we have fellowship with Him, and walk in darkness, we lie and do not practice the truth. But if we walk in the light as He is in the light, we have fellowship with one another, and the blood of Jesus Christ His Son cleanses us from all sin" (1 John 1:6-7).*

Fishers of men — A term Jesus first used to describe the soul-winning mission of his disciples. *"And He said to them, Follow Me, and I will make you fishers of men" (Matthew 4:19).*

Fornication — Any act of unsanctioned sexual behavior or perversion, especially used in association with sex outside the realm of marriage. *"But fornication and all uncleanness or covetousness, let it not even be named among you, as is fitting for saints;" (Ephesians 5:3).*

Fundamentalist — One who believes in the infallibility of the Bible as inspired by God and that it should be accepted literally.

Glossolalia — A theological term to describe the doctrine of speaking in tongues. *"And they were all filled with the Holy Spirit and began to speak with other tongues, as the Spirit gave them utterance" (Acts 2:4).*

Gospel — Literally, "good news." The story of Christ's life, His death and resurrection, as described from different perspectives by eye-witness authors, Matthew, Mark, Luke and John. Their four individual records of Christ are each called a Gospel, entitled with each authors name — which comprise the first four books of the New Testament. *"For I am not ashamed of the gospel of Christ, for it is the power of God to salvation for everyone who believes, for the Jew first and also for the Greek" (Romans 1:16).*

Hallelujah — A variation of a Hebrew word, *ALLELUJAH,* which means Praise the Lord. *"After these things I heard a loud voice of a great multitude in heaven, saying, Alleluia! Salvation and glory and honor and power to the Lord our God!" (Revelations 19:1).*

Heaven — The eternal realm and dwelling place of God. *"Assuredly, I say to you, unless you are converted and become as little children, you will by no means enter the kingdom of heaven" (Matthew 18:3).*

Hell — From the Greek, *GEHENNA* (valley of *Ge-Hinnom*) used figuratively to describe the place of everlasting punishment for the unrighteous. (Also used for *SHEOL* and *HADES*, "the abode of the dead.") *"And if your eye causes you to sin, pluck it out and cast it from you. It is better for you to enter into life with one eye, rather than having two eyes, to be cast into hell fire" (Matthew 18:9).*

Holy Roller — This term has been used as a reference to Pentecostal believers, who are often associated with more emotional, Charismatic displays of worship. It is believed the term was coined to describe those so overwhelmed by the Spirit, that they would fall to the floor and roll in the aisles.

Indulgence — A term used by the Roman Catholic church to describe a remission of temporal punishment due to sins. The sale of indulgences by the church was the one of the first issues refuted by Martin Luther which inadvertently brought about reformation.

Inspired — A term which means originated of God or God breathed. *"All Scripture is given by inspiration of God, and is profitable for doctrine, for reproof, for correction, for instruction in righteousness" (2 Timothy 3:16).*

Intercession — To intercede in behalf of another person or cause in prayer. *"...It is Christ who died, and furthermore is also risen, who is even at the right hand of God, who also makes intercession for us" (Romans 8:34).*

Jehovah (Yahweh) — The English rendering of the Hebrew consonants, JHVA. This is God's sacred name, used over 7,000 times in the Old Testament. The Jews considered this name to be so sacred that when reading scripture aloud, they preferred not to utter it, but would use the word Adonai, which means "Lord," in its place. The transliteral pronunciation, Jehovah, was formed from the Hebrew consonants JHVA and the vowels from Adonai. However, scholars of ancient Hebrew say that JHVA was originally pronounced as "Yahweh." The King James Version translated it as Jehovah, while new translations use Yahweh or Lord. *"That men may know that thou, whose name alone is JEHOVAH, art the most high over all the earth." (Psalms 83:18 KJV)*

Justified — To be made just and right in God's sight which occurs through our faith in Christ. *"...being justified freely by His grace through the redemption that is in Christ Jesus" (Romans 3:24).*

Laity — The laymen or non-clergy members of the church.

Lake of fire — The place of everlasting punishment — hell, GEHENNA. *"And anyone not found written in the Book of Life was cast into the lake of fire" (Revelations 20:15).*

Lamb of God — A figurative term to describe Jesus as the lamb sacrifice for our sins, relating from the lamb sacrifices of the Old Testament. *"The next day John saw Jesus coming toward him, and said, "Behold! The Lamb of God who takes away the sin of the world!" (John 1:29).*

Laying on of hands — The act of placing hands upon a person, in conjunction with prayer, to invoke God's blessing or anointing. *"...they will lay hands on the sick, and they will recover" (Mark 16:18).*

Litany — A prescribed form of prayer made by minister or priest with congregational responses.

Liturgy — This is a prescribed form or collection of forms for public worship. In liturgical churches, the rite and ceremony is more prominent than the emphasis on preaching, evangelism, or spontaneous expressions of worship.

Lord's Supper — A memorial meal for believers to commemorate Jesus' death and suffering, using bread and wine as symbols of His broken body and shed blood, as was portrayed at His last supper with His disciples. It is also referred to as Holy Communion. *"Therefore when you come together in one place, it is not to eat the Lord's Supper" (1 Corinthians 11:20).*

Lost — The state of not knowing God, unsaved, unregenerated. *"For the Son of Man has come to save that which was lost"* (Matthew 18:11).

Lucifer — The name of one of the Lord's three archangels, who rebelled and was cast out of Heaven to the earth, where he dwells as Satan or the Devil. *"How you are fallen from heaven, O Lucifer, son of the morning! How you are cut down to the ground, you who weakened the nations!"* (Isaiah 14:12).

Mainline — A reference to long-standing denominational establishments; mainline churches are those such as the Presbyterians, Episcopalians, and others.

Manifestation — The act of making obvious or bringing out in the open. *"In this the love of God was manifested toward us, that God has sent His only begotten Son into the world, that we might live through Him"* (1 John 4:9).

Maranatha — A Greek word which means "Our Lord comes," or the coming of the Lord, used literally in the King James Version. *"If any man love not the Lord Jesus Christ, let him be Anathema Maranatha"* (1 Corinthians 16:22 KJV).

Messiah — A reference to Jesus Christ. Literally, "The Anointed One" (Dan. 9:25).

Millennium — A word that literally means "thousand," referring to the future thousand years of Christ's reign upon the earth. *"Blessed and holy is he who has part in the first resurrection. Over such the second death has no power, but they shall be priests of God and of Christ, and shall reign with Him a thousand years"* (Revelations 20:6).

Minister — One who serves in a ministerial role of a church, as to preach sermons or conduct religious services, or to perform some service to the spiritual benefit of others. It literally means to serve, help or encourage. *"...I became a minister according to the gift of the grace of God given to me by the effective working of His power"* (Ephesians 3:7).

Monotheism — The belief in one God.

Move of God — A traditional term to describe a spiritual stirring among God's people, or the activity or manifestation of the Holy Spirit.

Mt. Zion — The mountain on which Jerusalem is built, where Solomon's Temple rested. Frequently used metaphorically as where God dwells. *"Beautiful in elevation, The joy of the whole earth, Is Mount Zion on the sides of the north, The city of the great King" (Psalms 48:2).*

Offering — A gift given from our own possessions or riches. *"Will a man rob God? Yet you have robbed Me! But you say, In what way have we robbed You? In tithes and offerings" (Malachi 3:8).*

Omnipotent — A theological term to describe the all-powerful characteristics of God.

Omnipresent — A theological term to express God's characteristic of being everywhere at once.

Omniscient — A theological term to describe God's all-knowing characteristics.

Ordained — Chosen, authorized or endorsed. Generally used to describe God's approval. Ordination of a minister is the act of recognizing God's endorsement upon an individual for a ministry office, implemented by the laying on of hands or the issuance of ministerial credentials. *"...He has appointed a day on which He will judge the world in righteousness by the Man whom He has ordained. He has given assurance of this to all by raising Him from the dead" (Acts 17:31).*

Ordinance — A religious rite or ceremony performed in obedience to scripture, but not considered a sacrament.

Orthodoxy — A belief in doctrines which are considered correct or sound.

Outpouring — A reference to a generous showering effect — often in association with the Holy Spirit. *"And it shall come to pass in the last days, says God, That I will pour out of My Spirit on all flesh; your sons and your daughters shall prophesy, your young men shall see visions, your old men shall dream dreams" (Acts 2:17).*

Parishioner — A constituent or member of a church congregation or parish.

Pastor — By modern tradition, a person who is a minister and spiritual overseer of a church congregation — an elder or bishop. A pastor literally means "a shepherd," a metaphoric description of one who cares for and leads a flock of God's sheep. One of five office gifts described in Ephesians 4:11.

Pentateuch — A reference to the first five books of the Old Testament: Genesis, Exodus, Leviticus, Numbers, & Deuteronomy.

Pentecostal — A believer who claims the same experience of the early disciples on the day of Pentecost — the infilling of the Holy Spirit with evidence of speaking in tongues *(Acts 2:1-4)*. The Pentecostal embraces the present-day operation of the gifts of the Spirit.

Pews — The traditional bench-long seats in churches. The term originated from the French word, PUIE, "a raised place," which was used to describe the boxed, balcony seats in a theater. In precolonial days, the term became identified with the enclosed boxed seats in a church sanctuary, and later to all church bench seats. Other tradition says that the term originated from pioneer days when bathing was sometimes infrequent, and the bench seats retained the odor from users.

Plead the blood — A term whose origin is associated with the story of the Passover, when the death angel passed over the home of Israelites who had wiped lamb's blood on their doorposts *(Exodus 12:1-15)*. It is sometimes used to describe a prayer appeal for God's protection, symbolically covering us with Christ's blood.

Polytheism — The belief in many Gods.

Pray-through — An older traditional term used to express earnest seeking of God in prayer until an inner confidence or peace is attained.

Preacher — One who proclaims monologues, or brings forth sermons or messages in relationship to the Bible. *"How then shall they call on Him in whom they have not believed? And how shall they believe in Him of whom they have not heard? And how shall they hear without a preacher?"* (Romans 10:14).

Protestant — A term which originated with regards to Martin Luther and his followers. Because they "protested" against certain non-scriptural practices of the Roman Catholic Church, they were called "Protestants."

Prophecy — The act of speaking from the mind of God. Either to forthtell or foretell. *"...for prophecy never came by the will of man, but holy men of God spoke as they were moved by the Holy Spirit"* (2 Peter 1:21).

Prophet — One who speaks in God's behalf, either to proclaim His written Word or to speak from His supernatural revelation. One of five office gifts described in *Ephesians* 4:11.

Pulpit — The podium from which a minister preaches. The term was used in the King James Version, where a pulpit was something stood on for elevation when speaking to a crowd. *"And Ezra the scribe stood upon a pulpit of wood..."* (Nehemiah 8:4 KJV).

Rapture — This term comes from the Latin word, RAPTO, to "seize" or "snatch," which was used in the Latin Vulgate version of the New Testament to describe the saints being "caught up" to meet the Lord in the air *(1 Thessalonians 4:17)*. This event will occur in the last days, preceding Christ's return to the earth. *"For the Lord Himself will descend from heaven with a shout, with the voice of an archangel, and with the trumpet of God. And the dead in Christ will rise first. Then we who are alive and remain shall be caught up together with them in the clouds to meet the Lord in the air. And thus we shall always be with the Lord"* (1 Thessalonians 4:16-17).

Rebuke — An expression of disapproval or reprimand. *"Take heed to yourselves. If your brother sins against you, rebuke him; and if he repents, forgive him"* (Luke 17:3).

Reconciliation — A term which means being brought back. *"And you, who once were alienated and enemies in your mind by wicked works, yet now He has reconciled"* (Colossians 1:21).

Redeemed — A term which means bought or purchased. *"...knowing that you were not redeemed with corruptible things, like silver or gold, from your aimless conduct received by tradition from your fathers, but with the precious blood of Christ, as of a lamb without blemish and without spot"* (1 Peter 1:18-19).

Regenerated — A theological term, describing the state of new life, resulting from the new birth in Christ.

Repent — To be remorseful for sin, and to turn around and go in a new direction. *"Repent therefore and be converted, that your sins may be* *blotted out, so that times of refreshing may come from the presence of the Lord"* (Acts 3:19).

Saints — Persons who are separated unto God. A term which refers to all believers. *"Now, therefore, you are no longer strangers and foreigners, but fellow citizens with the saints and members of the household of God"* (Ephesians 2:19).

Salvation — A term which describes the rescue of our soul from eternal death. *"For by grace you have been saved through faith, and that not of yourselves; it is the gift of God, not of works, lest anyone should boast"* (Ephesians 2:8-9).

Sanctified — To be made separate for holy use. *"For this is the will of God, your sanctification: that you should abstain from sexual immorality; that each of you should know how to possess his own vessel in sanctification and honor"* (1 Thessalonians 4:3-4).

Sanctuary — Often used to describe the auditorium used for church gatherings. The term originates from reference to the temple or tabernacle, coming from the term "sanctify," to set apart for the Lord's use. *"Lift up your hands in the sanctuary, And bless the LORD"* (Psalms 134:2).

Sawdust trail — A traditional term which refers to the aisles between seats in the revival preacher's gospel tents. Timber was cut to erect poles for the tents, leaving sawdust behind on the floor of the tent. Thus, the preacher would call for the lost to come down the aisles — the sawdust trail — to accept Christ.

Secular — That which is not sacred or ecclesiastical. It pertains to things not Christian or church related, such as unbelieving society.

Second Coming — A reference to the end-time return of Jesus Christ to the earth, His second appearance, which He promised and which is predicted throughout the Old and New Testaments. *"You also be patient. Establish your hearts, for the coming of the Lord is at hand"* (James 5:8).

Seeking God — A reference to praying to God or attempting to attain his attention or favor. *"Seek the LORD and His strength; seek His face evermore!"* (1 Chronicles 16:11).

Sermon — An oral presentation of teachings or inspiring thoughts.

Slain in the Spirit — An extrabiblical term used to describe a phenomenon which brings about an overwhelming awareness of the Holy Spirit, causing a person to fall prostrate. *"Then; when He said to them, I am He; they drew back and fell to the ground" (John 18:6).*

Soteriology — A theological term used to describe the doctrine of salvation. Taken from the Greek word for salvation, *SOTERIA.*

Soul-winner — A person who wins souls to Jesus Christ. *"...he who wins souls is wise" (Proverbs 11:30).*

Speaking in tongues — An utterance in another language supernaturally enabled by the Holy Spirit. *"And they were all filled with the Holy Spirit and began to speak with other tongues, as the Spirit gave them utterance" (Acts 2:4).*

Spirit-filled — To be full of the Holy Spirit. *"And do not be drunk with wine, in which is dissipation; but be filled with the Spirit" (Ephesians 5:18).*

Spiritual gifts — Manifestations or gifts of the Holy Spirit which provide ministry to the body of Christ. *"Now concerning spiritual gifts, brethren, I do not want you to be ignorant:" (1 Corinthians 12:1).*

Tarry — A term which means to wait, sometimes used to describe waiting on the Lord through prayer. *"Behold, I send the Promise of My Father upon you; but tarry in the city of Jerusalem until you are endued with power from on high" (Luke 24:49).*

Teacher — One who seeks to instill knowledge in others by methods of instruction. One of five office gifts described in Ephesians 4:11.

Testament — A sacred covenant or promise, as in the Old or New Testaments. *"But their minds were hardened. For until this day the same veil remains unlifted in the reading of the Old Testament, because the veil is taken away in Christ" (2 Corinthians 3:14).*

Testimony — A solemn affirmation of some fact. In modern church tradition this frequently describes a public testimonial of thanksgiving to God for an answered prayer. *"And they overcame him by the blood of the Lamb and by the word of their testimony, and they did not love their lives to the death" (Revelations 12:11).*

Theology — The study of God *(Greek, THEO).*

Throne of grace — A term which refers to God's presence and His character of granting undeserved favor through prayer. *"Let us therefore come boldly to the throne of grace, that we may obtain mercy and find grace to help in time of need" (Hebrews 4:16).*

Tithe — The first ten percent of our increase or income which God claims as His. *"Bring all the tithes into the storehouse, that there may be food in My house, and prove Me now in this, says the LORD of hosts, If I will not open for you the windows of heaven And pour out for you such blessing That there will not be room enough to receive it" (Malachi 3:10).*

Tract — A brief pamphlet designed to share Gospel truths or to invite persons to accept Jesus Christ.

Trespass — A sin or offense. *"And whenever you stand praying, if you have anything against anyone, forgive him, that your Father in heaven may also forgive you your trespasses" (Mark 11:25).*

Tribulation — Trouble or calamity. The "Great Tribulation" is a seven-year period of unparalleled calamity upon the earth, immediately prior to the return of Christ. *"For then there will be great tribulation, such as has not been since the beginning of the world until this time, no, nor ever shall be" (Matthew 24:21).*

Trinity — A theological term which describes the three persons of the Godhead, the Father, Son and Holy Spirit. A church which embraces this doctrine is called "Trinitarian." *"For there are three who bear witness in heaven: the Father, the Word, and the Holy Spirit; and these three are one" (1 John 5:7).*

Trouble-Maker — A term often used to describe a person who stirs up strife or causes tension or trouble in the church.

Unregenerated — A theological term referring to the natural, sinful state of man; without having been regenerated or born-again.

Wildfire — A traditional term which is sometimes used to describe spiritual disorder in a church service resulting from highly fanatical, emotional outbursts or sensational displays which are determined to be of a fleshly origin rather than inspired of the Holy Spirit.

Witness — To share the Gospel of Christ with others; to bear witness of His presence in our life. *"But you shall receive power when the*

Holy Spirit has come upon you; and you shall be witnesses to Me in Jerusalem, and in all Judea and Samaria, and to the end of the earth" (Acts 1:8).

Word — "The" Word, God's Word, the Bible. Jesus Christ is the Word who was made flesh. *"Therefore those who were scattered went everywhere preaching the word" (Acts 8:4).*

BIBLIOGRAPHY

All About the Bible, Sidney Collet
Assimilating New Members, Lyle E. Schaller
Anti-Nicene Church Fathers
Augustine
Baker's Dictionary of Theology, Harrison
Basics of Bible Interpretation, Bob Smith
Biblical Eldership, Alexander Strauch
Body Life, Ray Stedman
Deeper Experiences of Famous Christians, James Gilchrist Lawson
Dictionary of Pentecostal & Charismatic Movements, Zondervan
Cambridge History of the Bible
Christianity Through the Centuries, Earle E. Cairns
Eerdman's Handbook To The History Of Christianity
Effective Preaching, Deane A. Kemper
Evidence That Demands A Verdict, Josh McDowell
Foxe's Book of Martyrs, John Foxe
From Ancient Tablets to Modern Translations, David Ewert
God's Plan For Man, J. Finis Dake
Growing the Small Church, C. Wayne Zunkel
Halley's Bible Handbook
Handbook of Denominations, Frank S. Mead
History of the Christian Church, Philip Schaff
How to Prepare Sermons, William Evans
Is The Bible The Word Of God?, William R. Kimball
Kingdom of the Cults, Walter Martin
Larsen's Book of Cults, Bob Larsen
Leading Your Church To Growth, C. Peter Wagner
Lectures in Systematic Theology, Henry Clarence Thiessen
Man, Myth and Magic
Martin Luther, John Dillenberger
Nelson's Illustrated Bible Dictionary
None of These Diseases, Dr. S.I. McMillen
Preaching with Purpose, Jay E. Adams
Principles of Biblical Hermeneutics, J. Edwin Hartill
Protestant Christian Evidences, Bernard Ramm
Revival, Winkie Pratney

Revival Lectures, Charles Finney
Roman Catholicism, Loraine Boettner
Selecting a Translation of the Bible, Lewis Foster
Science Speaks, Peter W. Stoner
Solving the Ministry's Toughest Problems
Souer's History of the Christian Church
Textus Receptus, Allan A. MacRae
The American Almanac, 1995
The Book of Acts, Stanley Horton
The Book of First Corinthians, Paul A. Hamar
The Complete Book of Church Growth, Elmer L. Towns
The Christian Book of Why, John C. McCollister
The Decline and Fall of the Roman Empire, Edward Gibbon
The Encyclopedia Britannica
The English Bible/From KJV to NIV, Jack P. Lewis
The Foundations of Bible History, John Garstang
The Funk and Wagnall Encyclopedia
The Joy of Belonging, Richard L. Dresselhaus
The Measure of a Church, Gene A. Getz
The Merriam Webster Dictionary
The Multiple Staff and the Larger Church, Lyle E. Schaller
The Open Church, James H. Rutz
The Oxford Dictionary of the Christian Church
The Power of a Loving Church, Margaret & Bartless Hess
The Victor Bible Source Book, Stephen D. Swihart
The World Almanac, 1995
The World Book Encyclopedia
The Zondervan Pictorial Encyclopedia of the Bible
Today's Pastors, George Barna
Twenty Centuries of Christian Worship
What is the Church?, Bruce L. Shelley
What the Bible Teaches about the Church, John F. Balchin
Winning the Backdoor War, Johnathon Gainsbrugh
Your Bible, R. Laird Harris

Reference Notes:

Question 2.
1. Hartford Seminary's Hartford Institute for Religion Research,
hirr.hartsem.edu
2. What is the Church?, Bruce E. Shelley

Question 3.
1. Eerdmans Handbook to the History of Christianity
2. Kingdom of the Cults, Walter Martin
3. Larsen's Book of Cults, Bob Larsen
4. Armstrongism refers to beliefs that were originally held by the
Worldwide Church of God.

Question 9.
1. Hartford Seminary's Hartford Institute for Religion Research,
hirr.hartsem.edu
2. Duke University National Congregations Study,
www.soc.duke.edu/natcong/
3. 2012 Yearbook of American & Canadian Churches

Question 10.
1. Leading Your Church To Growth, C. Peter Wagner
2. Growing the Small Church, C. Wayne Zunkel
3. Winning the Backdoor War, Johnathon Gainsbrugh

Question 21.
1. The Oxford Dictionary of the Christian Church

Question 30.
1. Today's Pastors, George Barna
2. The Open Church, James H. Rutz

Question 32.
1. Today's Pastors, George Barna

Question 34.
1. Biblical Eldership, Alexander Strauch

Question 45.
1. Handbook of Denominations in the United States 13th Edition

Question 49.
1. Evidence That Demands A Verdict, Josh McDowell
2. Protestant Christian Evidences, Bernard Ramm
3. The Victor Bible Sourcebook, Stephen D. Swihart
4. None Of These Diseases, Dr. S.I. McMillen
5. Science Speaks, Peter W. Stoner
6. Rivers in the Desert; History of Negev, Nelson Glueck
7. The Foundations of Biblical History, John Garstang
8. Foxe's Book of Martyrs, John Foxe

Question 50.
1. Selecting a Translation of the Bible, Lewis Foster
2. Evidence that Demands a Verdict, Josh McDowell

Question 56.
1. The Decline and Fall of the Roman Empire, Edward Gibbon

Question 58.
1. The Victor Bible Source Book, Stephen D. Swihart

Question 60.
1. The Zondervan Pictorial Encyclopedia of the Bible
2. Deeper Experiences of Famous Christians, James Gilchrist Lawson

Question 61.
1. Baker's Dictionary of Theology
2. History of the Christian Church, Philip Schaff
3. The Open Church, James H. Rutz
4. Twenty Centuries of Christian Worship

Question 63.
1. Augustine, Vol. 4

Question 64.
1. Eerdman's Handbook to the History of Christianity
2. Revival Lectures, Charles Finney
3. Revival, Winkie Pratney

Question 65.
1. Refutation and Overthrow of False Doctrine
2. Anti-Nicene Church Fathers, Tertullian Vol. IV
3. Deeper Experiences of Famous Christians, James Gilchrist Lawson
4. The Encyclopedia Britannica
5. Souer's History of the Christian Church

Question 67.
1. De Trinitate, Augustine
2. The Christian Book of Why, John C. McCollister

Question 68.
1. The World Book Encyclopedia
2. Dictionary of the Occult and Paranormal
3. Man, Myth and Magic

Question 70.
1. Baker's Dictionary of Theology

Question 72.
1. The Oxford Dictionary of the Christian Church
2. Didache IXV
3. History of the Christian Church, Philip Schaff
4. Eerdman's Handbook to the History of Christianity

Question 75.
1. Preaching With Purpose, Jay E. Adams
2. Lectures on Preaching, Phillips Brooks

www.ingramcontent.com/pod-product-compliance
Lightning Source LLC
Chambersburg PA
CBHW060238050426
42448CB00009B/1490